Business Tax Deductons

2016

W. Murray Bradford, CPA

For one-owner and husband-and-wife owned businesses (proprietorships, S corporations, C corporations, limited liability companies, 1099, statutory employees)

*Clarifying Taxes
So You Take Control of
Your Money*

Workbook Price $397.50
With CDs $795.00
36th Edition

Bradford and Company, Inc
www.bradfordandcompany.com

Operations Center
1050 Northgate Dr., Ste. 351
San Rafael, CA 94903
(415) 446-4340

Editorial
1701 Pennsylvania Ave., N.W., Ste. 300
Washington, DC 20036
(202) 652-2293

Copyright 2016 by W. Murray Bradford, CPA

This material may not be reproduced, stored in a retrieval system, or transmitted in whole or in part, in any form or by any means (electronic, mechanical, photocopying, recording, or otherwise) without the prior written permission of the publisher and copyright holder.

The book is for use with the CDs and the on-line video that make up the *Business Tax Deductions* course. Neither the publisher nor the speakers are rendering tax, legal, accounting, or other professional advice. Users of this book and the accompanying CDs and on-line video must see their personal advisors to ensure proper implementation of ideas presented herein.

Table of Contents

Section 1
Why You Need This Course and What You Can Expect 5

Section 2
Travel Rule Basics and How to Put Them to Work for You 13

Section 3
Paying Mom and Dad or Friends or Relatives for Business Lodging at Their Homes 25

Section 4
How to Treat Two Regular Places of Business 27

Section 5
Entertainment Not Subject to the 50 Percent Cut 29

Section 6
Strategies to Capture More Entertainment Deductions 35

Section 7
Beware of the Entertainment Facility Rules That Kill Tax Deductions 43

Section 8
How to Build Audit-Proof Support for Entertainment 49

Section 9
New Law Makes Home Office Available to You 57

Section 10
Putting the IRS Audit Manual's Home-Office Section to Work for You 63

Section 11
Why Incorporation Makes Your Home-Office Deduction Less Subject to an IRS Audit 71

Section 12
Use Net Square Footage to Increase Home-Office Deductions 73

Section 13
Revenue Procedure Shows How Home Office Saves Extra Taxes with a 1031 Exchange 77

Section 14
Profit on Sale of Home with Office Sheltered by Exclusions 85

Section 15
Install a Section 105 Medical Plan Now 87

Section 16
Court Case Shows How a Wife's Business Covers the Husband with a Section 105 Medical Plan 101

Section 17
IRS Puts Screws to S Corporation Health Insurance 109

Section 18
Pocket Self-Employment Taxes by Renting from your Spouse 113

Section 19
Prepay Your Expenses 117

Section 20
Guide to Section 179 Benefits for Your Business Property 121

Section 21
Section 179 Recapture Problems Lurk in the Shadows 133

Section 22
Add to Your Net Worth with Cost Segregation 139

Section 23
Antiques Can Make Smart Assets for Your Business.. 147

Section 24
Should You Use IRS Mileage Rates or Actual Expenses?... 153

Section 25
Avoid Taxes with Section 1031 Exchanges of Vehicles 161

Section 26
What to Do When the Sale of Your Business Vehicle Would Produce a Loss Deduction 169

Section 27
To Buy or Lease Your Next Business Vehicle 171

Section 28
Building More Business Miles with Audit-Proof Records... 179

Section 29
Tax Breaks When You Total Your Vehicle......... 189

Section 30
Commission Rebate Deductions Allowed..... 191

Section 31
Save Big Tax Dollars—Hire Your Dependent Children 193

Section 32
Solo 401(k) Could Be the Perfect Retirement Plan 201

Section 33
Tips for Building Audit-Proof Support........... 209

Section 34
Choosing the Right Business Entity Can Be Critical to Your Business Health 213

Section 35
Single-Member Limited Liability Companies (LLCs) Are Simple to Operate 217

Section 36
The One-Person S Corporation...................... 221

Section 37
The One-Owner and Husband-and-Wife-Owned C Corporation 227

Section 38
Tactics for Paying the Owner of an S Corporation the Lowest Possible Salary........ 233

Section 39
Corporation Must Earn the Income; Assignment of Income Fails........................... 237

Section 40
Loans to Your Corporation Could Be Hazardous to Your Financial Health............... 241

Section 41
What Your Corporation Can Reimburse to You and Its Other Employees and Why That's Very Important.............................. 243

Section 42
Tax Plan Needed for Social Security Benefits 247

Section 43
Avoiding and Coping with the Dreaded IRS 255

Section 44
New Law Helps and Hurts Start-Up Deductions... 263

Section 45
Tax Planning in the Event Your Business Loses Money................................... 271

Section 46
Answers to Questions..................................... 275

Section 1

Why You Need This Course and What You Can Expect

Notes

Who You Are to Us

You are a client—not a customer—because, according to the eleventh edition of *Merriam-Webster's Collegiate Dictionary*:
- Clients are under the protection of another
- Customers purchase a commodity or service

Knowledge is protection. As a client, you can expect fully accurate information that you will understand, implement, and use to build your net worth.

Our Guarantee to You

If you have a question on your course materials, send your question to questions@bradfordandcompany.com

We guarantee that this tax strategies course:
- Will find you a minimum of $7,500 in new and usable tax deductions (probably $15,000 to $50,000)
- Will put a smile on your accountant's face as knowledge helps your accountant help you
- Will save you time keeping your tax records (when you know what you are doing, you spend a lot less time doing it)
- Will make your tax records far more audit-proof
- Will help you give your accountant ironclad supporting documentation for your tax deductions
- Is 100 percent accurate (if your accountant should have a technical disagreement about anything in our material, please arrange a three-way conference call with us to include you, your accountant, and W. Murray Bradford, CPA, the principal author of this work)
- Will be easy for you to understand and implement (if you have questions on the material in this course, please send your questions via email to questions@bradfordandcompany.com)

Because you are now our client, we are here for you.

Benefits Continue Year After Year

The effort you put into this course pays dividends year after year, all the years of your working life. Sure, tax laws change every year, but the general mind-set on how taxes interface with your business never changes, and basic principles of keeping good records never change.

To Do
1. Take CDs to vehicle--turn drive time into money time.
2. Check for updates: www.bradfordandcompany.com/2016
3. Watch the online video on how to audit-proof your tax records and save time: www.tax789.com/2016video

Notes

Many business-deduction strategies remain unchanged for dozens and dozens of years, so your efforts pay off for dozens and dozens of years. In a way, much of this knowledge is like an annuity, giving you an investment return for many years.

For Whom Is This Course Designed?

This course is for one-owner or husband-and-wife businesses. In general, the course applies to all
- Independent contractors
- Statutory employees
- Husband-and-wife businesses
- Partnerships owned by husband and wife only
- Corporations owned by one person or by a husband and wife
- LLCs owned by one person or by a husband and wife

The course is not designed for the W-2 employee who claims employee business expenses using a Form 2106. Further, although a useful reference, the course is not designed for the multiple-owner business because the strategies in this course are designed to benefit only the owner (one person or the husband-and-wife unit).

How the Course Works for You

The tax strategies course consists of three inextricably intertwined components:
1. The workbook reference source,
2. The audio CDs, and
3. An on-line video.

The three intertwined parts (workbook, CDs, and on-line video) work together in an easy and enjoyable way to produce the benefits you are looking for.

According to renowned consultant Jay Abraham, the audio CDs are about 667 percent more effective than a one-day live seminar. Abraham says that you leave a live seminar remembering about 15 percent of the information, even when you have a comprehensive supporting workbook.

Psychologists suggest listening to information multiple times to improve comprehension and integrate the information into your daily repertoire.

The retained comprehension part is a big reason we changed our educational strategy to this three-pronged approach. With the CDs, you can enjoy passive learning with excellent comprehension, by putting the CDs in your car and listening while driving (and while not driving, when waiting for the traffic to move).

You might want to use the CDs in concert with building endorphins, by listening while running or working out at the gym. This makes for happy tax advice.

The CDs are the first step to your understanding. The CDs, workbook, and on-line video are intertwined and interrelated, but not redundant. With the CDs, you will hear word-picture examples that make tax-saving strategies clear. Listen to the CDs first, with the workbook nowhere in sight.

We designed the CDs with tracks so you can skip around and choose the things you want to learn. Some sections contain several tracks so you can skip information inside a section as well as skip section to section. In general, sections and tracks give the complete story for a strategy or set of strategies, including the tax records needed. If a track is dependent on additional information, the track will direct you to that information.

You have probably heard the expression that a picture is worth a thousand words. We believe in the picture theory and use it extensively in the on-line video to show you ways to audit-proof your records. Tax law is very specific on the types of records you need. The on-line video makes it fast and easy for you to see how the records should look.

This reference book plays a vital role in the learning process, giving you easy-to-read breakdowns of the tax rules, followed by great examples. But the book does not stand alone in the tax-strategies course learning process.

Think of the book as one of three legs holding up a chair. Take away any of the legs and the chair falls over. It takes three legs to make the chair work, like it takes the three parts of this course to clarify taxes so that you take control of your money.

Note the extensive references at the end of most every section of this reference book. The annotations are for you. The annotations are for your tax advisors. The annotations show how each strategy complies with the law.

Why You Need This Course

When you went into business for yourself, you entered into a partnership agreement with the government. That partnership agreement, called the tax law, governs how you split the money you earn between yourself and the government.

The Tax Foundation, a think tank in Washington, D.C., says that taxes cost you more money than any other single expense, including housing and food. This is a lot of money, so it makes sense to pay attention to your taxes.

Notes

As a one-person or husband-and-wife business, it is doubtful that you could pay someone to take care of the taxes related to your business income. After all
- You are the one who spends the money.
- You are the one who needs to know what is deductible.
- You are the one who keeps the record of the expense.
- You are the one who has to comply with special requirements, like keeping a vehicle mileage log and recording the proper elements of support for travel and entertainment.
- You are the one who needs to ask the questions of your accountant.
- You are the one who provides the information to your accountant.

In other words, you are on the front-lines where most deductions are won and lost. This course gives you the weapons and tools you need to build your net worth and sleep better at night.

Why Your Accountant Cannot Do This for You

Your accountant does not know your business like you know your business. Your accountant does not care about your business like you care about your business. This is no fault of your accountant, who has many clients in many businesses. You are the expert on your business.

Expecting your accountant to take care of your taxes is like expecting your dentist to take care of your teeth. Your dentist could take care of your teeth. All your dentist would have to do is stop by your home every morning and evening to brush and floss your teeth for you.

Similarly, your accountant could take care of your taxes. All your accountant would have to do is follow you around all day and
- make notes every time you used something (noting both personal and business use in many cases),
- obtain receipts for your business purchases that require receipts as proof,
- make notes about certain expenditures that require specific notes, including those where receipts are not required,
- pay the bills,
- file the receipts, and
- summarize the information for your tax return.

To do all this, your accountant would have to have only one client—you!

In fact, how often do you see your accountant? Once a year? Even if you see your accountant often, like really often—say every day—you still need this course. Why? Your accountant does not have time to do what we do for you.

Here are four reasons your accountant does not do what we do (or you could say, four reasons you would not want to pay your accountant to do what this course does for you).

1. Research just for you: The principal author of this work, W. Murray Bradford, CPA, spends an average of 80 hours a month researching the tax law for benefits that the one-owner business can put to use. He also has a staff, outside writers, and a cadre of highly placed enrolled agents, CPAs, and tax lawyer colleagues he calls on for ideas and advice.

He charges $350 an hour for his time. The 80 hours is worth $28,000 a month! That's what it takes each month to put you under our protection as a client of this tax strategies course.

And it has taken us years to build this course. Mr. Bradford, just one of the contributors to this body of knowledge, has been researching, studying, and teaching tax strategies for small business people like you for the past 27 years. In other words, he alone has invested more than 25,000 hours in learning not only your tax issues, but how to make them come to life for your benefit.

Your accountant cannot do this on your behalf. First, your accountant must bill for time spent researching tax issues. It is unlikely that he or she has either the time available for non-billable research, or clients willing to pay for 80 hours of research a month.

Second, if for some strange reason your accountant had 80 hours of time for research during a month, that research would probably focus on far more issues than your small business deductions, including issues like
- Death and estate taxes
- Business reviews
- Audits
- Litigation support
- Sales taxes
- Payroll taxes
- Compliance with ERISA
- Gift taxes
- Acquisition reviews
- Compliance with general accounting principles
- Business valuations
- Workers' compensation
- State income taxes
- Financial statement preparation and review
- Personal property taxes
- Insurance

Notes

- Formal compliance reviews
- Loan covenant reviews and audits
- Unemployment
- The inner dealings of multi-owner corporations
- Internal control reviews
- Compliance difficulties with general and limited partnerships
- Foundation compliance
- Endowment reviews
- Grant writing, reviews, and audits
- Personal financial planning, plans, and investment reviews
- Divorce planning
- Succession planning

Most of these issues have nothing to do with you and your tax situation. Unlike your accountant, we do one thing and one thing only: We concentrate on the day-to-day small buisness tax issues that pertain to the one-owner or husband-and-wife-owned business.

2. Research for you from the best sources: In all likelihood, we subscribe to more and better tax services than your accountant subscribes to. In our headquarters office, we subscribe to U.S. Tax Reporter, RIA, BNA Tax Management Portfolios, Parker Tax, PPC, Tax Analysts Tax Notes, Tax Facts, Warren Gorham and Lamont, Matthew Bender, and LexisNexis. Most practicing accountants who deal with one-owner businesses subscribe to one service, maybe two at most.

Again, nothing against your accountant here, but your accountant has to do much more than just find deductions for you. The thousands we spend for such a wide variety of resources makes no sense in a private practice. Accountants in private practice spend most of their time doing the work and talking to the clients about a variety of issues.

We have only you, the one-person or husband-and-wife business. You are our one-and-only issue. We devote our time and resources to you.

3. Narrow definition makes our materials apply to you: You are like Mr. Bradford's dad. He operated a small business as a sole proprietorship. Mr. Bradford knows who you are and what you do from morning until night.

He has been studying you and the tax laws that apply to you since 1979, when he left the international accounting firm of Price Waterhouse to get into the business of supplying tax strategies for the small businesss. His definition of a small business is the one-owner or husband-and-wife-owned business.

We don't care how you operate this one-owner business. You can be a corporation, partnership, LLC, or proprietorship. You can even be a life insurance agent paid as a statutory employee (independent contractor for all purposes other than FICA, Medicare, and certain fringe benefits). We like salespeople, medical people, and franchise owners. You benefit from this course when you meet the criteria stated (i.e., you are the owner, or you and your spouse own the business together).

Our narrow definition of the small business gives us the ability to really focus on you. Many accountants do not like you as a client. In fact, very few accountants specialize in one-owner businesses, and even those that specialize are taken off track by the variety of other issues that arise, like death of the sole owner and inheritance by the three children (hence three owners).

4. Easy for you to understand and use: You will learn and apply the material in this course because we designed it for your understanding. This is not like talking taxes with your accountant.

Mr. Bradford has a unique ability to take complicated material and make it understandable. This "taking the complicated to comprehensible and usable" is what led to his highly regarded appointment to a tour of duty in the Washington, D.C., national office of Price Waterhouse many years ago. He did not disappoint. In an unusual move, Price Waterhouse extended his original tour from two years to four years.

During his tour of duty, his job was to write and teach complicated material to nonaccountants. He taught many groups, big and small, throughout the United States. He listened and learned a great deal. Then he took that knowledge with him; ever since, he has been applying it to your tax situation.

Professional educators and communicators have spent over 500 hours reviewing our materials for both accuracy and interest level. We keep you alert, enthused, and learning all of the time you have our materials in your hands.

As to quality of material and relevancy to your morning-to-night business activities, we average better than 9.67 on a 10-point scale. You will like our teaching style and you will thank us for your clear understanding of the materials.

Why Your Accountant Will Thank You for Taking This Course

Your accountant cannot do for you what this course does for you. In fact, your completion of this course will put a smile on your accountant's face because you will become

Notes

- an accurate record keeper who does not have to worry about documentation, and
- an informed taxpayer who now asks good questions.

People always complain that their accountants are never aggressive enough on their behalf. Would you be aggressive on behalf of someone you doubt? Would you be aggressive on behalf of the person you think has bad records? Of course not!

Your accountant may think (or know) that you are a terrible record keeper. Most taxpayers who have *not* had this course are bad record keepers. Why? Lack of knowledge! Tax rules on the required records vary by the type of deduction, but by following the principles in this course, you will have the records you need that allow your accountant to be aggressive on your behalf. Further, this course shows you how to keep those records in a minimum of time (probably far less than you are spending right now).

Have you ever asked a question that seems ridiculous to your accountant? Have you ever asked a question that makes your accountant think you want to circumvent the system? Such questions make your accountant really nervous. This can happen when you have no desire whatsoever to do anything wrong, but the question makes it appear so. No longer. This course gives you a base of knowledge that allows you to ask your accountant questions that lead to results. You get the tax savings you deserve and your accountant is confident about "locking it in" for you—both of you are happy.

Get Started Now!

Don't waste a minute. Get started now! Put the CDs in your car or other listening device and start listening. You do not need the workbook with you. The CDs stand alone. You can listen anywhere, anytime.

The CDs allow you to skip and jump around to topics of particular interest to you. You can start anywhere, right now.

Listen to the CDs before watching the on-line video. Why? The on-line video is a supplement that shows you how to document various deductions discussed in the CDs. Think of the CDs as the meat of the course, with the book and on-line video as condiments that make everything taste better.

Okay! Stop reading now. Pop in the CDs and start protecting yourself with knowledge! Start making and saving money right this minute!

Section 2

Travel Rule Basics and How to Put Them to Work for You

Definition: Tax law allows you to deduct travel expenses incurred while away from home in pursuit of business.[1] If your trip required you to sleep or rest away from your principal place of business, you were away from home and in travel status.[2]

Example 1: Homer Correll drove 150 to 175 miles a day in his sales territory. He traveled no farther than 55 miles from his home. He left home at 5:00 a.m. and returned at 5:30 p.m. He tried to deduct breakfast and lunch as travel expenses. The Supreme Court said "no deductions" because Correll did not require sleep or rest.[3]

Example 2: Frederick Barry, a consulting engineer, traveled three states to service his clients. He left home at 6:30 a.m. and returned at midnight. For a break, he stopped in rest areas and closed his eyes for 15 to 20 minutes. No deduction! The Tax Court ruled that Barry's sleep did not add to his expense or put him in travel status to deduct his meal expenses.[4]

Pursuit of business: You pursue your business when you pursue your current livelihood. This requires much more effort than entering an activity to make a profit.[5] You travel in pursuit of your business when your travel is:
- Appropriate and helpful to the development and maintenance of your business[6]
- With the intent to secure a business benefit[7]
- Customary and usual within your business community[8]

When you travel in pursuit of your existing business needs, your travel is deductible immediately as a business expense.[9] The law allows the deduction for "carrying on" the business and thus presumes that the business already exists.

Two categories of expenses: Your travel expenses fall into-one of two categories:
1. Transportation-to-business-destination expenses
2. Business-day expenses

You pay airfare and car expenses to transport yourself to a business destination. While there, you incur business-day expenses like eating food and sleeping in a hotel. You may deduct food and lodging on business days, even when your trip does not include enough business days to make it a business trip.[10]

Example: Your trip from New York to Phoenix lasts five days. You work only one day. You may deduct the costs of food and lodging for the one day of work, but you deduct nothing for transportation.

Deductible Business Days Come from a Variety of Sources

Rule: For each business day of travel, you may deduct lodging, 50 percent of your meal costs, and incidentals.

Foreign rules are clear: Tax law contains clear examples of business days for foreign travel. Although the definitions for foreign deductions are generally stricter than those for domestic travel, they provide a definition guideline that is highly useful. Following are the stricter foreign travel definitions for business days.

Work days: You count as a business day any day during which your principal activity during normal business hours is the pursuit of business.[11] In other words, you must work more than half of the work day.

Tried-to-work days: You count as a business day any day when circumstances beyond your control prevented you from actively pursuing your business objective.[12]

Weekends, holidays, and standby days: Weekends, holidays, and other necessary standby days count as business days when sandwiched by business days during a trip you conduct with reasonable dispatch.[13] The weekend rule applies only where it would not be practical to return home from your business destination for the weekend because of time required or expense involved.

Saturday night travel: Airlines generally charge you less if you stay at your destination over a Saturday night. If you save money by staying over Saturday night, you count the stayover days as business days.[14]

Travel days: Travel days are business days.[15] To ensure business-day status, your total portal-to-portal in-transit and business activity time for the day should exceed four hours.

Deductible Methods of Transportation

Rule: You may transport yourself to and from a business destination by:[16]
- Automobile
- Airplane

- Train
- Boat

It makes no difference if your car is large or small, if you fly coach or first class, or if it is a private plane. Transportation costs are deductible in full, except for luxury boats.

Car strategy—transport family 300 miles toward business destination:
Consider driving your car on a combined business and pleasure trip. When you drive 300 miles in a direct route toward the destination, the day counts as a business day, just as it does for an IRS agent.[17] Therefore, you:
- Count the day as a business day to satisfy the 51/49 test.
- Deduct costs for sustaining life while on the road that day.

Meals and lodging expenses of family members other than the taxpayer do not qualify for deduction. If the cost of lodging is $80 for one person and $95 for the family, you deduct only $80.

Example: You put the family in the car and drive from Chicago to Washington, D.C., for a three-day convention. The drive takes two days each way. You spend 6 days sightseeing. Your trip is primarily business because you spent 7 of 13 days on business. You deduct:
- 100 percent of the transportation, and
- 7 days of sustaining business life on the road costs (for yourself only).

Big Changes in Cruise Ship Deduction Limits for 2016

Say you are going to travel to St. Thomas in the Virgin Islands for a one-day business seminar and you are considering two choices for transportation: airplane or cruise ship. If you travel by airplane, you deduct what you spend. If you travel by cruise ship, you may not deduct more than the luxury water-travel limits that apply for each day of your travel to St. Thomas.

In 2016, the luxury water-travel daily limit varies from a low of $688 to a high of $856.[18]

You can find the current per diem rates at www.gsa.gov/perdiem. For those who enjoy business travel aboard a cruise ship, find your daily luxury water-travel limit by doubling the highest rate of per diem in this publication for your days of travel.

In 2016, the highest daily per diem limit is $428 in Telluride, Colorado. Two times the $428 produces a 2016 luxury water-travel limit of $856 a day for travel from January through March 2016.

When to Deduct Transportation to a Travel Destination

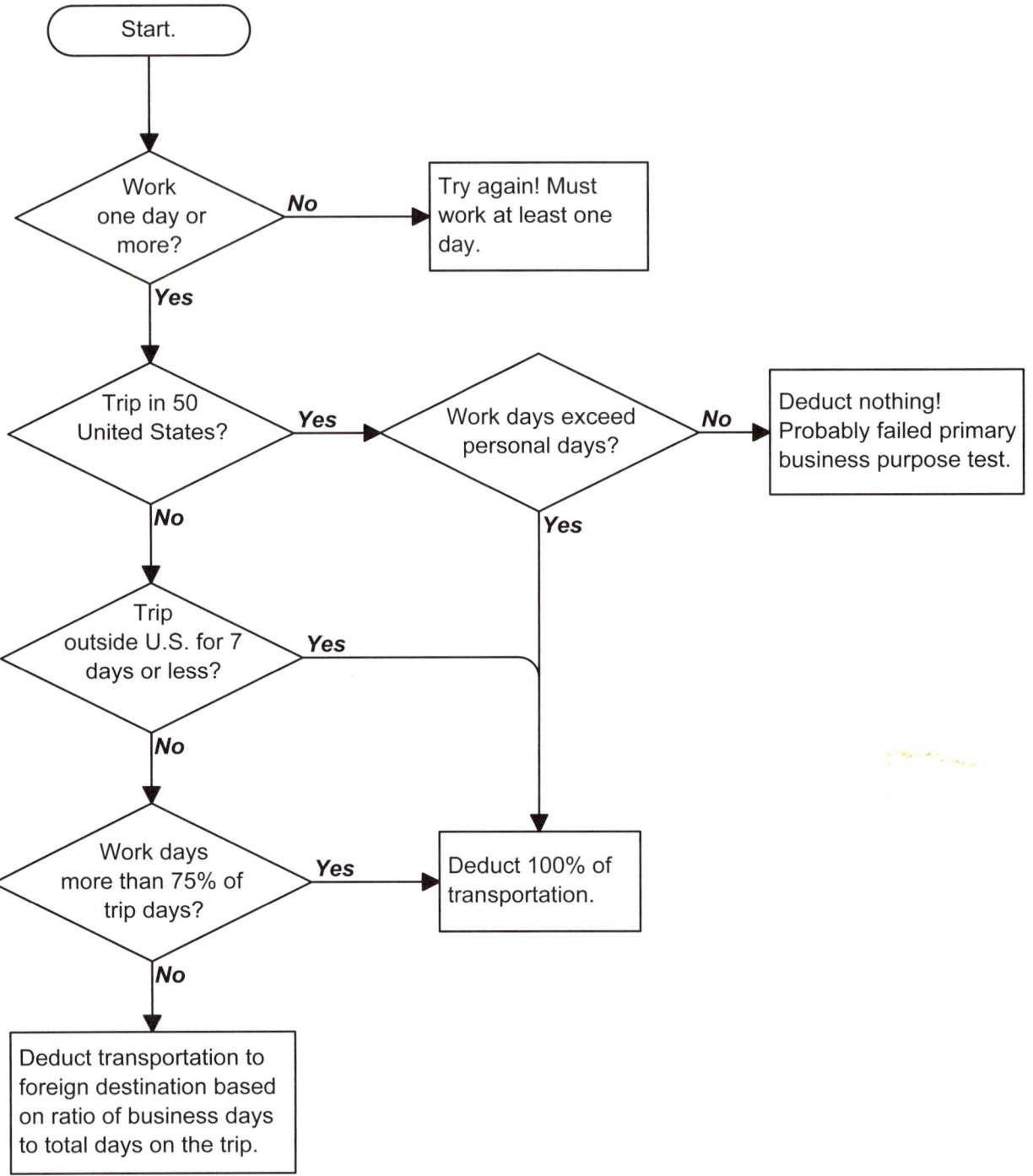

The following daily luxury water-travel limits apply in 2016. The IRS may adjust the rates for the last three months in its October 2016 revision of the per diem rates (see IRS publication 1542—this is simply a republication of the GSA rates cited earlier). If the rates change, an IRS transition rule allows you to choose the rates below or the updated rates. The current rates for 2016 are:
- $856 from 1/1 to 3/31 and 12/1 to 12/31[19]
- $752 from 4/1 to 4/30[20]
- $688 from 5/1 to 5/31[21]
- $700 from 6/1 to 8/31[22]
- $760 from 9/1 to 11/30[23]

Let's go back to your trip to St. Thomas. Say you're going to cruise to a seminar, attend the seminar, and cruise back. Let's assume that your cruise will take place in December and will take seven days. Your maximum write-off for your cruise ship business travel to and from the seminar is $5,992 per business traveler ($856 x 7 days).

Deduct Your Transportation Cost by Using the Trip-Day Rules

Rule: You deduct business transportation expenses to the extent that your trip passes a test for deducting transportation. See the flowchart at the left for an easy overview.

Work days exceed personal days: The work-days-exceed-personal-days (primary purpose) test applies to the costs of transporting yourself to and from a business destination within the 50 United States or the District of Columbia. Under this test, if you spend more days on business than you spend on pleasure, you deduct 100 percent of your transportation.[24] If your trip is not primarily business, you may deduct nothing for transportation.

Foreign-travel test: If more than 75 percent of your days are business days, you may deduct 100 percent of the costs of transporting yourself to a foreign destination. A foreign destination is outside the 50 United States and District of Columbia.[25] If you spend 75 percent or less of your days on business, you may deduct transportation expenses based on the ratio of business days to total trip days.[26]

Trip outside the U.S. for seven days or less: You may deduct 100 percent of the transportation to a foreign destination when your trip involves one business day and is less than seven days, excluding the day of departure.[27]

Notes

Think of the primary purpose test as the 51/49 test with 51 as the business part!

Notes

Reasons for Business Travel

Travel to start a new business: See the discussion in the start-up section of this program.

Travel for your hobby: Should you travel for your hobby, your expenses, including travel, may not exceed your income from the hobby.[28] Worse, you may not deduct any hobby losses—not in the current year or against income of a future year.[29]

Example: You raise dairy cows for a hobby. Your gross income from sales is $1,000. You spend $500 in interest to finance the cows and $900 to feed them. Your $400 loss is not deductible this year[30] or in any future year.[31]

Licenses in more than one state: See the discussion in Section 4 on how to treat two places of business.

Get educated out of town: You may deduct the travel costs necessary to obtain education or attend a meeting or convention.[32] Tax law does not require study in your backyard, even when the same courses are available there. The Senate noted that a French scholar may deduct his travel to study at the Sorbonne.[33] Similarly, a Texas professor deducted the costs of travel and living in Hawaii while studying for her Ph.D. in Hawaii.[34]

Meet with colleagues: You could travel to meet with colleagues in other parts of the country to learn new skills.

Job hunting trips: You want business deductions. Job hunting produces personal deductions, but when you are desperate, this beats nothing.

Deducting the cost of bringing your spouse to the convention: Tax law gives no deduction for travel of a spouse, dependent, or other individual accompanying the taxpayer on business travel unless:[35]
- The spouse, dependent, or other companion is an employee of the taxpayer
- The travel of the spouse, dependent, or other companion is for a bona fide business purpose
- Travel expenses of the spouse, dependent, or other person would otherwise be deductible

The law makes it clear that your spouse not only must be an employee, but also must travel for a bona fide business purpose. You get no travel deduction when you bring your spouse to:
- Be the socially gracious spouse[36]
- Staff the hospitality suite[37]
- Be the assigned fraternizer[38]
- Type notes, eat lunches and dinners[39]

The presence of your children at the travel site helps negate the business aspects of your spouse's travel.[40]

Videotapes at resorts: You get no deduction for a business seminar that gives you a videotaped lecture that you may watch at your convenience.[41] If you must watch the tape at the seminar or convention site, the videotape counts just as if you attended a live lecture.[42]

Observation: You obviously invite more scrutiny if you attend a resort-based session that consists solely or primarily of videotape.

Convention delegate: You may deduct the costs of attending a convention as a delegate if you can show that attendance advanced your personal business interests.[43]

Example: You attend the Toastmasters International convention as a delegate. You can prove that such attendance generated more revenue than you spent at the convention. You may deduct the costs.

Special Rules for Conventions

U.S. cruise ship conventions: You may deduct up to $2,000 for the cost of a cruise ship convention or meeting, provided:
- The meeting relates directly to the active conduct of your business.[44]
- The ship is a registered U.S. vessel.[45]
- All ports of call are in the United States or its possessions.[46]
- You attach written statements, signed by you and the program sponsor, to your tax return.[47]

North American conventions: You may not deduct a foreign convention unless it is as reasonable for the convention to be outside the United States as to be within the United States. "Reasonable" is the basic rule. Of course, the law contains exceptions! Convention trips to defined North American destinations do not have to pass the foreign trip reasonableness test.[48] The defined North American area includes:[49]
- American Samoa
- Antigua
- Aruba
- Bahamas
- Baker Island
- Barbados
- Barbuda
- Bermuda
- Canada
- Costa Rica

Notes

- Dominica
- Dominican Republic
- Grenada
- Guam
- Guyana
- Honduras
- Howland Island
- Jamaica
- Jarvis Island
- Johnston Island
- Kingman Reef
- Marshall Islands
- Mexico
- Micronesia
- Midway Islands
- Netherlands Antilles
- Northern Mariana Islands
- Palau
- Palmyra Atoll
- Panama
- Puerto Rico
- Trinidad and Tobago
- U.S. Virgin Islands
- USA
- Wake Island

Tax law treats travel to any North America location listed to the left under the same rules it applies to travel to Chicago (or any other U.S. destination).

To deduct a convention trip to the above destinations, you must make the trip during the ordinary and necessary course of your business. For example, you must have a business reason to attend the convention.

Foreign conventions: Tax law states:[50] "In the case of any individual who attends a convention, seminar, or similar meeting which is held outside the North American area, no deduction shall be allowed under Section 162 for expenses allocable to such meeting unless the taxpayer establishes that the meeting is directly related to the active conduct of his trade or business and that, after taking into account in the manner provided by regulations prescribed by the secretary:

1. the purpose of such meeting and the activities taking place at such meeting,
2. the purposes and activities of the sponsoring organization or groups,
3. the residences of the active members of the sponsoring organization and the places at which other meetings of the sponsoring organization or groups have been held or will be held, and
4. such other relevant facts as the taxpayer may present,

it is as reasonable for the meeting to be held outside the North American area as within the North American area."

Travel outside the North American area for sales dollars.

Technical note: The Senate committee report from which the foreign convention rules originate states: "The bill makes clear that the foreign convention provisions do not apply to normal business meetings for employees of a company."[51]

Applying the Rules to Some Example Trips

Example 1: You travel from Seattle to Miami Thursday, work Friday, stand by Saturday and Sunday, work Monday, and return home Tuesday. The six days qualify as business days. You deduct 100 percent of your transportation to and from Miami. You also deduct your costs of sustaining life for each of the six business days.

Example 2: Same as Example 1, except you vacation for four days at the end of your stay. Again, you deduct 100 percent of your transportation. You also deduct the same costs for the six business days. You do not deduct any costs for the four vacation days.

Example 3: You travel from Miami to Seattle Wednesday, work Thursday, layover Friday and Saturday to save travel costs with a lower airfare, and return home Sunday. You deduct 100 percent of your transportation. You also deduct your costs of sustaining life for each of the five days.

Example 4: You travel from San Diego to Philadelphia and spend 3 days working and 15 days playing. You deduct your costs of sustaining life for the three work days and nothing (zero, zip) for transportation.

Building Audit-Proof Support for Your Travel Deductions

Timely records required: Tax law effectively requires you to record travel expenditures "at or near the time" you incur the expenses.[52] Timely records have a "high degree of credibility not present with respect to a statement prepared subsequent thereto when generally there is a lack of accurate recall."[53]

Diary entries needed: Generally, when taxpayers lose court cases involving travel, they lack proper documentation, mainly entries in a diary.[54]

Notes

In other words, taxpayers not in control of meeting locations may deduct the costs of such meetings under the "not in my control" standard. (Document your work effort to ensure deductions.)

Diary Entry for a Travel Day

To do's	
2	
3	
4	
5	
6	
7	

Appointments		car miles	bi pc
7:00			
8:00	Meet with Sam Smith's office - dis-		
9:00	sect operations. Review observa-		
10:00	tions with Sam		
11:00			
12:00			
1:00			
2:00			
3:00			
4:00			
5:00			
6:00			
7:00			
8:00			
9:00			
10:00			

Business (b)	Total miles this day	
Investment (i)	Circle car driven this day 1 2 3	
Personal (p)	End Odometer	
Commuting (c)	Beg Odometer	
Total miles	Total miles	

TODAY'S ACTION
Action: Review monthly goals before making your to-do list!
Result: Your list will reflect the important things you need "to do" to realize your goals.

Copyright 1998 by W. Murray Bradford, CPA

Tax Diary System 1

Circle month of year and day of week
Jan Feb Mar Apr May Jun   Sun Mon Tue Wed
Jul Aug Sep Oct Nov Dec   Thu Fri Sat

CARS		Car 1 exp	
For each vehicle, enter all (100% of) monies spent for gas and oil, tires, insurance, car washes, repairs, and other out-of-pocket expenses.		Car 2 exp	
		Car 3 exp	
		Parking/tolls	
TRAVEL		Air/rail/boat	
Where (city)	Wash DC	Rental car/bus/taxi	57 00
Why (business reason)		Lodging	120 00
Learn Smith's business tactics		Tips, laundry, other	12 00
		Total trv day (no meals)	189 00
MEALS/ENTERTAINMENT/ETC		Trv brkfst	15 00
Who		Trv lunch	19 00
Where		Trv dinner	66 00
Why		Snacks/drinks	10 00
		Ent meals	
		Associated ent	
		Total trv meals & ent	110 00
		Presentation exp	
		Special sporting events (100%)	
MISCELLANEOUS		Supplies	
For Business Gifts To whom		Postage	
Why		Business gifts	
		Other	
		Other	
		Other	

What to write down: You must prove for each travel expenditure:[55]
1. Amount: Amount of each separate expenditure for traveling away from home, such as cost of transportation or lodging, except that daily cost of a traveler's own breakfast, lunch, dinner, and incidentals may be aggregated, if set forth in reasonable categories, such as meals, gas and oil, and taxi.
2. Time: Dates of departure and return for each trip away from home, and number of days away from home spent on business.
3. Place: Destination or locality of travel, described by name of city or town or other similar designation.
4. Business purpose: Business reason for travel or nature of the business benefit derived or expected.

See the entry on the left for an easy way to meet the requirements. Note the answers to the questions: Where (city)? Why (business reason)?

Receipts required: Tax law requires documentary evidence, such as receipts, paid bills, or similar evidence sufficient to support expenditures for:[56]
- Lodging
- Any expenditure of $75 or more

Hint: Keep receipts for all expenses and record the places where you eat the meals, e.g., hotel, McDonald's, etc.

Categories of travel: The IRS lists the following recognized categories of travel expenses:
- Meals and lodging, both en route and at the final work destination;[57]
- Transportation costs, including air, rail or bus fares, and the costs of transporting baggage, sample cases, or display materials;[58]
- The allocable portion of operating and maintenance expenses of automobiles, house trailers, and airplanes;[59]
- Cleaning and laundry;[60]
- Telephone;[61]
- Public stenographer costs;[62]
- Costs of transportation between an airport or station and hotel, from customer to customer, and from one place of business to another;[63] and
- Tips incidental to the above expenses.[64]

Cleaning and laundry: To deduct the cost of cleaning your clothes, you must get the clothes dirty while in travel status (out of town overnight).[65] The rules do not require that you get your travel clothes cleaned while out of town.

Notes

Endnotes–Section 2

1. IRC Section 162(a)(2).
2. Rev. Rul. 54-497; Rev. Rul. 75-432 as modified by Rev. Rul. 63-145, Rev. Rul. 75-169, and Rev. Rul. 76-453.
3. Homer O. Correll v U.S., 389 U.S. 299, rev'g CA-6, 68-1 USTC ¶9101.
4. Frederick J. Barry v Commr., CA-1 (aff'g TC per curiam), 71-1 USTC ¶9126 435 F2d 1290.
5. E.g. A.J. Whipple v Commr., Sct. - (vacating and rem'g CA-5), 63-1 USTC ¶9466; 373 U.S. 193; 83 Sct. 1168; Ct D 1882; 1963-2 CB 641.
6. Welch v Helvering, 290 U.S. 111, 113.
7. Interstate Drop Forge Co. v Commr., 326 F.2d 743 (7th Cir. 1964), aff'g T.C. Memo. 1963-149.
8. Welch v Helvering, 290 U.S. 111, 113.
9. IRC Section 162(a)(2).
10. Reg. Section 1.162-2(b)(1).
11. Reg. Section 1.274-4(d)(2)(iii).
12. Reg. Section 1.274-4(d)(2)(iv).
13. Reg. Section 1.274-4(d)(2)(v).
14. PLR 9237014.
15. Reg. Section 1.274-4(d)(2)(i).
16. IRS Pub. 463, Travel, Entertainment, and Gift Expenses.
17. 41 CFR 302-4.201
18. IRS Pub. 463, Travel, Entertainment, Gift, and Car Expenses.
19. U.S. General Services Administraton (GSA) Per Diem Rates for Fiscal 2016; $428 (per diem for Telluride, Colo.) x 2.
20. Ibid.; $376 (per diem for Key West. Fla.) x 2.
21. Ibid.; $344 (per diem for New York City) x 2.
22. Ibid.; $350 (per diem for Martha's Vineyard, Mass.) x 2.
23. Ibid.; $380 (per diem for New York City) x 2.
24. Reg. Section 1.162-2(b)(2).
25. IRC Section 274(c)(2)(b).
26. Reg. Section 1.274-4(g), Example 7.
27. IRC Section 274(c).
28. IRC Section 183.
29. IRC Section 183(b).
30. Reg. Section 1.183-1(b)(3) Example (1).
31. IRC Section 183(a) and (b).
32. IRC Section 274(h); Reg. Section 1.162-5(e)(1).
33. S. Rep. No 313, 99th Cong., 2d Sess. 75 (1986).
34. Johnson v Commr., T.C. Memo. 1988-177.
35. IRC Section 274(m)(3).
36. Marion T. Weatherford v Commr., CA-9 (rev'g and rem'g DC) 69-2 USTC ¶9723 418 F2d 895.
37. Grace Shantz Est. v Commr., T.C. Memo. 1983-743.
38. David J. Hosbein v Commr., T.C. Memo. 1985-373.
39. Rev. Rul. 56-128.
40. Charles R. Hefti v Commr., T.C. Memo. 1988-22.
41. Conf. Rep. No. 841, 99th Cong., 2d Sess. 31, 32.
42. Ibid.
43. Rev. Rul. 59-316; Rev. Rul. 63-266.
44. IRC Section 274(h)(2).
45. IRC Section 274(h)(2)(A).
46. IRC Section 274(h)(2)(B).
47. IRC Section 274(h)(5).
48. Rev. Rul. 94-56.
49. Rev. Rul. 2011-26.
50. IRC Section 274(h).
51. S. Rep. No. 1031, 96th Cong., 2d Sess. 11.
52. IRC Section 274.
53. Reg. Section 1.274-5T(c)(1).
54. See, e.g., Tyler v Commr., T.C. Memo 1982-160; McDougal v Commr., T.C. Memo 1980-289.
55. Reg. Section 1.274-5T(b)(2).
56. IR-95-56; $25 before September 30, 1995, per Reg. Section 1.274-5(c)(2)(iii).
57. Reg. Section 1.162-2(a).
58. IRS Pub. 463 Travel, Entertainment, and Gift Expenses.
59. For autos and house trailers, see IRS Pub. 463 Travel, Entertainment, and Gift Expenses. For airplanes, see Hitchcock v U.S., 12 AFTR 2d 5801 (E.D. Wash. 1963); Gibson Products Co. v Commr., 8 TC 654 (1947), acq., 1947-2 C.B. 2.
60. Rev. Rul. 63-145, 1963-2 C.B. 86.
61. Reg. Section 1.162-2(a).
62. Reg. Section 1.162-2(a).
63. IRS Pub. 463, Travel, Entertainment, and Gift Expenses.
64. IRS Pub. 463, Travel, Entertainment, and Gift Expenses.
65. Rev. Rul. 63-145.

Section 3

Paying Mom and Dad or Friends or Relatives for Business Lodging at Their Homes

You travel on business to the city where your mother and father live. Can you stay with mom and dad and then count that day as a deductible business travel day even if you do not have a lodging receipt? Can you take your mom and dad to dinner and deduct the dinner as a cost of lodging? Can you pay your mom and dad for your night's lodging and deduct that payment? This section shows you the best financial result for both you and your mom and dad.

If you stay with mom and dad and do not pay them for the stay, you still have a deductible travel day for your other expenses. Further, you do not need to jump through any special hoops to support your trip. You will probably already have a plane ticket, fees paid for seminars and meetings, rental car, etc., that help support your stay in town.

Should you stay at mom's and dad's for free and then take them to dinner as a repayment for free lodging, you obviously have a business reason for the entertainment. Should the dinner cost less than the value of the lodging, the dinner should be deductible as business entertainment.

The best strategy is the rental strategy. Tax law ignores the rental of a principal home when the rental days during a tax year total less than 15 days.[1] Thus, your mom and dad could collect up to 14 days of rental income and report zero rental income subject to income tax. Is this good, or is this good!

Make sure you pay a "fair rent" to your mom and dad for the period of your stay. Without a fair rent, the IRS could disallow the transaction as a sham.

Perhaps there are some hotels and motels near your parents' home. You might collect hotel rate sheets and make copies for your mom and dad (think evidence here). The rates should be for accommodations similar to those you experience when staying with your mom and dad. Photos of mom's and dad's guest room and maybe a brochure with pictures from the hotel can make great evidence in your tax file.

Notes

With respect to your trip, you may deduct your cost of lodging when you have a business day.[2] Business days include not only days when you attend seminars, but also those days between meetings when it is more cost-effective to stay where you are than to return home.

Regardless of where you stay on a trip, tax law requires receipts for all lodging deductions, no matter the cost.[3] If you pay mom and dad, you need to obtain a receipt. This does not need to be formal: a simple handwritten receipt can do just fine.

Say that during the year you stay at your mom's and dad's home for 11 nights while visiting town on business. Based on evidence, you can prove that mom's and dad's guest room is about equal to the motel down the street that rents for $119 a night. If you pay mom and dad $119 a night for 11 nights, you may deduct the $1,309 you paid for lodging.

Your mom and dad collect the $1,309 as tax-free income because they rented their home for less than 15 days during the tax year. The rules state that they do not have to report the $1,309 in rent receipts to the IRS.

However, there is some required paperwork. Even though mom and dad do not pay taxes on this rental income, they will list the rent from the IRS Form 1099 on their tax return. In this case, you have to give your mom and dad an IRS Form 1099 for the rents.[4] Tax law says that when you pay business rents of $600 or more to an individual during a tax year, you must report the total of those business rents to the IRS.[5]

If your parents get an IRS Form 1099 for rental income, you know that the IRS expects to find that number in their tax return. Do not let your parents disappoint the IRS! Mom and dad should report the rental income from the Form 1099 on their Schedule E for the year. Then, because the amount is not taxable, they should subtract that amount in the expense section of Schedule E and add a supporting statement that states: "Taxpayers rented their personal residence for less than 15 days during the tax year. Such rent is exempt from tax under IRC Section 280A."

Endnotes–Section 3

[1] IRC Section 280A(g)(2).

[2] Reg. Section 1.162-2(a).

[3] Reg. Section 1.274-5T(c)(2)(iii)(A).

[4] Reg. Section 1.6041-1(a)(2).

[5] IRC Section 6041(a

Section 4

How to Treat Two Regular Places of Business

Florida in the Winter and Wisconsin in the Summer

If you have two or more regular places of business, your tax home is at your principal place of business.[1] You may deduct expenses traveling to discharge duties at your non-principal place of business.[2]

Example: Your tax home is in Wisconsin. You may deduct as a business expense your three-month stay to work at your secondary location in Florida.

The location of your principal place of business is a question of fact; important factors include:[3]
- Total time ordinarily spent at each business post
- Degree of business activity at each post
- Financial return attributable to each post

Example: Your nine-month stay in Wisconsin generates 70 percent of your gross income and 72 percent of your total financial return from all endeavors. Your tax home is in Wisconsin.

When you travel away from home overnight on business, you need to keep a good diary book. Records you keep must prove amounts, time, place, and business purposes for travel expenditures.[4]

You do not need receipts for travel expenses less than $75, provided such expenses are not for lodging.[5]

Our new, friendly IRS says that a log maintained weekly, which accounts for use during the week, is a record made at or near the time of such use.[6] By keeping the weekly record, you meet the IRS test for maintaining a diary, travel log, trip sheet, or similar documentation while you have current knowledge of your travel expenditures.[7]

You have to love this simple set of rules for running businesses in more than one location. As they say, location is everything.

Notes

Endnotes–Section 4

1. Revenue rulings 93-86 and 75-432; Markey v Commr., 490 F. 2d 1249 (6 Cir. 1974).
2. IRC Section 162(a)(2).
3. Revenue ruling 54-147.
4. IRC Section 274(d).
5. Regulation Section 1.274-5(c)(2)(iii).
6. Regulation Section 1.274-5T(c)(2)(ii)(A).
7. Ibid.

Section 5

Entertainment Not Subject to the 50 Percent Cut

Special Sporting Events

Special "sporting event" tax rules: If it qualifies as deductible entertainment, you may deduct 100 percent of the cost of tickets to a sporting event that benefits a charity, if the event:[1]
- Is organized for the primary purpose of benefiting the charity
- Gives the entire net proceeds to the charity
- Uses volunteers to perform substantially all of the event's work

Deduct the works: The deduction includes the cost of the ticket package, including amounts spent for:[2]
- Seating
- Use of entertainment areas
- Contestant positions
- Meals furnished at or as part of the event
- Parking

Golf tournament example: You buy four tickets to the Booz Allen Classic golf tournament in Washington, D.C. You use the tickets to take three clients and yourself. You discuss business during lunch. That discussion qualifies the entertainment as a deduction under the "associated entertainment" rules. You may deduct 100 percent because:
- The tournament donates its net proceeds to charity.
- The tournament uses 1,200 volunteers and only 5 paid employees (volunteers do substantially all the work).
- The tournament is organized by the PGA tour for the primary purpose of benefiting 501(c)(3) charities.

Charity golf outing example: You play in a golf event where the net proceeds of the tournament go to your church. You buy two $150 tickets, one for you and one for your business prospect. The church sends you a notice that, of the $150, $110 goes for greens fees, carts, prizes, etc., and your deduction is only $40. How much can you deduct for the two tickets?

Result 1: If you do not have a business discussion with your business prospect over breakfast, lunch, or dinner, you deduct $80 as a charitable contribution.

Result 2: If you have a substantial and bona fide business discussion and the golf qualifies as associated entertainment, you deduct $300—the full ticket price. Also, this golf event qualifies for an exemption from the percentage reduction in entertainment expenses (currently 50 percent).

Notes

Planning note: Charity golf for business produces double the deductions of regular business golf (100 percent versus 50 percent).[3] Also, the full deduction applies to the full ticket package, including related services such as parking, use of entertainment areas, contestant positions, and meals furnished as part of the event.[4]

Planning tip: Make sure you identify the $300 deduction to your accountant as not subject to the 50 percent rule. Otherwise, your accountant will put the $300 in the spot where he or she automatically cuts it with the 50 percent rule.

Party With Your Employees for 100 Percent

Employee recreation produces 100 percent deductions not subject to the 50 percent rule on entertainment: Tax law does not apply the 50 percent entertainment rule to recreational expenses for employees.[5] In most cases, your deductible entertainment is cut by 50 percent when you file your tax return. The 50 percent rule does not apply to recreational expenses for employees.

Cruises for employees: American Business Service Corporation, a Southern California temporary employment agency, has about 100 employees. On 41 occasions during the year, the corporation charters a 53-foot powerboat for one-day recreational cruises for its employees.

The boat can safely and comfortably accommodate about 30 people. Employees, owners, and executives who want to play on the boat for a day have to sign up in advance. This is a "first-come, first-served" event.

The corporation has one central office and about 25 branch offices, located primarily in central and southern California. The corporation's "ordinary and necessary" business purpose for the cruises is to bring together and create social interaction among its
- branch employees,
- central office employees,
- managers, and
- executive employees.

During a recent year, the corporation paid $41,000 for 41 excursions. The court ruled that the corporation could deduct all of the $41,000, without worrying about the 50 percent cut for entertainment, because the cruises[6]
- were primarily for the employees,
- did not discriminate in favor of the owners and highly compensated employees,
- were documented as to who cruised and when,
- passed the ordinary and necessary business purpose test,
- were exempt from the 50 percent cut in entertainment rule, and
- were exempt from the directly related entertainment rule.

Primarily for employees: To qualify for the 100 percent deduction, the recreation, the recreational event or facility must primarily benefit your employees, other than those who
- own 10 percent or more of the business, or
- are in the highly compensated group.

10 percent test: For purposes of the 10 percent test, an employee is treated as owning any interest owned by a member of his or her family. The family includes brothers and sisters, spouse, ancestors (like parents and grandparents), and lineal descendants (like children and grandchildren).[7]

Technical note: American Business Service Corporation won its deductions for the cruises because it could prove that it conducted the cruises primarily for the benefit of its employees and that it did not discriminate in favor of 10 percent owners or highly compensated employees.

Highly compensated employees are those employees who during the current or preceding year[8]
- own 5 percent or more of the business,
- receive pay greater than $120,000 and rank by pay in the top 20 percent of all paid employees, or
- are officers of the corporation.

Primary: In tax law, the term "primary" or "primarily" means "more than 50 percent."[9] For employee recreation, that means the rank-and-file employees have to use the facility more than 50 percent of the time. You could measure this by days of use, time of use, or any other reasonable method.

How McReavy got a zero deduction: In *McReavy*,[10] a corporation owned by William and Kathleen McReavy owned a one-bedroom lake cabin on a four-acre island in Minnesota. The McReavys often had deductible business parties for their friends at this cabin. They also, supposedly, made this lake cabin available to their employees and claimed that the cabin was a recreational facility primarily for the benefit of the employees. However, the employees seldom used this cabin and that limited use caused loss of the recreational facility deductions.

Those McReavy employees who did use the island cabin had to agree that they would help maintain it. During the summer months, some employees visited the property every other week to perform maintenance, mow the grass, and water the flowers. On two or three occasions over a two-year period, the McReavys invited employees to the cabin for a steak fry.

The court noted that, other than those occasional steak fries and whatever minor recreational use might have been enjoyed while carrying out maintenance assignments, the McReavy employees did not use the property for recreational purposes during the years at issue. Therefore, the court denied the

Notes

Notes

McReavy deduction for its employee recreational facility because the cabin was used primarily by the owners of the corporation.

Court's rationale: The court noted that "actual use of the facility" controls this deduction, not availability of the cabin for employee use.

What do you do? What things do you do, or could you do, primarily for the benefit of your employees? Remember, primary means more than 50 percent. Say you have a beach home. Say that, during the year, your employees use the beach home on more days than you use the beach home. Presto, with an ordinary business-use reason, you have a beach-home deduction on your Schedule C. That's the beauty of the 50 percent test—you can measure it directly. The law contemplates that your recreational activities for your employees will include things like Christmas parties, annual picnics, summer outings, and facilities for the employees like swimming pools, baseball diamonds, bowling alleys, and golf courses.

Your ordinary and necessary business reason: You must have an ordinary and necessary business reason for your partying with the employees. The phrase "ordinary and necessary" has a specialized definition in tax law, and one that you will like. Here is what the court said about the terms "ordinary and necessary" in the Capital Video case.[11]

The term "necessary" imposes "only the minimal requirement that the expense be "appropriate and helpful" for "the development of the [taxpayer's] business." An expense need not be recurring in order to be considered ordinary.

There are many cases that use similar definitions, but the bottom line is that "ordinary and necessary" is easy. Even though it's easy, it requires action. Think about your ordinary and necessary reason and document it.
Your reason might be as simple as improving employee morale and binding employees to your business because you offer more fun and better working conditions than the competition. Obviously, that's what the law had in mind when it named the summer picnic as a deductible employee party.

The Making-Presentations Exception Grants 100-Percent Deductions for Entertainment

Example 1: In Matlock, the court ruled that Matlock could deduct 100 percent of the refreshments he served to prospects during sales seminars he conducted in his home.[12] The court concluded that the refreshments were a cost of his sales seminar and not entertainment. Matlock sold solar heating and cooling systems. He installed a unit in his home. He used the sales seminars in his home to show the system. Because the meals were integral to the sales presentation, the court ruled that Matlock could avoid the 50 percent reduction. Thus, Matlock deducted 100 percent of the meal costs as business promotional expenses.

Example 2: IRS regulations state that the cost of a fashion show is not entertainment when put on by a manufacturer of dresses for its prospective store buyers.[13] On the other hand, the IRS notes that the appliance distributor who conducts a fashion show for the wives of his retailers incurs entertainment expenses.[14]

Example 3: The IRS says that although attending a theatrical performance is generally entertainment, this is not true for a professional theater critic who attends in his or her professional capacity.[15]

Example 4: In a private ruling, the IRS concluded that the taxpayer who provided free dinners to his prospects before his sales presentations incurred 100 percent deductible costs, not costs subject to the 50 percent limit.[16] In this ruling, the taxpayer earned commissions on his sales of real property. He invited prospects to a free dinner, after which he made his sales presentations. The IRS concluded that the meals were associated with the taxpayer's business, but not subject to the ceiling on entertainment deductions.

Example 5: In its explanation of the entertainment rules, the Senate noted that the cost of food served by a wine merchant to show how wines are suitable for particular meals does not incur entertainment expenses but regular promotional expenses.[17]

Do I Have to Invite the General Public?

In Matlock, the court ruled that Robert Matlock incurred presentation expenses and not entertainment expenses at the solar heating and cooling seminars he conducted in his home.[18] At these presentations, Matlock had food and beverages. He found his customers in various ways, including telemarketing. We assume that he sold to anyone he could find (i.e., the public).

In Matlock, the court stated that its task was to decide whether the solar energy sales talks at Matlock's home were entertainment. The court concluded that the talks were not entertainment but presentations. The court said Matlock's talks were like the IRS regulation example in which the manufacturer of dresses does not entertain when he conducts fashion shows to introduce his products to groups of store buyers.

In Private Letter Ruling 9414040, a real estate broker provided free meals to prospects who attended his sales presentations. The attendees entered drawings at trade shows, conventions, and the state fair. The broker then used telemarketing to invite the prospects to the free dinners. The IRS ruled that the dinners were not entertainment subject to the limit but rather were 100 percent deductible (like Matlock's presentation expenses).

Notes

In this ruling, the IRS cited the example in which a wine merchant has a wine tasting that includes both the wines and the foods that show the suitability of each wine for particular meals.

In both Matlock and the IRS ruling, the taxpayers were marketing to the general public. So first you will have to say that you make your presentations to the general public. If your audience is made up of relatives and close friends, they are not the public; but if your audience is made up of prospects and customers with whom you have no personal relationship, they are obviously the public.

Cruise Ship Entertainment

If the cruise line breaks out the cost of meals and entertainment from the other costs of the cruise, you have to apply the 50 percent cut to those meals before you apply the daily limits to the trip.[19] That's the bad news.

The good news is that if the cruise ship fare does not break out the costs of meals and entertainment, you deduct 100 percent of your cruise ship fare up to the amount of the daily limits.

Line of attack. Cruise only on cruise ships that do not break out the costs of meals and entertainment.

Endnotes–Section 5

1. IRC Section 274(l).
2. P.L. 99-514, H.R. 3838, 99th Cong., General Explanation Prepared by the Staff of the Joint Committee on Taxation, 55-70 (May 4, 1987).
3. IRC Section 274(n)(2)(C).
4. P.L. 99-514, H.R. 3838, 99th Cong., General Explanation Prepared by the Staff of the Joint Committee on Taxation, 55-70 (May 4, 1987).
5. IRC Sections 274(n)(2); 274(e)(v).
6. American Business Service Corporation v Commr., 93 T.C. No. 36 (October 3, 1989).
7. Reg. Section 1.267(c)-1(a)(4).
8. IRC Section 414(q); IRS News Release 2015-118 (adjusted for inflation for 2016).
9. For example, see Revenue Ruling 63-144, Questions and Answers 60 through 66.
10. William L. McReavy et ux. v Commr., T.C. Memo. 1989-172.
11. Capital Video Corporation v Commr., 90 AFTR 2d 2002-7429 (CA1) November 27, 2002.
12. Robert Matlock v Commr., T.C. Memo 1992-324.
13. Reg. Section 1.274-2(b)(1)(ii).
14. Ibid.
15. Ibid.
16. Plr 9414040.
17. S. Rep. No. 313, 99th Cong., 2nd Sess., 72 (1986), 1986-3 (Vol. 3) C.B. 1, 72.
18. Robert Matlock v Commr., T.C. Memo. 1992-324. The court stated that, unlike sales seminars in the home, a restaurant meal is generally considered entertainment. Private Letter Ruling 9414040 makes no such distinction, and the meals in this ruling appear to take place in a restaurant. Thus, we do not think a restaurant meal destroys the ability to make a presentation.
19. Notice 87-23.

Section 6

Strategies to Capture More Entertainment Deductions

Deduct "Dutch Treat" Business Entertainment

General Dutch treat rule: IRS regulations state that the taxpayer may deduct entertainment "even though the expenditure relates to the taxpayer alone."[1] The IRS says its objective test precludes arguments that "entertainment" means only entertainment of others.[2] Further, the IRS acknowledges that business entertainment may include an activity that satisfies a personal, family, or living expense.[3] The IRS notes that an individual in business may deduct the entertainment cost, including his personal benefit, as a business expense.[4]

Example: Wilson and Jones go to lunch to discuss prospecting methods. The lunch costs $32. Wilson pays his $16 share. Jones pay his $16 share. Both Wilson and Jones may deduct their $16 shares.

Urbauer case: Charles Urbauer used both the "directly related" and the "associated" entertainment rules to further his business, play golf, and bowl. Urbauer, an eight-handicap golfer, waited on the first tee for prospects to arrive, played golf with them, and then discussed business over drinks and dinner. He achieved deductions for both the golf and the dinners.[5] The dinners met the "directly related" test because he actively pursued future benefit over dinner. His golf occurred on the same day. He did not pay either for the others to play golf or for their dinners. The court also allowed Urbauer to deduct his bowling league fees.

O'Donoghue case: Laurie O'Donoghue sold commodities. After work, she and her colleagues stopped by the local pub to down a few drinks and talk about the market. Sometimes they had dinner later. O'Donoghue claimed $6,500 for expenses, including taxi fares. O'Donoghue made a tragic mistake in recording her business entertainment: she did not always write down the business reason for the entertainment (remember—note "future business"). The court allowed her Dutch treat drinks and meals to the extent she met the five elements of support.[6]

Notes

Frequent Lunches with Office Manager

Can you take your office manager to lunch four times a week and deduct them?

No, you violate the "too many lunches" rule. In your case, you are absorbing too much of your personal, family, and living expenses by having too many of these lunches.

You are like Richard Hankenson, MD, who had 174 lunches with his staff and other doctors. The court ruled that the lunches were personal.[7]

The IRS may invoke the Sutter Rule (named after this taxpayer) if it believes you are having too many business meals that absorb your otherwise personal living expenses.[8]

As a rule of thumb, limit your entertainment for a single person to 30 times or less during a year. Call this the tax-strategies-gut-check rule for entertainment with the same person. Also, you'll want to follow our other gut-check rule of no more than 100 deductible breakfasts, 100 deductible lunches, and 100 deductible dinners per year.

Deduct the Cost of Entertaining Closely Connected Spouses and Family Members

Deductions for spouses: If you bring your spouse to the entertainment and you meet the rules for deducting the entertainment with a business discussion, you may deduct your cost and the cost for your spouse.[9] The rules clearly state that entertainment associated with the taxpayer's active conduct of business may include deductions for those "closely connected" with the taxpayer.[10] The IRS says your spouse is closely connected![11] Thus, should you and your spouse entertain another couple and should you meet the rules for business discussion, you may deduct the costs of entertaining the spouses.[12]

Closely connected rule restated: If entertainment of a business guest qualifies as "directly related entertainment," the "closely connected" rule allows you to deduct the costs of entertaining the spouses.[13]

Other closely connected persons: The IRS states that the same rule applies to all who are closely connected, but it fails to specify other possibilities, such as children, Mom and Dad, and significant others.[14] The IRS does include "family" in its definition of entertainment, and thus it seems reasonable to consider children and other family members as closely connected under the proper circumstances.[15]

Do Not Entertain for Goodwill Reasons

Goodwill entertainment not deductible: Auto Zapper & Towing, Inc., repossessed autos, boats, and motor homes. Auto Zapper got its business from various financial institutions. To promote its business, Zapper chartered three buses to transport its employees and their prospects from Los Angeles to Las Vegas for a weekend of gambling. Zapper provided refreshments during the five-hour trip and paid the hotel bills for all participants.

The trip had a significant upward impact on Zapper's business. One bank supervisor testified that his employees liked the trip enough to want to give Zapper the bulk of the bank's repossession activity. During the trip, the buses stopped twice so that Zapper employees could switch buses and mingle more.

Zapper claimed $9,300 as its deduction for the trip. The court ruled that the expenses passed Test One because they were ordinary and necessary. But then the court ruled that the expenses failed Test Two because there were no "directly related" business discussions. The employees did not write down what they discussed with whom during the trip. The court ruled that the $9,300 was nondeductible "goodwill" entertaining because there was no business discussion before or after the goodwill entertainment.[16]

Planning tip: Make your goodwill entertainment "associated entertainment" with meetings or discussions that precede or follow the entertainment.

Deduct Season Ticket Cost Based on Ticket Use

Season ticket rule: When you hold season or series tickets to events, like the home games of the baseball team, you treat each ticket as a separate item, and deduct the tickets based on how you used the tickets.[17]

Example: You buy four season tickets to the eight scheduled games (32 tickets). You and your spouse take the Nelsons to the first game after a business discussion at dinner. The cost of the four tickets is deductible as entertainment associated with the directly related business dinner.

Give Gifts of Entertainment to Avoid $25 Cap on Gifts

Gift versus entertainment rule: For business gifts, you may deduct up to $25 a person a year.[18] For entertainment, you may deduct whatever the

Notes

entertainment rules allow, like 50 percent of the amount spent for a business meal.[19] If you give your ticket to a prospect and do not accompany the recipient to the entertainment, you may treat the cost of an admission ticket as either a gift or an entertainment expense.[20]

Example: You give season tickets to the ballet to a new client. You may deduct the $275 cost of the tickets as entertainment.

Rebates: See the section on rebates for a complete discussion of this topic.

Deduct the Cost of Entertaining Prospects and Clients in Your Home

Home entertainment rule: The law contains no special rules for home entertainment. You may deduct directly related home entertainment. You may deduct associated home entertainment. In other words, the business discussion must take place either in your home or within 24 hours of the home entertainment.

Example: You invite Mr. and Mrs. Johnson to dinner to ask them for referrals. Your grocery and beverage bills total $120. You may deduct the $120 cost for entertaining Mr. and Mrs. Johnson, your spouse, and yourself.

Receipts required: You need receipts to support home entertainment expenses of $75 or more. You could make separate purchases of your business groceries. You also could circle the business items on a combined business and personal grocery receipt.

Deduct the Cost of Small Dinner Parties in Your Home

Dinner party rules: The IRS presumes a social gathering with little or no possibility of business discussion when you have a large group gathered in your home.[21] You can use directly related business discussions to overcome the no-business presumption.[22]

Example: You invite seven couples to your home for dinner. You have directly related business discussions with five couples. Include yourself, and then deduct 6/8 of the cost.

Deduct the Cost of Large Parties

Planning tip: See the section in this book on presentation expenses on how to make large meetings 100 percent deductible and not subject to the 50 percent cut that applies to entertainment.

The IRS notes that you do not meet the "directly related" test in settings where it is impossible to have meaningful business discussions.[23] This clearly applies where the distractions are substantial, such as when the meetings or discussions occur at nightclubs, theaters, sporting events, cocktail parties, or social gatherings.

The IRS cites Israelson[24] as an example of how to disallow a deduction. Israelson, a lawyer, gave a party at the country club. He invited clients, referral sources, colleagues, and other business associates. He discussed no business at the party. The court ruled that Israelson gets no deduction for the party.

Big NO-NO: You may not deduct the cost of a party to build goodwill.[25]

Rule: You may deduct the cost of a large party when:
- The cost is not lavish or extravagant.[26]
- You meet the "directly related" or "associated" standard for business guests.[27]
- You have the party for employees.[28] (Note—employee parties are 100 percent deductible.)
- There is a proper allocation of costs to business and personal guests.[29]
- There are receipts, invoices, canceled checks, and charge-card slips to support monies spent.[30]

Big hurdle: Your primary motivation for the party must be future business.[31] You automatically get credit for future business motivation for the employees you invite to the party.[32]

Solution: Make your home a clear business setting for the Christmas party. You do this when you:[33]
- Let attendees know that you are directly furthering your business
- Display your products
- Discuss your products
- Have as your clear purpose business publicity rather than goodwill

Example: You sell insurance for a living. On a bulletin board near the bar, you post product broadsides and other descriptions of IRAs, private pensions, insurance, etc. You discuss the products with anyone who has questions. The bulletin board display establishes a clear business setting and sets the stage for making a large party deductible.

Notes

Building proof: You help prove active business pursuit when your invitation contains your business name and states something like: "Please come for holiday cheer and help me celebrate 15 years in the insurance business." Take photos of attendees viewing that bulletin board covered with your product brochures. Take candid shots of attendees viewing other product literature. Process your film or digital images at a store where they stamp the date processed on the side or back of the photo. Next, jot down in your diary as many business conversations as you can remember from the party. Finally, keep receipts for the costs of the party. If you bought both business and personal groceries, circle the business items on the receipt and keep it.

Like You, Tiger Woods May Not Deduct His Golf-Club and Similar Dues

In *Garcia*,[34] the court stated, "No one, including golf professionals or instructors, may deduct club dues" (dues paid to a private country club). In other words, not even Tiger Woods may deduct his country club dues.

In tax law, we call this "overkill". In 1993, when lawmakers were attempting to balance the budget by finding more tax money, they decided that they could get some easy cash by eliminating the club dues deduction. Rather than allow any bona fide business use of clubs or consider any type of fairness or equity, lawmakers instead opted for what they called "strict nondeductibility," regardless of circumstances.[35]

Therefore, the law says that dues paid to a private country club are not deductible, period. No business reason overcomes this no-deduction-under-any-circumstances rule.

Planning note: The no-deduction-under-any-circumstances rule applies to membership in any club organized for pleasure, recreation, or other social purpose. The purposes and activities of a club, and not its name, determine whether it is organized for pleasure, recreation, or other social purpose. Clubs organized for pleasure, recreation, or other social purposes include, but are not limited to,[36]
- country clubs,
- golf and athletic clubs,
- airline clubs,
- hotel clubs, and
- luncheon and dinner clubs.

Exceptions: In general, the law does not consider the following clubs as organized for pleasure, recreation, or other social purposes:[37]

- business leagues,
- trade associations,
- chambers of commerce,
- boards of trade,
- real estate boards,
- professional organizations (such as bar associations and medical associations), and
- civic or public service organizations.

Are Dues to the Shriners or Masons Deductible?

Good question! Neither the law nor the regulations provide a definitive answer. In its preamble to the regulations, the IRS states that the rules that disallow deductions for club dues do not apply to the Kiwanis, Lions, Rotary, or Civitan.[38] The preamble goes on to state the general rule that you may not deduct club dues paid to any membership organization, a principal purpose of which is to conduct entertainment activities for its members.[39]

Thus, are the Shriners and Masons like the Kiwanis, Lions, Rotary, or Civitan? If you can say "yes" to this question, you probably qualify for a deduction. Next, do the Shriners or Masons have a purpose of entertainment that is greater than the Kiwanis, Lions, Rotary, or Civitan? If no, then you probably qualify for a deduction.

Your Shriners or Masons club dues are one of those deductions where you have to use judgment until you can find precedent.

Deduct Expenses to Entertain Clients on Boats

General rule: When you entertain on your boat, you may deduct only the out-of-pocket expenses.[40] Examples include the money you spend for:
- Gas and oil
- Food and beverages

You may not deduct any slip rental fees, maintenance, or depreciation on the boat.[41] Tax law treats the boat as an "entertainment facility" and disallows all boat expenses.[42]

Planning tip: Use the boat (like a car) primarily for transportation and you do not trigger the entertainment-facility rules on the transportation part. See the entertainment-facility section for more rules on how to make entertainment facilities deductible.

Endnotes–Section 6

1. Reg. Section 1.274-2(b)(1)(ii).
2. Ibid.
3. Reg. Section 1.274-2(b)(1)(i).
4. Ibid.
5. Charles F. Urbauer, T.C. Memo. 1992-170.
6. James M. O'Donoghue, 47 T.C.M. 1563 (1984).
7. Richard Hankenson v Commr., T.C. Memo. 1984-200.
8. Richard Sutter v Commr., (1953) 21 TC 170, acq; see also, Harry LaForge v Commr. (1970, CA2) 26 AFTR 2d 70-5768, 434 F2d 370, 70-2 USTC ¶9694.
9. Rev. Rul. 63-144, 1963-2 C.B. 129, questions 18 and 19.
10. Reg. Section 1.274-2(d)(4).
11. Ibid.
12. Ibid.
13. Reg. Section 1.274-2(d)(4).
14. Reg. Section 1.274-2(d)(2), (4).
15. Reg. Section 1.274-2(b)(1)(i).
16. Auto Zapper & Towing, Inc. v Commr., T.C. Memo. 1992-662.
17. Rev. Proc. 63-4, 1963-1, C.B. 474, Q&A 17.
18. IRC Section 274(b).
19. IRC Section 274(n).
20. Reg. Section 1.274-2(b)(1)(iii)(b)(2).
21. Reg. Section 1.274-2(d)(3)(i)(a).
22. Howard v Commr., T.C. Memo 1981-250.
23. 60IRS Market Segment Specialization Program Paper, Attorneys, Training 3149-102, TPDS 83183A; June 1, 1994.
24. Israelson v United States, 74-1 U.S.T.C. 9150 (1973 DC Md).
25. Leon v Commr., T.C. Memo. 1978-367.
26. IRC Section 274(k)(1).
27. IRC Section 274.
28. IRC Section 274(n)(2).
29. Lewis v Commr., 560 F.2d 973 (9th Cir., 1977), reversing T.C. Memo. 1974-59.
30. Luetzow v Commr., T.C. Memo 1973-63; aff'd in unpub. op. (7th Cir., 1974).
31. Pelowski v Commr., 605 F. Supp. 65 (N.D. Ohio 1985).
32. IRC Section 274(n)(2).
33. Reg. Section 1.274-2(c)(4).
34. Rodolfo Garcia, Jr. v Commr., T.C. Summary Opinion 2005-2.
35. See H. Rept. 103-111, at 646 (1993), 1993-3 C.B. 167, 222.
36. Reg. Section 1.274-2(a)(2)(iii)(a).
37. Reg. Section 1.274-2(a)(2)(iii)(b).
38. Treasury Decision (TD) 8601, 7/18/1995.
39. Ibid.
40. Reg. Section 1.274-2(e)(3)(iii)(a).
41. Reg. Section 1.274-2(e)(3)(i).
42. IRC Section 274(a)(2).

Section 7

Beware of the Entertainment Facility Rules That Kill Tax Deductions

Ugly words: Two words—entertainment facility—make for misleading and ugly tax results.

Common usage: For most people, and even Webster's dictionary, the word "facility" indicates real property. Webster defines facility to mean "something (as a hospital) that is built, installed, or established to serve a particular purpose."[1]

Uncommon usage: Tax law has a far more expansive definition of "facility." The ugly "entertainment facility" rules prohibit deductions, except for things discussed later, for any real or personal property owned, rented, or used by a taxpayer in connection with an entertainment activity.[2] The legislative history says this includes, among others,[3]
- hunting lodges,
- airplanes,
- beach cottages,
- automobiles,
- fishing camps,
- hotel suites,
- swimming pools,
- ski lodges,
- tennis courts, and
- bowling alleys.

The entertainment facility rules are deadly. With exceptions discussed later, the general rule is NO deduction for any real or personal property used for entertainment. Further, ONE entertainment use can DESTROY ALL of the deductions for that real or personal property.

One entertainment is fatal: James Gordon argued that his boat was not an entertainment facility because he used it only incidentally during the year in connection with entertainment. The court noted that the law says that any use of that boat for entertainment is fatal to Gordon's boat deductions.[4]

Notes

Technical note: Although Gordon may have qualified for one of the exceptions below, he never made those claims at trial.

Applying the one-taint rule: With certain exceptions, as we will discuss in a moment, any use of real or personal property for entertainment destroys all deductions for that real or personal property.

The Ireland case: Thomas Brown Ireland held various meetings at his three-acre beachfront property. He met with investment advisors and with current and prospective clients to discuss business opportunities. He also met with salesmen, trainees, and other partners in his business. The court noted that these activities are valid business activities, not entertainment. However, on occasion, the business guests brought their families with them to the meetings. Often, the meetings lasted three days. The family members did not attend the meetings. The court noted that the family members probably played on the beach and spent the night at the beach home partying. The court noted that any use of this beach home for entertainment, no matter how small, is fatal to the claimed deduction because IRS Code Section 274(a)(1)(b) operates as an absolute bar to a facility deduction when there is any entertainment.[5]

Golf clubs provide another example: Say you are a sales person who periodically plays golf with prospects. You may qualify to deduct the cost of golf as an entertainment expense, but you may not deduct the golf clubs, because your entertainment use makes the golf clubs a nondeductible entertainment facility.

Planning note: Although you may not deduct the golf clubs, you may deduct the cost of greens fees and other non-property items, including golf lessons. The legislative history specifically exempts out-of-pocket entertainment costs from the disallowance rules.[6]

Another bad rule: If the facility rule disallows any deductions, the taxpayer must treat the facility as an asset used by the individual for personal, living, and family purposes.[7] Thus, if you operate your business as a C corporation and you lose a deduction under the entertainment facility rule,
- your corporation gets taxed on the disallowance, and
- you get a constructive dividend equal to the disallowance.

In other words, both you and your corporation get taxed. Yes, that's right, double taxation—the worst possible result!

Make Your Entertainment Facility Immune from the "No Deduction" Rules

In addition to out-of-pocket costs, tax law grants immunity from the 100 percent entertainment facility disallowance rule to certain types and uses of facilities. Following are six common immunities that may fit in your planning.

1. Transportation immunity: You may deduct the transportation component of your automobile or airplane or other transportation facility.[8] Other transportation property could easily include a boat or a horse.

Entertainment use of transportation assets does not produce deductions. In general, the IRS ignores incidental entertainment use of transportation assets, like using your car a minimal percentage of the time for transportation to and from entertainment activities. However, if you had a truck that you used only for hunting, the entertainment facility rules would destroy your truck depreciation deductions.

Planning tip: Although the law destroys your truck depreciation deduction, it does not destroy your deductions for gas, oil, and other out-of-pocket costs for the entertainment use.

Horse example: If you use a horse to walk the borders of the properties that you sell, that horse is a business transportation horse. If you also use that horse 30 percent of the time for business entertainment, you then have a 70 percent transportation horse and a 30 percent nondeductible entertainment facility horse.

Airplane example: If you use an airplane 80 percent for business trips and 20 percent for hunting trips with your clients, you may deduct only 80 percent of the airplane.[9] The remaining 20 percent is a nondeductible facility expense.

Need more than 50 percent business use: Both the legislative history[10] and Technical Advice Memorandum 9608004 state that transportation facilities, like airplanes and automobiles, must be used more than 50 percent for business to qualify for the transportation exception to the entertainment facility disallowance rules. Therefore, make sure that you have more than 50 percent business use of your transportation property.

2. 1099 immunity: If you put the cost of using your entertainment facility on IRS Form 1099 and consider it compensation for services rendered, or as a prize or award to the recipient, you deduct your entertainment facility expenses as compensation to the recipient. To make this work, the statute and the regulations require that you file all the required IRS Forms 1099.[11]

Note: you must file a Form 1099 when the value of entertainment compensation is $600 or more. If the value of the entertainment is less than $600, no Form 1099 is required to make the entertainment deductible.
In Sutherland Lumber-Southwest Inc., the court allowed Sutherland to de-

Notes

duct its entire cost of providing the company plane to its employees for vacation use, even though the cost exceeded the amount treated as compensation by the regulations. In making this ruling, the court noted the interpretation of the "to the extent that" language found in the legislative history. This means "to the extent" you call it compensation to the user, the facility is exempt from the entertainment facility rules.[12]

In the Sutherland case, the court cited the legislative history example of the manufacturer who allowed use of its entertainment facility by its dealers. In the example, the manufacturer is not subject to the entertainment facility limits because the manufacturer includes the value of the entertainment facilities in the income of the dealers. In other words, the entertainment facility rules do not apply "to the extent that" the use is included in the dealer's income.

3. The W-2 immunity: You may deduct your entertainment facility "to the extent that" you treat the use of that facility as compensation to an employee, with proper[13]
- classifications on your original tax return, and
- proper payroll filings of the W-2, 941, etc.

4. Immunity for the employee entertainment facility: You could make your entertainment facility an employee fringe benefit. If you have an entertainment facility that is for use by your employees generally, like a swimming pool, baseball diamond, bowling alley, or golf course, you may deduct the cost of that entertainment facility as an employee welfare benefit.[14] However, any expenditure for an activity that discriminates in favor of employees or officers, shareholders or other owners, or highly compensated employees is not made primarily for the benefit of employees generally.

5. Immunity for employee, stockholder, and other business meetings: The entertainment facility rules do not apply to bona fide business meetings with your employees, stockholders, agents, or directors.[15] This break applies only when your principal purpose of the meetings is bona fide business discussions.[16]

Examples: The IRS says that you meet this exception when you gather your employees for a bona fide meeting to instruct them in a new procedure for conducting your business.[17] Similarly, the IRS says that you meet this exception when you hold a bona fide meeting of the stockholders to elect directors and discuss corporate affairs.[18] These are just two examples, but that should give you some ideas.

6. Lodging immunity: The legislative history of the entertainment facility law says that the entertainment facility rule does not disallow otherwise allowable deductions for items related to bona fide business expenses incurred while away from home overnight.[19]

How the Entertainment Facility Rules Apply to a Hunting Lease

What works? The "no-deduction-for-entertainment-facilities rules" do not apply to regular business entertainment activities. For example, if you take a customer hunting for a day at a commercial shooting preserve, you deduct the expenses of the hunt, like the costs for the[20]

- hunting rights,
- dogs, and
- guide.

Of course, you must properly document the entertainment deductions as provided under current law.

You qualify for deduction of this commercial hunt because you do not have exclusive use of the commercial hunting preserve for just one day. Thus, the expenses you incurred for this one day are out-of-pocket expenses.

What does not work? On Shore Quality Control Specialist, Inc. entered into an oral hunting lease with Mr. Robert Carr. On Shore renewed the hunting lease annually for 13 years, paying Mr. Carr $10,000 annually for the "right to hunt" in years 12 and 13. On Shore had the exclusive right to hunt on the ranch, with the limited exception that Mr. Carr could also hunt on the ranch and allow some of his friends and business acquaintances to hunt.

The tax court ruled that On Shore may not deduct its hunting lease because its "exclusive lease" makes the hunting lease an entertainment facility.[21]

In addition, if On Shore owned its guns, dogs, and other personal property used for hunting, the "exclusive use" rules would kill deductions for the guns, dogs and other personal property.

Planning tip: Make your hunting lease payments on a short-term, out-of-pocket basis to protect your tax deductions.

Consider Incorporating Your Entertainment Facility as a Second Business

Blanche and Harry Mellon own 100 percent of Tennis Now, Inc., an S corporation that operates a tennis club. The facility is not open to the public. It makes all of its money from charity tennis events, a few tennis tournaments, and fees from Mellon Corporation for use of the tennis facility by Mellon employees and clients. The Mellon Corporation is another S corporation owned 100 percent by Blanche and Harry.

Mellon Corporation pays Tennis Now, Inc., whenever Mellon's employees or clients use the tennis facility. Mellon Corporation deducts the tennis fees as entertainment expenses subject to the 50 percent limit on entertainment expenses.

Notes

Blanche uses the facility every week, but Harry uses the facility only occasionally.

The IRS field office questioned the close relationship between the two entities and worried that the transactions between these two entities, both owned 100 percent by Blanche and Harry, were designed to negate the rules that prohibit deductions for entertainment facilities.

In technical advice, the national office told the field office that Tennis Now, Inc., is a bona fide second business operated by an independent entity, the S corporation owned by Blanche and Harry Mellon.[22] Accordingly, Tennis Now, Inc., could report its income and deductions as a separate business not subject to the entertainment facility rules because it had a profit motive. Mellon Corporation could deduct each use of the facility as entertainment, subject to the regular entertainment rules.

Planning tip: Consider a separate corporation for your entertainment facility.

Endnotes–Section 7

[1] Merriam-Webster's Collegiate Dictionary, Tenth Edition, 2000.

[2] Senate Finance Committee Report (S. Rep. No. 1263, 95th Cong., 2d Sess. (1978)).

[3] Senate Finance Committee Report (S. Rep. No. 1263, 95th Cong., 2d Sess. (1978)).

[4] James R. Gordon v Commr., T. C. Memo. 1992-449.

[5] Thomas Brown Ireland v Commr., 89 T.C. No. 978.

[6] Conference Committee Report, H.R. Rep. No. 1800, 95th Cong., 2d Sess. 251.

[7] IRC Section 274(g).

[8] Reg. Section 1.274-2(b)(1)(iii)(c)(1).

[9] Technical Advice memorandum 9608004.

[10] Senate Finance Committee Report (S. Rep. No. 1263, 95th Cong., 2d Sess. (1978)).

[11] Reg. Sections 1.274-2(f)(2)(iii)(B) and 1.274-2(f)(2)(iv)(c).

[12] Sutherland Lumber-Southwest Inc. v Commr., 88 AFTR 2d 2001-5026, 2001-2 USTC ¶50,503 (CA8, 7/3/2001) Acq., 2002-06 IRB, affirming 114 TC 197, TCR ¶114.14 (3/28/2000).

[13] Reg. Sections 1.274-2(f)(2)(iii)(A)(2) and 1.274-2(f)(2)(iv)(b). Although the regulations make the "original-return" requirement, the IRS has no basis in the law or legislative history for this requirement.

[14] Reg. Section 1.274-2(f)(2)(v).

[15] Reg. Section 1.274-2(f)(2)(vi).

[16] Ibid.

[17] Ibid.

[18] Ibid.

[19] Senate Finance Committee Report (S. Rep. No. 1263, 95th Cong., 2d Sess. (1978)).

[20] Conference Committee Report, H.R. Rep. No. 1800, 95th Cong., 2d Sess. 251.

[21] On Shore Quality Control Specialist, Inc., v Commr., T. C. Memo. 1996-95. Also, see Harrigan Lumber Co., Inc., v Commr., 88 T.C. No. 88 (1987) where the "exclusive use" produced a nondeductible entertainment facility hunting lease.

[22] Private Letter Ruling 200214007 (as we discuss this ruling in the text, we made up the names to make the ruling easier for you to read)

Section 8

How to Build Audit-Proof Support for Entertainment

Definition of entertainment: The IRS states: "The term 'entertainment' means any activity which is of a type generally considered to constitute entertainment, amusement, or recreation, such as entertaining at nightclubs, cocktail lounges, theaters, country clubs, golf and athletic clubs, sporting events, and on hunting, fishing, vacation, and similar trips, *including such activity relating solely to the taxpayer or the taxpayer's family.*"[1] [Emphasis added]

Conflict: Tax law does not allow a deduction for personal, family, or living expenses.[2]

Technical note: The entertainment rules allow personal absorption of expenses. IRS regulations state that entertainment may include an activity, the cost of which is claimed as a business expense by the taxpayer, that satisfies the personal, living, or family needs of any individual.[3]

Documentation required: For each element of entertainment, you must prove five elements:
- Amount of each separate expenditure except incidentals that can be aggregated.[4] The IRS allows you to prove amounts less than $75 simply by making an entry in your tax diary.[5] For amounts of $75 and over, you must have receipts.[6]
- Date of entertainment.[7]
- Place. Name, address or location, and type of entertainment, such as dinner or theater, if such information is not apparent from the name.[8]
- Business purpose. The business reason or business benefit derived or expected from the entertainment.[9]
- Business relationship. Occupation or other information relating to the person or persons entertained, including name, title, or other designation sufficient to establish business relationship to the taxpayer.[10]

Planning tip: Make your diary entries stand up! Enter your specific business purpose for the entertainment. Let your entry show how you tried to achieve that specific business purpose. For example, "Asked for referrals—got none!" Or "Learned Matt's close—revised mine!"

Recording the Five Elements for Entertainment

To do's	
2	
3	
4	
5	
6	
7	

Appointments		car miles	bi pc
7:00			
8:00			
9:00			
10:00			
11:00			
12:00			
1:00			
2:00			
3:00			
4:00			
5:00			
6:00			
7:00	Bill Hart	26	b
8:00			
9:00			
10:00			

Business (b)		Total miles this day	
Investment (i)		Circle car driven this day 1 2 3
Personal (p)		End Odometer	
Commuting (c)		Beg Odometer	
Total miles		Total miles	

TODAY'S ACTION — **Action:** Review monthly goals before making your to-do list! **Result:** Your list will reflect the important things you need "to do" to realize your goals.

Copyright 1998 by W. Murray Bradford, CPA

Tax Diary System **1**

Circle month of year and day of week
Jan Feb Mar Apr May Jun   Sun Mon Tue Wed
Jul Aug Sep Oct Nov Dec   Thu Fri Sat

CARS
For each vehicle, enter all (100% of) monies spent for gas and oil, tires, insurance, car washes, repairs, and other out-of-pocket expenses.

Car 1 exp	
Car 2 exp	
Car 3 exp	
Parking/tolls	6 00

TRAVEL
Where (city)
Why (business reason)

Air/rail/boat	
Rental car/bus/taxi	
Lodging	
Tips, laundry, other	
Total trv day (no meals)	

MEALS/ENTERTAINMENT/ETC
Who Bill Hart
Where Tommy Toys
Why Sell 2548 Florida Street

Trv brkfst	
Trv lunch	
Trv dinner	
Snacks/drinks	
Ent meals	96 00
Associated ent	
Total trv meals & ent	
Presentation exp	
Special sporting events (100%)	

MISCELLANEOUS
For Business Gifts
To whom
Why

Supplies	
Postage	
Business gifts	
Other	
Other	
Other	

Time saver: You do not need an essay to support your entertainment deductions, but you do need to be specific about your hoped-for future benefit.

Failure to satisfy the documentation standards means you lose the deduction.[11]

Diary entry: Tax law expects you to record your entertainment expenses at or near the time of expenditure, when you have full present knowledge of the elements.[12] You may record the expenses in an appointment book or any record. You generally meet the rules when you record
- who you entertained,
- where you entertained, and
- why you entertained.

General rules: You may deduct entertainment only if it meets either:[13]
- the directly related test or
- the associated test

Directly related entertainment either (1) meets four requirements or (2) occurs in a clear business setting.

The four requirements are:
1. At the time you committed to spend the money, you had more than a general expectation of future business.[14]
2. During the entertainment, you actively discussed the topic that could produce future business benefit.[15]
3. Your principal reason for the activity was the active conduct of your business.[16]
4. You incurred the expense to speak with the person who produced your general expectation of future business.[17]

If you intended to do the items above, but circumstances beyond your control prevented you from doing so, you still may deduct the costs as directly related entertainment.[18]

Clear setting: You do not have to meet the four requirements above if you spent the money in a clear business setting. The clear business setting exception makes the entertainment automatically deductible as directly related entertainment.[19] Entertainment occurs in a clear business setting when:[20]
- The person with whom you have the business discussion knows you are spending your money on the entertainment to directly further your business.
- You spend your money in a hospitality room at a convention where you display your products to further your business.

Diary Entry - Directly Related Entertainment

To do's			
2			
3			
4			
5			
6			
7			
Appointments		car miles	bi pc
7:00			
8:00			
9:00			
10:00			
11:00			
12:00	Lunch - Jones	6	b
1:00			
2:00			
3:00			
4:00			
5:00			
6:00			
7:00			
8:00			
9:00			
10:00			

Business (b)	Total miles this day	
Investment (i)	Circle car driven this day 1 2 3	
Personal (p)	End Odometer	
Commuting (c)	Beg Odometer	
Total miles	Total miles	

TODAY'S ACTION — **Action:** Review monthly goals before making your to-do list! **Result:** Your list will reflect the important things you need "to do" to realize your goals.

Copyright 1998 by W. Murray Bradford, CPA

Tax Diary System — 1

Circle month of year and day of week

Jan Feb Mar Apr May Jun   Sun Mon Tue Wed
Jul Aug Sep Oct Nov Dec   Thu Fri Sat

___

CARS For each vehicle, enter all (100% of) monies spent for gas and oil, tires, insurance, car washes, repairs, and other out-of-pocket expenses.	Car 1 exp	
	Car 2 exp	
	Car 3 exp	
	Parking/tolls	1 00
TRAVEL Where (city) Why (business reason)	Air/rail/boat	
	Rental car/bus/taxi	
	Lodging	
	Tips, laundry, other	
	Total trv day (no meals)	
MEALS/ENTERTAINMENT/ETC Who Sam Jones Where Leah's place Why Learn Sam's referral tactics	Trv brkfst	
	Trv lunch	
	Trv dinner	
	Coat check ~~Snacks/drinks~~	1 00
	Ent meals	16 00
	Associated ent	
	Total trv meals & ent	
	Presentation exp	
	Special sporting events (100%)	
MISCELLANEOUS For Business Gifts To whom Why	Supplies	
	Postage	
	Business gifts	
	Other _____	
	Other _____	
	Other _____	

- You have no meaningful social or personal relationship with the people with whom you have the business discussion.

Business setting: You do not qualify for directly related entertainment when the entertainment takes place in a setting where you have little possibility of engaging in an active business discussion.[21] Locations that make a business discussion unlikely include nightclubs, theaters, sporting events, and cocktail parties.[22] For directly related entertainment, the surroundings should be such that you have no substantial distractions to discussion.[23] The IRS considers as conducive to business discussion a restaurant, hotel dining room, or similar place that does not involve distracting influences, such as a floorshow.[24]

Associated entertainment: If your entertainment is not directly related to the active conduct of your business, you may not deduct that entertainment unless:[25]
- The entertainment is associated with the active conduct of your business, and
- The associated entertainment directly precedes or follows a substantial and bona fide business discussion.

Associated entertainment does not have to involve a business discussion. It takes place in a setting not conducive to a business discussion. To deduct associated entertainment, you must have a substantial and bona fide business discussion before or after the entertainment.

Place for associated business discussion: The business discussion may occur in the office or in any other business setting, like during a directly related entertainment meal. In such cases, you may deduct the associated entertainment with no further action on your part.[26] In other words, if you have your substantial and bona fide business discussion over dinner and then go to the theater, you deduct both the dinner and the theater.

Timing of associated discussion: How soon before or after the associated entertainment must you have the substantial and bona fide business discussion? The same day always qualifies.[27] If the entertainment does not occur on the day of the business discussion, all circumstances are considered, including the reasons for not entertaining on the day of the business discussion. The IRS says that entertainment of an out-of-town customer qualifies as associated if you have the business discussion on the day before or day after the entertainment.[28]

Example: You and your spouse take the Nelsons to dinner and discuss an investment program with them. After dinner, you and your spouse take the Nelsons to the ballgame, where no business discussions take place. You deduct the entire cost of the $250 dinner and the $150 spent at the ballgame.

Notes

Diary Entry for Dinner Followed by Associated Entertainment

To do's			
2			
3			
4			
5			
6			
7			
Appointments		car miles	bi pc
7:00			
8:00			
9:00			
10:00			
11:00			
12:00			
1:00			
2:00			
3:00			
4:00			
5:00	Jim and Jane Nelson	96	b
6:00	Dinner Discussion		
7:00	O's Game		
8:00			
9:00			
10:00			
Business (b)	96	Total miles this day	96
Investment (i)		Circle car driven this day 1 2 3	
Personal (p)		End Odometer	
Commuting (c)		Beg Odometer	
Total miles	96	Total miles	

Audit-proof "associated entertainment" by adding the "duration" of the business discussion as required by the latest IRS regulations.

TODAY'S ACTION — **Action:** Review monthly goals before making your to-do list! **Result:** Your list will reflect the important things you need "to do" to realize your goals.

Copyright 1998 by W. Murray Bradford, CPA

Tax Diary System — 1

Circle month of year and day of week
Jan Feb Mar Apr May Jun   Sun Mon Tue Wed
Jul Aug Sep Oct Nov Dec   Thu Fri Sat

CARS		
For each vehicle, enter all (100% of) monies spent for gas and oil, tires, insurance, car washes, repairs, and other out-of-pocket expenses.	Car 1 exp	
	Car 2 exp	
	Car 3 exp	
	Parking/tolls	12 00
TRAVEL Where (city)	Air/rail/boat	
	Rental car/bus/taxi	
Why (business reason)	Lodging	
	Tips, laundry, other	
	Total trv day (no meals)	
MEALS/ENTERTAINMENT/ETC	Trv brkfst	
Who Jim / Jane Nelson	Trv lunch	
Where Dinner at Palm; followed by O's game	Trv dinner	
Why	Snacks/drinks	
Dinner discussion - sell 64T annuity	Ent meals	250 00
	Associated ent	150 00
	Total trv meals & ent	400 00
	Presentation exp	
	Special sporting events (100%)	
MISCELLANEOUS	Supplies	
For Business Gifts To whom	Postage	
Why	Business gifts	
	Other _____	
	Other _____	
	Other _____	

No business discussion at the O's game. You deduct the O's game because it is associated with your business discussion at the Palm restaurant.

How the IRS looks at entertainment: In an audit of entertainment, the IRS tells its examiners to look for:[29]
- An ordinary and necessary business reason for the entertainment
- A directly related business discussion (about a product, request for referrals, or other future business)
- Substantiation (who, where, why)

The IRS notes that entertainment, promotion, and advertising expenses are areas that give rise to audit issues. In one case, the IRS found a taxpayer who claimed over $60,000 in deductions for front-center seats to rock concerts. The taxpayer took prospects, colleagues, and clients to concerts to gain exposure to rock groupies, roadies, and stars that might produce music business clients. The IRS tells its examiners that they should argue the reasonableness of that assertion!

We more than agree. You need to write down why you entertained someone after each entertainment. You should directly relate your "why" to your business, and the associated "rock concert" should follow or precede your bona fide directly related business discussion. The business discussion should take place in surroundings conducive to business discussions (like at a table in a quiet restaurant).

Notes

To visualize how the audit-proofing process works, see the online video: www.tax789.com/2015video

Endnotes–Section 8

1. Reg. Section 1.274-2(b)(1)(i).
2. IRC Section 262.
3. Plr 8937029; Reg. Section 1.274-2(b)(1)(i).
4. Reg. Section 1.274-5T(b)(3)(i).
5. Reg. Section 1.274-5(c)(2)(iii)(B).
6. Ibid.
7. Reg. Section 1.274-5(b)(3)(ii).
8. Reg. Section 1.274-5(b)(3)(iii).
9. Reg. Section 1.274-5(b)(3)(iv).
10. Reg. Section 1.274-5(b)(3)(v).
11. E.g., Dowell v U.S., 522 F.2d 708 (5th Cir. 1975), cert. denied, 426 U.S. 920 (1976), rev'd 370 F.Supp. 69 (N.D. Tex. 1974).
12. Reg. Section 1.274-5T(c)(2)(ii)(A); e.g., Blake v Commr., T.C. Memo 1981-579, aff'd 697 F.2d 473 (2d Cir. 1983).
13. IRC Section 274(a)(1)(A).

Notes

14. Reg. Section 1.274-2(c)(3)(i).
15. Reg. Section 1.274-2(c)(3)(ii).
16. Reg. Section 1.274-2(c)(3)(iii).
17. Reg. Section 1.274-2(c)(3)(iv).
18. Reg. Section 1.274-2(c)(3).
19. Reg. Section 1.274-2(c)(4).
20. Ibid.
21. Reg. Section 1.274-2(c)(7).
22. Reg. Section 1.274-2(c)(7)(ii)(a).
23. Rev. Rul. 63-144, 1963-2 C.B. 129, Answer 16.
24. Ibid.
25. Reg. Section 1.274-2(d).
26. Reg. Section 1.274-2(d)(4).
27. Rev. Rul. 63-144, 1963-2 C.B. 129, Answer 24.
28. Ibid.
29. IRS Market Segment Specialization Program Paper, Attorneys, Training 3149-102, TPDS 83183A; June 1, 1994

Section 9

New Law Makes Home Office Available to You

Eliminates commute: The IRS says, "If you have an office in your home that qualifies as a principal place of business, you can deduct your daily transportation costs between your home and another work location in the same trade or business."[1]

You may have more than one office: Then, in its business use of home publication, the IRS says, "You can have more than one business location, including your home, for a single trade or business."[2]

Put an administrative office in your home to produce a principal office: The IRS goes on to say, "Your home office will qualify as your principal place of business for deducting expenses for its use if you meet the following requirements:[3]
1. You use it exclusively and regularly for administrative or management activities of your trade or business.
2. You have no other fixed location where you conduct substantial administrative or management activities of your trade or business."

This is the word: Note that these are exact quotes from the IRS. What this means is that if you do your administrative work at home and not at your other office or offices, your home office is your principal office. If your home office is your principal office, your other office is a secondary office. The IRS says that you can deduct your vehicle expenses for trips from your administrative office to your secondary office.

Administrative or managerial activities: The IRS says, "There are many activities that are administrative or managerial in nature. The following are a few examples:[4]
- Billing customers, clients, or patients.
- Keeping books and records.
- Ordering supplies.
- Setting up appointments.
- Forwarding orders or writing reports."

What do you do? Do you pay the bills for your business? Keep the financial records and take care of the business plan? Order supplies and equipment? Read the business mail? These are the types of things that qualify as administrative or management activities.

Notes

Your choice: The IRS gives you lots of flexibility with your home office. For example, if you have suitable space at one of your outside-the-home offices to conduct administrative or management activities, but choose to use your home office instead, no problem. Your choice does not disallow the home office.[5]

Administrative in secondary office: The IRS says that you can occasionally conduct minimal administrative or management activities at a fixed location outside your home, for example, in one of your satellite offices.[6] No problem. This does not hurt your home office.

Helpers don't hurt: Similarly, you may have others conduct your administrative or management activities, for example, using a bookkeeper or an outside billing company.

Sales office does not hurt: You qualify for the principal office in your home even when you conduct substantial nonadministrative or nonmanagement business activities at a fixed location outside your home.[7] For example, you meet with or provide services to customers, clients, or patients at a fixed location of the business outside your home.

An "on-point" example: The IRS uses an anesthesiologist example in its publication, which is pretty much on point and follows:[8]

Paul is a self-employed anesthesiologist. He spends the majority of his time administering anesthesia and postoperative care in three local hospitals. One of the hospitals provides him with a small shared office where he could conduct administrative or management activities.

Paul does not use the office the hospital provides. He uses a room in his home that he has converted to an office. He uses this room exclusively and regularly to conduct all the following activities:
- *Contacting patients, surgeons, and hospitals regarding scheduling.*
- *Preparing for treatments and presentations.*
- *Maintaining billing records and patient logs.*
- *Satisfying continuing medical education requirements.*
- *Reading medical journals and books.*

Paul's home office qualifies as his principal place of business for deducting expenses for its use. He conducts administrative or management activities for his business as an anesthesiologist there and he has no other fixed location where he conducts administrative or management activities for this business. His choice to use his home office instead of one provided by the hospital does not disqualify his home office from being his principal place of business. His performance of substantial nonadministrative or nonmanagement activities at fixed locations outside his home also does not disqualify his home office from being his principal place of business. He meets all the qualifications, including principal place of business . . .

You probably are just like Paul!

Three Easy Rules Give You the Home Office

The new law rules became effective on January 1, 1999—and they are easy. To gain the benefits described in this section, you must use your home office:[9]
- For administrative or management duties
- Exclusively for business
- Regularly for business

Rule 1—Administrative or management use: See the discussion at the beginning of this section.

Rule 2—Use the office regularly for business: You must exclusively use your home office on a regular basis for this administration or management activity. The court ruled in Green that Green's use of the home office for a little more than 10 hours a week met the regular-use test.[10] Unlike some cases where the courts found the use not regular, Green used his office every week, except for vacations. So make your use repetitive and frequent to ensure that it is regular.

Proving regular use: How do you prove "regular use"? One clear way to make your presentation is to make entries in your appointment book, as we did below. When you do the 90-day test for your car and other listed property, simply track your body, too. It's easy. Below, we logged our body as it used the office in the home. The logging clearly shows the home office use.

Appointments		car miles	bi pc
7:00	Open mail		PO
8:00	Respond to mail		
9:00			
10:00	Meet with Lyons		
11:00			
12:00			
1:00	Telemarketing calls		
2:00			
3:00			
4:00	Jones - 15 Park Place	15	b

Notes

Note for coporate owners: IRC Section 280A(c)(6) prohibits claiming deductions for the rental of your home office to your corporation. Therefore, the corporation should:

1. require you to find an office for the convenience of the corporation, and
2. reimburse you for your home office expenses (use IRS Form 8829 to figure the reimbursement).

When reimbursed, the corporaton gets the deduction and you, the employee, do not report the reimbursement as income. This gives you the home office deduction on the corporation's books.

Reg. Section 1.62-(d)(1) allows reimbursement of home office, including depreciation and Section 179 deductions.

Overview Calculation of Home Office Monetary Benefits

	Gross	% Office	Deduction	Tax Rate	Cash
Mortgage interest	$15,400	17%	$2,618	15.3%	$401
Property taxes	1,500	17%	255	15.3%	39
Utilities	2,105	17%	358	47.8%	171
Homeowner's ins.	317	17%	54	47.8%	26
Repairs, paint, etc.	800	17%	136	47.8%	65
Pest control	480	17%	82	47.8%	39
Repairs to office part	230	100%	230	47.8%	110
Depreciation - equip	1,350	100%	1,350	47.8%	645
Depreciation - home	6,800	17%	1,156	47.8%	553
Cash from the home office deduction					2,049
Eliminate 9-mile commute			3,150	47.8%	1,506
Annual cash from office and vehicle					$3,555

25% federal taxes, 7.5% state taxes, and 15.3% self-employment taxes make up the 47.8% rate

Eliminates Commuting and Takes Advantage of Your Living Costs

The administrative home office eliminates commuting. Smith, our example taxpayer, erases 9 miles of commute a day. That's 18 miles round trip, 90 miles a week, 4,500 miles a year converted from ugly personal to beautiful business miles. In Smith's case, the 4,500 miles increased his car deductions by $3,150 a year.

You need a place to live—why not deduct part of that place? It makes no difference if you own or rent. With the home office deduction, you convert otherwise personal expenses to business deductions.

Most of these expenses are expenses you have no matter what. Mortgage interest, property taxes, utilities, homeowners insurance, pest control, repairs, and paint are all common home expenses.

Extra benefits from mortgage interest: On the mortgage interest you already pay, you convert the home office part (17 percent in this case) to business and deduct it against your self-employment income. If your business income is:
- Under the Social Security maximum, you gain 15.3 percent in extra tax benefits.
- Over the Social Security maximum, you gain 2.9 percent Medicare tax benefit.

More cash from the phaseouts: Then, no matter if you are over or under the Social Security maximum, you gain on those sneaky phaseout taxes that apply to:
- Reducing your itemized deductions
- Reducing your personal exemptions
- Limiting your real estate rental deductions
- Cutting back your child credits

The phaseout tax benefits alone could produce 20 percent or more in benefits depending on your situation. To calculate the true after-tax benefit in your individual case, do your tax return two ways—with and without the home office and vehicle benefits.

Cash benefits from depreciation: Depreciation on this home produces $553 in annual after-tax cash benefits. When Smith sells, he will pay a recapture tax of $289 (25 percent x $1,156), pocketing $264 on the depreciation deduction.

Claim office until death: When you die, the law forgives the home office and marks up the home to fair market value for estate tax purposes. The markup for estate tax purposes does not trigger any depreciation recapture or capital gains taxes on the death transfer.

Keep correspondence: Do one more thing. Keep incoming correspondence and photocopies of outgoing correspondence. Just toss it in a file or a box by date. Don't spend time on it, unless you need it. Then, if you ever need supporting evidence, the correspondence file will prove itself a gold mine.

The correspondence file often produces highly beneficial documents that you can use for far more than your taxes. Simply get in the habit of copying all written documents that you send out, even thank-you notes.

Rule 3—Use the office exclusively for business: The final hurdle to claiming the home office deduction is "exclusive use." You must use the room, rooms, or area exclusively for qualifying business use as an office and for no other purpose.[11]

Think proof! How do you prove exclusive business use?

Curphey proved his exclusive use by showing that the room he used as an office contained only business furniture and no personal-use furniture like a television, sofa, or bed. What would be good proof in this situation? Photographs! How could you prove when you took them? Have them developed by a processor that dates the photos.

The business bed: If your room has a bed or other indications of potential personal use, again, think proof. Photos of the bed covered with files can help prove business use of the bed. If you have no storage area for the bed and the bed is simply too good to give away, you have additional evidence. Neither of these by itself will prove exclusive use, but both help.

Is the Home Office a Big Red Flag?

Home office deduction does not cause an audit. We asked about 3,000 self-employed taxpayers who claimed the home office if the IRS had audited them during the past five years. Their answers showed that the IRS had audited almost none of them.

Further, this is a new law, and there really is no audit history yet. Under the old law, it was very difficult to qualify for the home office deduction. You had to assume that ultra-strict tax rules would have caused lots of audits, which, of course, we now know is not what happened at all.

Summary

The new rules on the home office deduction put cash in your pocket from the place where you live and the vehicle you drive. You don't need to find a different place to live. You don't have to buy a more expensive vehicle.

You need to spend a little time building proof. Get serious here! Only a few hours a year building proof for tax benefits can, in just five years, put $21,242 (more or less) in after-tax cash in your pocket.

Let's face it. You already work at home and do most of what's needed to meet the rules. Your effort to pocket this cash is nothing compared with the benefits.

Keep this workbook handy. Read the rules several times and get started. Then put the workbook in a place where you can read it once a year, so that you remember what you have to do and why you want to do it.

Endnotes–Section 9

[1] *IRS Publication 17, Your Federal Income Tax* (2014), p. 182.

[2] *IRS Publication 587, Business Use of Your Home* (2014), p. 3.

[3] Ibid.

[4] Ibid.

[5] Ibid.

[6] Ibid; however, we must point out that the word "occasional" is probably an understatement as Congress said that you qualify for the home office if you do not conduct substantial administrative or management activities for this business at any other office. "Substantial" is a far different word from "occasional." See Statement of Managers; House Report No. 2014; July 31, 1997; paragraphs 743 to 745.

[7] *IRS Publication 587, Business Use of Your Home* (2014), p. 4.

[8] Ibid, ps. 4-5.

[9] IRC Section 280A(c)(1).

[10] Green v Commr., 78 T.C. 428 (1982), Rev'd on other grounds, 707 F.2d 404 (9th Cir. 1983).

[11] Reg. Section 1.280A-2(g)(1)

Section 10

Putting the IRS Audit Manual's Home-Office Section to Work for You

The IRS audit manual contains not only information on how to audit your tax returns but also boilerplate language for auditors to use when they disallow your deductions. The boilerplate disallowance explanations are instructive because they
- help you focus on the rules,
- highlight common mistakes your fellow taxpayers are making, and
- help you develop an audit-proof plan.

With respect to the home office, the IRS audit force has 19 boilerplate paragraphs that explain why the IRS is not going to give you some or all of your claimed home-office deductions.[1] We dissected those 19 paragraphs and built 11 audit-proofing tactics to ensure that you get every single deduction you deserve. We discussed the first 3 of the 11 tactics in the previous section of this course. Here, we will discuss the remaining eight, plus new rules on cell phones.

Remember, when you claim the home-office deduction, you achieve two valuable monetary results:
1. The home office produces tax benefits for money you would spend on your home, no matter what.
2. As an administrative office in your home, the home office becomes your principal office, which eliminates commuting to work. With no more commuting, you put more after-tax benefits from your vehicle in your bank account.

Benefit example 1. You make $10,000 worth of repairs that benefit your entire home. Without the home office, you can deduct nothing. Repairs to a home are not deductible. With an office that takes 20 percent of your home, you deduct $2,000 ($10,000 x 20 percent).

Benefit example 2. You drive a $50,000 vehicle that you will sell for $10,000 after you use it in your business. With no home office, you have 60 percent business use—deductions of $24,000 on the cost of this vehicle. With an administrative office in your home that eliminates commuting, you now have 90 percent business use—deductions of $36,000 on the cost of this vehicle, a $12,000 improvement.

Notes

You can see that establishing a home office adds to your bank account. But you cannot depend on that extra cash making it into your account unless your home office is audit-proof.

Here are the eight remaining tactics you need to make sure all your deductions make it to your bank account.

1. Pass the Convenience-of-Employer Test If You Operate as a Corporation

If you operate your business as a corporation and claim the home-office deduction, you need to prove that you use the home office for the *convenience* of the employer, your corporation.

Before the home-office rules changed in 1997, the convenience of the employer test was pretty wide open. However, with the new rules, the legislative history has modified the convenience test in the following manner:[2]

In the case of an employee, the question whether an employee chose not to use suitable space made available by the employer for administrative activities is relevant to determining whether the present-law "convenience of the employer" test is satisfied.

The IRS had this interpretation of the legislative history paragraph quoted above:[3]

One warning here: an employee's decision not to use suitable space made available by the employer can affect the deductibility.

This means that as an owner-employee of your corporation, you need to meet both the basic rules for the home office and the additional convenience-of-the-employer rule. The basic rules say that you may claim a home office if you

- use the office for administrative or management activities;
- have no other fixed place where you conduct substantial administrative or management activities; and
- use the office exclusively and regularly as a place of business.

Once you establish that you meet the basic rules, you need to spend some time documenting how and why you meet the convenience-of-the-employer test. Your best bet is to have the corporation write you a letter requiring you to do your administrative or management activities at home for a valid business reason. For example, your corporation might require your administrative or management work be carried out at home

- to protect the confidentiality of the payroll and accounting records;
- to ensure that your work at the office focuses on sales (patient care, production);
- because the office has inadequate space to accommodate the payables records, invoices, receipts, and so on; or
- to facilitate uninterrupted attention to business plans and budgets.

This list is by no means exhaustive, but it should help you target viable reasons you need to do your administration or management at home.

Planning note. You must pass the convenience-of-the-employer test whether or not you are having the corporation reimburse you for home-office expenses. If you are going to have your corporation reimburse home-office expenses to you as an employee of the corporation, see the next section of this course for important details.

2. Don't Even Think About Renting Your Home Office to Your Employer

If you claim the home-office deduction as an employee business expense, you place that deduction in the miscellaneous itemized deductions category. This is a bad place. Here, your miscellaneous deductions are going to suffer either
- a reduction of up to 2 percent of adjusted gross income, or
- elimination, if you are subject to the alternative minimum tax.

As you can see, this bad place produces bad results.

You *cannot* avoid these bad results by renting your home office to your employer. Section 280A(c)(6) prohibits the home-office deduction for rentals of a home office to an employer.

The perfect solution. Have the corporation reimburse you for the home-office deduction. This gives the corporation the deduction. You get cash as a reimbursed employee expense, and that cash reimbursement is not taxable to you. With the reimbursement, you also avoid both the 2 percent problem and the alternative minimum tax problems. The reimbursement gives you the best result if you operate your business as a corporation.

3. Don't Fret About the Gross Income Limit

Your home-office deduction is limited to the income from your business. It's simple. No income, no deduction. Little income, little deduction.

Regardless, you should claim the home office if you can. Why? Expenses disallowed by the income limit this year, because you did not make enough money, carry over to next year, and the year after, and every year thereafter until you make enough money to use them. You don't lose the deductions. Think of the disallowed deductions as going into a holding tank where they wait for release; when you *do* have income, they can attack and reduce that taxable income.

4. Classify Your Repairs Properly

You incur three types of repairs:
- Repairs that benefit the entire house
- Repairs that benefit only the personal part of the house
- Repairs that benefit only the office part of the house

Notes

You may deduct the business percentage of the repairs that benefit the entire house and the repairs that benefit only the office part of the house.

- **Example 1.** You paint the outside of the home. This benefits the entire house. You deduct your business percentage of this repair.
- **Example 2.** You add electrical outlets to the room you use as an office. You expense the entire cost of this electrical repair.
- **Example 3.** You repair the floor in the kitchen. This repair gives you zero home-office benefit.

Build better records of your repairs by making brief notes on the repair invoices and receipts indicating the area benefited (entire house, personal part, or office part).

5. Prove Your Expenses

You need receipts and canceled checks to back up your home-office expenses. Keep your mortgage payment statements, property tax statements, and utility bills, and obtain receipts for repairs and maintenance and all other claimed expenses and improvements. Receipts and invoices prove what you bought.

Canceled checks and online payments prove that you paid the money.

You need both kinds of proof: what you bought and the fact that that you paid for your purchases.

6. Take Advantage of Lawn Care and Landscaping Issues

The IRS does not want your home-office deduction to include any landscaping or lawn care. In fact, the IRS has a proposed regulation disallowing landscaping and lawn care as part of the home office. This proposed regulation was issued on August 7, 1980, although it has never made it to a final regulation.
The IRS audit manual tells IRS agents and auditors not to allow your lawn care and landscaping. That's the IRS's side of the story. There is another side of the story.

Charles Hefti faced and beat the proposed regulations in court. He got the court to look at the proposed regulation and conclude that his lawn care and landscaping costs were deductible to the extent of his business-use percentage. The court found that Hefti had clients visiting on a regular basis and that the appearance of the residence and the grounds were of significance to Hefti's business operation.[4]

In *Rhoads*, the court allowed the lawn-care deduction and stated that although the home-office regulations had not been a subject of the case, the court felt that the ruling was correct given the regulations.[5]

In *Neilson*, the IRS disallowed the lawn-care deduction in its audit, but the court overturned the disallowance and allowed the lawn-care deduction for the Neilsons' child-care center operated out of their residence.[6]

Two of these cases confronted the proposed regulations directly, and both taxpayers won. The IRS has yet to win a lawn-care-deduction-denial case under its 1980 proposed regulations.

What does this mean to you? It means you should claim the lawn care if you have significant justification. As in the court cases cited above, the exterior appearance of your home office needs to be of enough value to your business to demonstrate a business incentive for the work. Should you face the IRS on this issue, one of the following three things will happen:
- You will back down and give up the deduction.
- The IRS will back down and give you the deduction.
- You and the IRS will duke it out in court.

7. Identify Your Depreciable Basis

The basis of your home is original cost, plus improvements, minus depreciation. If your home has declined in value, you must use the lower market value as your basis. Also, if you used the section 1034 tax-deferred rollover rules that existed before 1999, your basis was adjusted in the rollover.

You depreciate the building, not the land; therefore, your first step to claiming the home-office deduction is to divide the basis of your home between building and land. An appraisal or the tax assessor's statement makes good evidence for allocating basis between land and building.

Example. You are going to claim the home-office deduction for the first time this year. You bought your home in 1999 for $250,000. You have a tax assessor's property tax statement for your 1999 property taxes that shows the value of the land to be equal to 20 percent of the total value. On the basis of this statement, you allocate 80 percent of the $250,000 to the building and start depreciating your business percentage of the $200,000 cost this year.

In your tax file, you should have documents that prove your acquisition cost, improvements, and allocation between land and building.

8. Deduct the Proper Amount of Your Phone Bill

Lawmakers enacted section 262(b), which states that you must treat as a personal expense any charge for basic local telephone service to any residence. However, long-distance business phone calls on the first telephone line, as well as the cost of a second line used exclusively for business, are deductible business expenses.[7] Further, charges for optional services offered by the telephone company, such as call waiting, call forwarding, speed or three-way calling, extra directory listings, and equipment rentals are deductible to the extent of business use.[8]

Cell Phones (New Rules)

Break for Employees, Including Corporate Owner-Employees

In IRS Notice 2011-72, the IRS said
- it will not tax the value of employees' personal use of employer-provided cell phones, and
- employees and employers do not have to keep any records of their cell phone use.

To qualify for this tax-favored treatment, the employer must provide the employee with a cell phone primarily for "noncompensatory business purposes" such as the following (and you are going to love these):

1. The employer needs to be able to contact the employee at all times in case of work-related emergencies.
2. The employer requires that the employee be available to speak with clients when away from the office.
3. The employee needs to speak with clients located in other time zones at times outside of the employee's normal workday.

If you operate as a corporation, you should have no problem satisfying one or more of the three criteria above.

Your corporation need not buy you a cell phone. Instead, it can pay you a cash allowance and/or reimburse you for your personal cell phone use.[9] If you pay a flat monthly fee for your cell phone service, your corporation can reimburse you for the entire amount even though you use the phone for both personal and business calls.[10]

Caution. Cell phones given to an employee solely to boost morale or to serve as additional compensation create taxable income for the employee.[11]

Cell Phones for the Sole Proprietor and the Single-Member LLC

The IRS's no-hassle cell-phone break applies to your employees, but not to you if are a sole proprietor or the owner of a single-member LLC.

If you are in the out-of-favor group, you deduct your monthly business-related cell phone costs the same as any other business operating expense, such as rent or utilities. You depreciate the cost of the cell phone itself, just like any other capital property, such as computers.

Your sole piece of good news comes from the change in the law, not from the IRS. Cell phones are no longer listed property. That makes things easier.

But unlike those who own corporations, you are required to offer proof of your percentage of business use. If you use the cell phone 75 percent for business and 25 percent for personal, your deduction for depreciation and monthly charges is based on your 75 percent business use.

To prove the 75 percent, you need to keep track of your calls. One easy method is to simply tally the business and personal calls that show on your cell phone bill as proof of your business and personal use.[12]

You don't necessarily have to go through every cell phone bill for the entire year and categorize each and every call. If you make about the same number of calls every month, you can use a sampling method, say, for three months.[13]

If you hate the idea of checking off the calls on your phone bill, consider acquiring two phone numbers for your cell phone: one for business and one for personal use.[14] Technology now makes this possible.

Special Category for Independent Contractors

The IRS grants independent contractors tax-free, tax-favored employee status for cell phones given to them or reimbursed to them by their employers (clients, customers, brokers, etc.).[15]

This favored-employee status does not apply to independent contractors who are not reimbursed by an employer. Unreimbursed independent contractors are proprietorships for cell phone use and thus subject to the prove-your-cell-phone-use rules.

Phone is a Utility

Although you'll find the phone disallowance paragraph in the home-office section of the IRS audit manual and in the IRS publication on the home office, the IRS makes it clear that phone charges are not home-office expenses. According to the IRS, you should label your phone charges as utilities.[16]

Summary

Remember, the eight tactics above and the three in the prior section were derived from the 19 standard paragraphs in the audit manual that IRS personnel use when they tell you why the IRS is not going to give you some or all of your claimed deductions. Pay attention and put into practice those parts of the 11 tactics that apply to your home-office deduction.

Think of the home-office deduction as a money stream to your bank account. You need a place to live, so you incur these expenses no matter what. When you claim the home-office deduction, the law grants you deductions for monies that you are going to spend whether or not you are in business.

Notes

Another major benefit of the home office is that it eliminates commuting from a principal office in your home to an office outside your home. Any reduction in your commuting mileage is a good thing.

The benefits make keeping the right records a highly profitable effort. Now that you know what records to keep, you'll find that it takes little time to actually keep them. And that little time is time well spent.

Endnotes–Section 10

1. Internal Revenue Manual, Exhibit 4.10.10-2 (04-04-2008) Standard Explanations.
2. JCS-23-97, Joint Committee on Taxation, General Explanation of Tax Legislation Enacted in 1997, Title IX, D2. (Section 932 of the Act and Section 280A of the Code).
3. IRS Pub. 1049B, Business Taxpayers Should Look for Tax Changes.
4. Charles Hefti v Commr., TC Memo 1988-22, on issues unrelated to the landscaping and lawn care deductions—affd without op (1989, CA8) 894 F2d 1340, cert den (1990, S Ct) 495 US 933.
5. Cecil Rhoads v Commr., TC Memo 1987-335.
6. Robert Neilson v Commr., 94 TC 1 (1990).
7. IRS Pub. 587, *Business Use of Your Home* (2011), p. 9.
8. RIA Checkpoint; COMREP ¶ 2621 Deduction denial for certain residential phone service. ('88 TAMRA, PL 100-647, 11/10/88).
9. IRS Memorandum for All Field Examination Operations, Sept. 14, 2011.
10. Ibid.
11. IRS Notice 2011-72.
12. Umit Tarakci, T.C. Memo. 2000-358.
13. Reg. Section 1.274-5T(c)(3)(ii)(C), Example 1.
14. One way to accomplish this is to use a GSM cell phone with slots for two SIM cards. See Lee, "Cell phones with two numbers," http://reviews.cnet.com/2795-6454_7-654.html. Alternatively, software is available that can add a second number to a cell phone; see http://www.line2.com/.
15. IRS Regulation 1.132-1(b)(2)(iv).
16. IRS Pub. 587, *Business Use of Your Home* (2011), p. 10.

Section 11

Why Incorporation Makes Your Home-Office Deduction Less Subject to an IRS Audit

If you filed your business income and expenses as a proprietor and reported $100,000 or more in gross receipts, your chances of being selected for an IRS audit the following year were 3.52 percent.[1] Had you reported this income as an S corporation, your chances of audit were only 0.40 percent.[2]

You have probably read that the home office increases your chances of IRS audit. We've read that, too, but we don't believe it. Regardless, let's assume that you're a little paranoid about audits, and you want to claim the home office in a way that doesn't attract the attention of the IRS.

If you operate as a corporation, your home-office deduction does not show up on either your personal return or your corporate return if you have the corporation reimburse the office as an employee expense. With reimbursement, the corporation claims the deduction for the expenses it reimburses to you. The corporation probably puts the reimbursement into a category called "office expenses" or something similar. Thus, the home-office deduction does not appear in the corporate return.

You receive the reimbursement from the corporation as a reimbursed employee expense. You do not report employee-expense reimbursements as taxable income on your personal return. Thus, you do not identify the home office on your personal return.

The easy method to find the reimbursement amount for the corporation is to complete the IRS home-office deduction Form 8829. With this form, the corporate reimbursement to you includes the home-office percentage of amounts you spend for mortgage interest and property taxes. Because the amounts are reimbursed to you by the corporation, you do not deduct them on your personal return.

Example. Your mortgage interest for the year is $10,000, and 10 percent of your home is office. Your corporation reimburses $1,000 (10 percent times $10,000), so your net mortgage interest expense for the year is $9,000 ($10,000 minus $1,000). You deduct the $9,000 as an itemized deduction on Schedule A of your 1040.

Notes

When you sell your home, you treat it as though you had taken the home office as a personal deduction. Your corporation reimbursed you for depreciation, and since depreciation is subject to the recapture tax, you must consider the depreciation recapture problem in your home-selling strategy.

The corporation may reimburse expenses only if it has adequate proof of the expenses. Therefore, make your corporation demand proof that substantiates your administrative use, regular use, and exclusive use of the home office. Think of your corporation as an IRS auditor who's making sure that the expenses meet the requirements of the law. If you fail the adequate-proof part, your corporation will have to include the expense reimbursements in your W-2 income.[3] You do not want that.

With proper proof, your corporation gets the tax deduction and you, the employee, get an employee reimbursement that is not taxable income to you.[4] A win-win situation!

If you want the home-office deduction but are paranoid about claiming it, consider the corporate form of business. It does a fantastic job of hiding the deduction.

However—remember—we do not consider the home office to be an audit flag at all. Thus, we would not incorporate just to remove the home office from our tax returns.

We also understand and appreciate a certain amount of IRS-induced paranoia.

Endnotes–Section 11

[1] Internal Revenue Service, Data Book 2008, Publication 55B, Washington, DC March 2009, Table 9a., p. 23.

[2] Ibid.

[3] Reg. Section 1.62-2(c)(5).

[4] Reg. Section 1.62-2(c)(4).

Section 12

Use Net Square Footage to Increase Home-Office Deductions

Have you ever wondered why it's called the *practice* of accounting? Like the practice of medicine, it's never perfect.

What can happen under generally accepted accounting principles varies widely. For example, one airline may depreciate an airplane over 7 years, while another airline depreciates the identical aircraft over 17 years. Both approaches may meet generally accepted accounting principles, although they produce far different earnings-per-share numbers.

Cost accounting, too, contains variations. Public Law 100-679 requires educational institutions to complete a Cost Accounting Standards Board disclosure statement for government grants. In the disclosure statement, the educational institution explains its methodology for allocating indirect costs when seeking reimbursement under government grants.

For example, the University of Delaware allocates its operations and maintenance pool costs on the net-square-footage basis. The expenses in this pool include the following:[1]
- Building services
- Repairs and maintenance
- Utilities
- Heating and cooling plants and functions
- Grounds upkeep and services
- Janitorial services

The University of New Hampshire also uses net square footage to allocate its facility service costs. The university defines net square footage as gross square footage minus common areas such as[2]
- halls,
- bathrooms,
- stairways,
- and foyers.

Notes

When you decide what percentage of your home is devoted to the home office, do you use gross square footage or net square footage? In its ("I'm here to help you") publication on the home office, the IRS says this:[3]

To find the business percentage, compare the size of the part of your home that you use for business to your whole house. Use the resulting percentage to figure the business part of the expenses for operating your entire home.

The publication further states that you can use any reasonable method to determine your business percentage, including the method just described, the "number of rooms" method, or any other reasonable method. Under the number of rooms method, if all the rooms in your home are about the same size, the IRS says you can divide the number of rooms used for business by the total number of rooms in your home to find your business percentage. If you use the number of rooms, you exclude hallways, bathrooms, stairways, and foyers, just as the University of New Hampshire excludes them when asking the government for grant reimbursements.

The number-of-rooms method will probably give you the most bang for your buck. Unfortunately, it has two problems. Problem #1: When you complete IRS Form 8829, the home-office deduction form, line 2 asks for the "total area of your home." That's not compatible with the number of rooms, and probably scares people away from using the number-of-rooms method.

Further, the instructions for Form 8829
- never mention the number-of-rooms method, and
- simply state that you may use "square feet or any other reasonable method."

The form gives you no place to disclose that you are using the number-of-rooms method or any other method.

Problem #2: If your home is like most homes, your rooms are not approximately the same size; therefore, logic tells you simply to take a pass on the number of rooms method.

This brings us to the net-square-footage method, our method of choice for avoiding the problems you encounter in the number-of-rooms method, while still keeping its bang. First, this method is compatible with the tax form where you enter the total area of your home, because the form is looking for square feet. You enter net square footage on this line (the appropriate measure of the usable square footage of your home).

Let's do this with an example. Say you measure the outside dimensions of your home and that measure produces 3,500 square feet. Say further that the inside dimensions of your office measure 280 square feet, making your office 8 percent of the whole house. That's what you claim if you simply read the IRS instructions and do not pay attention to your taxes.

Now let's remake that space using the net-square-footage method. Here you subtract from the gross square footage the footage consumed by
- outside walls,
- hallways,
- bathrooms,
- stairways,
- foyers,
- water heaters,
- crawl spaces, and
- the heating and cooling plant.

The result will be your net usable square feet.

Say your measure produces 2,500 net square feet. Divide the 280 square feet of office space by the 2,500 net square feet and you have an office equal to 11.2 percent of your home.

Comparing Square Footage Methods

Gross method	
Net square feet of office	280
Gross square feet of home	3,500
Office as a percentage of gross square footage	8%
Net method	
Net square feet of office	280
Net square feet of home	2,500
Office as a percentage of net square footage	11.2%
Increase in deductions with net-square-footage method	40%

Congratulations! You've just won yourself a 40 percent increase in deductions, just for knowing what you're doing. That means you now deduct 40 percent more of your
- mortgage interest (which reduces your self-employment and phaseout taxes),
- property taxes (which also reduces your self-employment and phaseout taxes),

Notes

Notes

- utilities,
- insurance,
- rent (if you are renting your home),
- pest control,
- maintenance and repairs (those benefiting the entire house),
- lawn care (the IRS says no to lawn care, but the courts have allowed lawn care when clients and prospects visit the home office on a regular basis[4]), and
- depreciation.

If you claim a deduction for an office in your home and you would like to increase the size of that deduction, you need to seriously consider the net-square-footage method. It approximates the number-of-rooms method championed by the IRS, but it overcomes the impediments.

New Optional Method

In lieu of actual expenses, you may use the IRS's new optional home-office deduction method rather than calculate, allocate, and prove your home-office expenses.[5]

The new IRS optional method is easy. There are two steps:[6]
1. Identify the square footage of your home office (limited to a maximum of 300 square feet).
2. Multiply the square footage times $5 a foot.

Example. You have a deductible home office in a room that measures 15' x 12', which gives you 180 square feet of home-office space. Your IRS optional home-office tax deduction is $900 (180 times $5).

Endnotes–Section 12

[1] www.udel.edu/Treasurer/CASB_Disclosure.pdf.

[2] www.unh.edu/rcm/manual11facilitieser.htm.

[3] IRS Publication 587, *Business Use of Your Home* (2011), p. 6.

[4] Charles Hefti v Commr., TC Memo 1988-22, aff'd 894 F2d 1340 (CA8, 12/18/1989); Celil Rhoads v Commr., TC Memo 1987-335.

[5] Rev. Proc. 2013-13.

[6] Ibid.

Section 13

Revenue Procedure Shows How Home Office Saves Extra Taxes with a 1031 Exchange

Tax knowledge is powerful stuff! Taxpayers in the know will stop selling their homes and start using 1031 exchanges.

In Revenue Procedure 2005-14, the IRS lays out new, helpful rules for combining
- Section 1031 tax-deferred exchanges on the office part of the home with
- Section 121 home-sale exclusions that allow qualified taxpayers to sell their homes and exclude gains of up to $250,000 if single and $500,000 if married filing joint returns.

Combining Code Sections 121 and 1031 can produce spectacular results, allowing you to
- avoid taxes on the sale of your home,
- avoid taxes on the sale of the office part of your home,
- avoid taxes on the sale of the rental part of your home,
- avoid taxes by converting your home to a rental property, and
- defer taxes on the depreciation recapture part caused by the office or rental.

Think of it! Zero taxes this year when you use the right combination of Sections 121 and 1031. You can use this combination to defer and avoid recapture, regular, and capital gains taxes on a home
- in which you claimed a home office deduction, or
- that you used as a rental property.

The word "exchange" in Section 1031 is misleading. To effect an exchange under this section of the law, you "sell" your old property and "buy" a replacement property. Note the words "sell" and "buy." To get the tax-favored treatment, you simply engage an intermediary who becomes both
- the substitute seller of your existing home, and
- the substitute buyer of your replacement home.

Think of the intermediary as a puppet: You hold the strings and tell the intermediary exactly what you want. With a little effort, you can set this up so you notice almost nothing, except the tax-favored treatment. And the right intermediary might do all the work for a fee of $750 or so.

Avoiding and deferring taxes is impressive. But the combination of Sections 121 and 1031 has an even more impressive side. How would you like, say, a $50,000 tax-free profit? That's what you get with Section 121. But then it's possible to make the $50,000 tax-free profit part of your depreciable basis on the replacement property. Now that's impressive!

Here's how it works with this $50,000 gain. The 121 and 1031 combination allows you to
- pay no taxes on the $50,000 home office gain;
- add the $50,000 gain to your basis in the replacement office (located in the replacement home); and
- depreciate the depreciable part of the $50,000.

This is a classic example of having your cake and eating it too. It doesn't get much better than this: having your *tax-free gains* turn into depreciation deductions. Wow!

In this section, we'll show you how the new rules work and how they can provide huge benefits for you.

How to Put the Rules to Work on Your Home Office

The IRS uses six examples and does a nice job in Revenue Procedure 2005-14 of explaining how you can combine Sections 121 and 1031 to reduce or eliminate taxes. In general, when you sell your home, Section 121 grants tax-free treatment to gains of up to $250,000 (single) or $500,000 (married).

Home office inside the dwelling: Section 121 allows you to apply the tax-free treatment to the gain on an office located *inside the walls* of the dwelling unit. Thus, if one-third of your house is office space, you may apply one-third of the $250,000 or $500,000 exclusion to the home office profits.

Example: The office, which you have claimed as a deduction for each of the past 10 years, takes up one-third of your dwelling. You and your spouse sell this home for a $300,000 profit (ignoring depreciation recapture). You and your spouse may use the Section 121 exclusion to
- make $200,000 of the home sale profit tax-free, and
- make $100,000 of the personal office profit tax-free.

In this case, all your profit from appreciation is tax-free.

Next, you must consider the depreciation-recapture tax (generally 25 percent) on the depreciation that you claimed on the office part of your home. No problem. Simply use the 1031 exchange to defer the recapture taxes.

Office outside the dwelling: You may not apply Section 121 to any profit on the sale of an office that's part of your home but located outside the walls of the dwelling unit.

Example: For the past 10 years, you've had an office in the guesthouse, which is located on your property about 13 feet from the main house. You sell this property, including the guest house, for a $300,000 profit. The guest house makes up one-third of the property. You and your spouse
- may use the Section 121 exclusion to make $200,000 of the home sale profit tax-free, but
- may not use any of the Section 121 exclusion on the $100,000 of home office gain (ignoring, for the moment, depreciation).

To the rescue: Don't worry about that $100,000 profit. Under Revenue Procedure 2005-14, you can use the 1031 exchange to defer taxes on both
- the taxable $100,000 profit from the sale of the guest house, and
- the depreciation recapture attributable to the guest house.

In summary, when you have a home office, inside or outside the dwelling, Revenue Procedure 2005-14 shows you
- How to use the 1031 exchange to defer the depreciation recapture tax (which applies to depreciation of the office part of your home claimed after May 6, 1997).[1]
- How to use Section 121 to make the gain on the office part of the home tax-free (assuming you meet the two-year test discussed below).
- How to use the 1031 exchange to defer taxes on the home office gain to which Section 121 does not apply (like the office in the guest house).

Real-World Example of the Benefits

Revenue Procedure 2005-14 contains six examples. We are using the third example to illustrate the benefits of the combined strategy.

Facts. Say you bought your home in 2001 for $210,000. You have used one-third of the building as an office and the other two-thirds as a residence. Today, the home is worth $360,000 and carries $30,000 in depreciation subject to the recapture tax.

Notes

Outcome: By following these steps and using the 121 and 1031 combination, you will
- avoid the recapture tax on the $30,000, and
- increase your basis in your new office by $50,000.

Step 1: You engage an exchange intermediary who charges about $750 to facilitate the exchange.

Step 2: The exchange intermediary sells your existing home for $360,000.

Step 3: You identify your replacement home, and the exchange intermediary buys it for $360,000.

Refer to the exhibit below to see how you pay zero tax on the exchange of your old home for the replacement home:
- Note the three columns for total, home, and office.
- Observe the first line, the replacement property line, which is the "amount realized" in this exchange.
- In the first gray area, look at the office column to see how depreciation reduces the basis of the office part of the home.
- In the second gray area, see how you apply $150,000 of the $250,000 exclusion to *eliminate* capital gains taxes on both the home and office.
- Also, see in the second gray area how the 1031 exchange takes care of depreciation recapture.
- Finally, go to the bottom of the exhibit and note that the gains subject to current-year taxation are ZERO.

How the $250,000 Exclusion and the 1031 Exchange Eliminate Taxes on the Home

	Total	Home	Office
Replacement property (Amount realized)	$360,000	$240,000	$120,000
Unadjusted basis of property relinquished	210,000	140,000	70,000
Depreciation on the home office	(30,000)		-30,000
Adjusted basis of property relinquished	180,000	140,000	40,000
Realized gain	180,000	100,000	80,000
Apply exclusion ($250,000 max/person)	(150,000)	(100,000)	(50,000)
Apply 1031 exchange	(30,000)		(30,000)
Gain subject to current-year taxation	Zero	Zero	Zero

Four Rules That Make You Want to Kiss the IRS

Rule 1: Revenue Procedure 2005-14 requires that you apply Section 121 before applying Section 1031. Excellent! You get the tax-free part first.

Rule 2: You may not apply the $250,000 or $500,000 exclusions to any gain attributable to post-May 6, 1997, depreciation claimed on a home office, rental, or other commercial use of the home.[2] No problem! You use the 1031 exchange to defer taxes on this part.[3]

Rule 3: The cash you receive in the combined 121 and 1031 exchange is not taxable until it exceeds the gain you exclude under the $250,000 or $500,000 exclusions.[4] Free cash is a very nice break.

Rule 4: You increase the basis of your replacement property by the gain that Section 121 excludes on your relinquished property.[5] Wow! First you exclude the gain from taxation; then you add this gain (on which you paid no taxes) to the cost basis of the replacement property and start depreciating it.

Take a look at the exhibit at the bottom of this page. Look at the Office column. See how you add the $50,000 gain from the gain on which you paid no taxes to the $40,000 adjusted basis to get a new $90,000 basis in the replacement office.

Let's look at this $50,000 in a different light. Say you pay taxes at the following federal rates:
- 15 percent on capital gains, and
- 31 percent on ordinary income.

Section 121 applies the exclusion to the $50,000 of capital gain attributable to the office part of the sale. That saves you $7,500 in capital gains taxes. Next, you depreciate the $50,000. That saves you $15,500 in ordinary income taxes. This little gift puts $23,000 in your pocket. That kind of savings makes you want to kiss the IRS.

How to Find Basis in the Replacement Home

	Total	Home	Office
Adjusted basis of property relinquished (Exhibit 1)	$180,000	$140,000	$40,000
Add gain from $250,000 exclusion	150,000	100,000	50,000
Adjusted basis of replacement property	$330,000	$240,000	$90,000

Notes

Your savings may be more or less depending on
- the ratio of land to building,
- your federal tax brackets, and
- your state brackets, and how the state treats capital gains.

Regardless, you will save big with this and the other breaks.

Convert Your Home to a Rental Property for More Happy Results

Sally and Bill Smith bought a $420,000 house that they used as their principal residence for 10 years, when they converted it to a rental property. After the conversion, the Smiths rented the house for 27 months, claimed $23,000 in depreciation, and then sold the house for $980,000 (using a 1031 exchange intermediary to sell it).

Within the proper 45- and 180-day periods laid out in the law, the exchange intermediary executed the sale of the rental house and used the proceeds to buy a $960,000 four-plex rental. This delayed exchange is often called a "Starker" exchange, after the taxpayer who won his court case, causing lawmakers to enact the delayed-exchange rules.[6]

Now that the exchange is complete, the Smiths have
- $20,000 in cash, and
- a $960,000 four-plex apartment building.

Revenue Procedure 2005-14 says the following:
- The Smiths may use the $500,000 exclusion on their old home, because in the Section 121 look-back period of five years, they used it as their principal residence for at least two years.
- The old home became a rental property and was a rental property at the time of the exchange.
- The $20,000 cash boot is not taxable because it is less than the $500,000 exclusion.

Here are the results:[7]

Replacement property	$960,000
Cash received	20,000
Amount realized	980,000
Cost of original home	420,000
Less depreciation	(23,000)
Adjusted basis	397,000
Realized gain	583,000
Apply $500,000 exclusion	(500,000)
Apply 1031 exchange	(83,000)
Gain subject to tax in current year	ZERO

Tax knowledge helps the Smiths pay zero tax on the sale of their old home and pick up a four-plex rental as well. If they had preferred, they could have received up to $500,000 cash and still not paid any taxes, because they used the combined 121 and 1031 strategy.

The basis of the four-plex after the exchange is as follows:

Adjusted basis of property relinquished (the old home/rental)	$397,000
Add Section 121 exclusion	500,000
Less cash received	(20,000)
Adjusted basis of replacement four-plex	$877,000

Two things to note here: First, the $500,000 cut the taxes on the first exchange and then created another tax benefit by becoming part of the replacement property's basis. Second, the $83,000 deferred by Section 1031 is only that—deferred—thus, it does not add to the Smith's basis in the replacement property.

When the Smiths plan their disposition of the four-plex, the $83,000 is nowhere to be found. It reduced the basis of the replacement property. Of course, with good planning, the Smiths can again avoid taxes on the sale, exchange, or other disposition of the four-plex.

Summary

When it's time to get rid of your home, you may want to do a little planning to make sure your tax bite disappears. The first step, of course, is to know what the tax bite is now.

Notes

Note that this rental is during the 5-year period and after use as the principal residence in compliance with Section 121(b)(4)(C)(ii)(I).

Notes

Revenue Procedure 2005-14 is powerful stuff. It illustrates how the use of Sections 121 and 1031 can produce spectacular results in which you
- avoid taxes on the sale of your home,
- avoid taxes on the sale of the home office part,
- avoid taxes on the sale of the rental part,
- avoid taxes on the exchange of a home that you converted to a rental property, and
- defer taxes on the depreciation recapture part.

To get the tax-favored treatment, you simply engage an intermediary, who may charge you a fee of $750 or so, to become
- the substitute seller of your existing home, and
- the substitute buyer of your replacement home.

Finally, you have to really like the part where the tax-free profit becomes part of the basis of the replacement property. That's impressive!

Endnotes–Section 13

[1] IRC Section 121(d)(6).

[2] IRC Section 121(d)(6) and Revenue Procedure 2005-14, Section 4.

[3] Revenue Procedure 2005-14, Section 4.

[4] Ibid.

[5] Ibid.

[6] Starker, T. J. v U.S., 44 AFTR 2d 79-5525, 602 F2d 1341, 79-2 USTC ¶9541 (CA9, 8/24/1979).

[7] Revenue Procedure 2005-14, Section 5, Example 1, gives these results for a single taxpayer. We simply increased the numbers from Example 1 in the Revenue Procedure to create this illustration.

Section 14

Profit on Sale of Home with Office Sheltered by Exclusions

Happy Holidays: A few years ago on Christmas eve, the IRS issued its new rules on sales of home offices.[1] Like a holiday gift that you really like, you are going to be most pleased with these new rules.

Retroactive: You may apply the new rules retroactively to amend any of your open tax years.[2] Generally, your tax return is open for three years from the day you send it to the IRS.

Overall rule: You may sell your main home for a profit of up to $250,000 ($500,000 if you file jointly) without owing a nickel to the IRS. This is a major tax-saving break for individuals. To cash in, you must:[3]
- own the property for at least two years out of the five years ending on the date of sale, and
- use it as your principal home for at least two years during this five-year period.

Husband and wife: For a husband and wife to qualify for the $500,000 exclusion, both must meet the use test, but only one has to meet the ownership test.[4]

Only once every two years: If you excluded the gain from an earlier home sale, you generally must wait two years before again taking advantage of the gain exclusion.[5]

The holiday present: Under the new rules, if you sell a home that contained an office inside the dwelling, you do not make any allocation of appreciation to the office part of your home.[6] You may have some depreciation recapture tax (very minor), as we will discuss later. But with an office inside the dwelling, you treat the appreciation on the sale of the home as if no office exists. Wow!

Example: Harry Miller bought his home 17 years ago for $65,000. He used 21 percent of his home as an office and deducted that office on his tax return every year. After making no improvements to the home for 17 years, Harry sells his home for $565,000. The Millers need not allocate any of the $500,000 to the office. Therefore, when Harry files jointly with his wife, they may exclude the entire $500,000 profit from taxation.

Thank the new rules: Before the new rules, Harry and his wife would have paid capital gains taxes on $105,000 of the appreciation (the 21 percent office part of the $500,000 gain).

Notes

Amended return: If Harry and his wife paid home office taxes on the $105,000 during any of the last three tax years, they may amend those returns and get a refund of the taxes paid.[7]

Tax on depreciation: Although you may exclude the appreciation from taxation, you may not exclude home office depreciation taken after May 6, 1997.[8] This is no big deal because
- the capital gains tax rate on this recaptured depreciation is only 25 percent (far less than the benefit rate), and
- you do not pay the 25 percent recapture tax until you sell the home (thus, you benefit by the time value of money).

Example: Betty Bestor is in the 43 percent tax bracket. She claims $1,000 in home-office depreciation and that puts $430 in her pocket. She takes this money and invests it at 5 percent, after taxes. In 10 years, when Betty sells her home, the original $430 has grown to $700. The sale of her home causes Betty to pay $250 in depreciation recapture taxes (25 percent x $1,000 original deduction). This is a good deal: pocket $700, pay $250, and make a profit of $450.

Office outside the house: If the office is not inside the house, you do not get the big appreciation break. Instead, you must pay taxes on the appreciation profits that you allocate to the office.[9]

Example: You have your office in a detached garage. Your condition is identical to Harry's above, except that your office is not inside the house. You owe tax on the $105,000 of gain that the law allocates to the office in your detached garage.[10]

Planning tip for the detached office: Eliminate the detached office and make it part of your home two years before sale of your home! This way you pass the two-out-of-five years test for exclusion of gain.

Example: You eliminate the detached office and make it part of your home two years before you sell. When you sell, the entire $500,000 profit qualifies for exclusion and you pay no taxes on the appreciation of your home.

Endnotes–Section 14

[1] The IRS made its final regulations on the sale of a home with an office effective on December 24, 2002. The new regulations replace the proposed regulations that were issued in October of 2000. Treasury Decision 9030, December 23, 2002.

[2] Reg. Section 1.121-1(f).

[3] IRC Section 121(a). To qualify for the $500,000 joint return exclusion, at least one spouse must meet the ownership test, and both must meet the use test [IRC Section 121(b)(2)].

[4] IRC Section 121(b)(2).

[5] IRC Section 121(b)(3)(A). The $500,000 joint return exclusion is available only when neither spouse claimed an exclusion for an earlier sale within the two-year period [IRC Sec. 121(b)(2)(A)(iii)].

[6] Reg. Section 121-1(e)(1).

[7] Reg. Section 1.121-1(f).

[8] Reg. Sections 1.121-1(e)(1); 1.121-1(d).

[9] Reg. Section 1.121-1(e)(1).

[10] See Reg. Section 1.121(e)(4), Examples 1 and 2

Section 15

Install a Section 105 Medical Plan Now

Because you are self-employed, Uncle Sam allows you to deduct 100 percent of your health insurance on your 1040. On the surface, this sounds like a great deal; after all, 100 percent is the WHOLE thing. But this 100 percent is sneaky. It does not produce like a 100 percent business deduction.

First, even if you qualify for the 100 percent, and health insurance is your only medical cost for the entire year, you win more cash with a Section 105 medical plan. Why? The Section 105 medical plan produces business deductions, whereas the 100 percent insurance deduction produces only a personal deduction on your Form 1040.

Second, you may not qualify for the 100 percent self-employed medical deduction. The 100 percent is not available to everyone. If either you or your spouse gets health insurance from an employer plan, you do not qualify for the 100 percent self-employed insurance deduction.

Third, without a Section 105 plan, you claim much of your medical on your personal return as an itemized deduction. Here you get crushed twice. First, the adjusted gross income (AGI) floor jumps up and takes a big bite out of your deductions. Second, the surviving deductions produce tax benefits only at your lowly personal rate.

This section shows how you win with the Section 105 medical plan and the steps you must take to put the plan in place.

How the Section 105 Plan Puts Money in Your Pocket

Example 1: You are self employed and your spouse is not an employee of another company. Say that your family medical is $6,000 each year for health insurance and $4,000 for deductibles, co-pays, eyeglasses, braces for Sally, prescription drugs, and mileage to and from the doctor. Say further that the 10 percent floor on itemized medical destroys your $4,000 deduction. In this situation, your tax benefit from the 100 percent self-employed health insurance deduction is $1,500 in your 25 percent federal tax bracket.

Notes

If you have two or more employees in your business, Obamacare complicates, and perhaps does away with, your Section 105 medical plan. See the updates page at www.bradfordandcompany.com/2016 for details and solutions.

The Section 105 plan (an HRA plan) kills both the 7.5 and 10 percent AGI problems and puts more money in your pocket.

7.5 percent problem. If you or your spouse is age 65 or older in 2016, you deduct itemized medical expenses only to the extent such expenses exceed 7.5 percent of your AGI.

10 percent problem. If both you and your spouse are younger than age 65 in 2016, you deduct itemized medical expenses only to the extent such expenses exceed 10 percent of your AGI.

You avoid the AGI floor with a 105 plan.

Notes

With a self-employed plan, you deduct the entire $10,000 as a business expense at your business tax rate, say 40.3 percent (15.3 percent self-employment tax plus the 25 percent income tax). Your tax benefit is $4,030.

You win by $2,530 ($4,030 minus $1,500) with the Section 105 medical plan. Keep in mind that the winnings come from money you already spend, and would spend regardless of how you deduct it. In other words, the Section 105 plan produces a $2,530 windfall simply for knowing what to do. You might save more.

Example 2: Employer plan involved. Say your situation is as above, but that you get your health insurance through an employer plan, either your employment or your spouse's employment, or even prior employment if you or your spouse is retired. In this case, you do not qualify for the self-employed insurance deduction. Thus, the entire $10,000 in medical shows up on your Schedule A as an itemized deduction subject to the 10 percent adjusted gross income floor. Let's say further that the floor eats your deductions and you get no benefit from your medical as an itemized deduction. (Yikes!)

Here comes the Section 105 medical plan to the rescue. With the plan, you deduct on your Schedule C all the medical as a business expense. At your benefit rate of 40.3 percent, you pocket $4,030—that's $4,030 more than you pocketed without the Section 105 plan.

Your actual circumstances may produce larger or smaller benefits, but one thing is for sure: You pocket more money with a Section 105 medical plan. What is a Section 105 medical plan?

Medical as compensation: The law says that you may deduct all the ordinary and necessary expenses to carry on your business, including a reasonable allowance for salaries and other compensation for personal services.[1] The regulations expand on "other compensation" to include[2]
- sickness,
- accidents,
- hospitalization, and
- medical expenses.

Tax-free fringe benefit: Section 105 makes the benefits of employer-provided health care a tax-free fringe benefit to the employee. The care that qualifies for this tax-free treatment may be for the employee, the employee's spouse, and the employee's dependents. Further, qualifying care is any care or treatment otherwise deductible as an itemized deduction and includes the diagnosis, care, mitigation, treatment, or prevention of disease, or treatment affecting a structure or function of the body.[3] It includes both transportation costs and the costs of insurance.

Spectacular results: What makes the medical reimbursement plan spectacular is the tax deduction for the business, combined with the tax-free benefits to the employee.

Example: Say that you are the owner of the business and your spouse is your only employee. You cover your spouse with a Section 105 family medical reimbursement plan. Here's the result:
- You, the employer, deduct the medical.
- Your employee-spouse obtains the medical as tax-free fringe benefits.

You deduct the cost. Your spouse has no taxable income from the medical reimbursement. You cannot find a better tax shelter.

Your Spouse as an Employee

The IRS says that the cost of health coverage is deductible by the employer-spouse if she provides it to her employee-spouse.[4] Further, the employee-spouse may exclude from his gross income both the cost of the health insurance coverage and the medical reimbursements.[5]

The employer may provide health coverage for not only the employee, but also the employee's spouse and dependents. With this family plan, you (the employer-spouse) obtain coverage as the employee's spouse.

For Employees Only

For purposes of the Section 105 medical plan, you, the self-employed individual, are not an employee.[6] To get around this problem,
- the married individual hires her spouse, and
- the single person either creates a C corporation or makes an arrangement with another self-employed person.

With an arrangement, the single person has a friend hire her and cover her with a medical plan. In turn, the single person hires the friend and covers her with a medical plan.

Three Great Things for Husbands and Wives to Know

1. No W-2 required for the family plan: The IRS does not require a W-2 to evidence employment of the spouse.[7]

2. Medical as sole remuneration: The IRS recognizes that often in Section 105 plans involving husbands and wives, the sole remuneration to the employee-spouse is the cost of the medical coverage.[8]

Overview Eligibility Flowchart

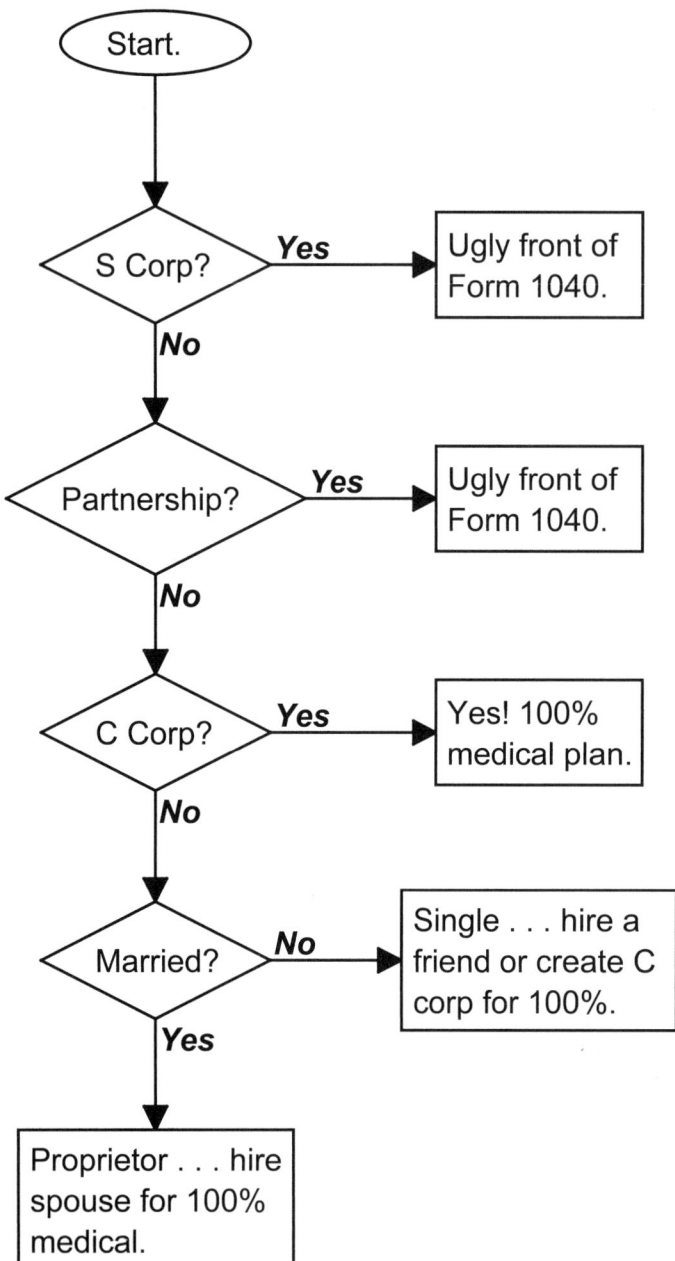

Special problems for the S corporation: See the S corporation 105 Plan section of this course for the special problems and solutions that S corporation owners face with their medical deductions.

3. Spouse medical approved: The IRS's position is that the cost of the Section 105 medical plan covering the employee-spouse is deductible by the employer-spouse.[9]

Bad News for S Corporations and Partnerships

The spouse of a more-than-2 percent owner of an S corporation or a partnership is treated as a more-than-2 percent owner; therefore, that spouse is not eligible for the Section 105 medical plan. In effect, this rule considers the spouse the same as the owner by attributing the owner-spouse's ownership to the employee-spouse.[10] Therefore, the Section 105 plan strategy does not work for husband-and-wife partnerships and S corporations.

Hot Issues with the IRS

Hot issue 1—Employee status: The hottest issue with the IRS is the bona fide employment of the spouse. If the employee-spouse is not a bona fide employee, the health coverage is a personal expense. Here are three tips on how to help ensure employee status:

Tip—No employment contract: Do not use an employment contract to prove employment status. The IRS does not believe the employment contract and finds it a useful tool to prove that employee status is lacking. Often, the husband-and-wife team violates the terms of their written employment contract, allowing the IRS to make unkind and damaging assertions.

Tip—Require a time sheet: Require the employee-spouse to submit a weekly time sheet showing the work completed. Time sheets are great evidence.

Tip—Maintain corroborative evidence: Do not destroy corroborative evidence. If your spouse typed letters or created a newsletter, you have corroborative evidence when you keep copies of the correspondence and newsletters. You might print this evidence and put it in a box, simply keeping it in case you ever need it.

Planning note: We used to be really hot on the W-2 as proof. But the fact that the IRS does not give weight to a W-2 makes us relax this belief and recommend that you make your record-keeping life easier. From a proof standpoint, the W-2 is excellent proof that you intended your spouse to be an employee. But the W-2 only helps with intent—the real proof is the time sheet. Besides, doing a payroll is a pain in the neck, and it's expensive and time-consuming.

Section 105 Medical Plan
Eligible reimbursements include:*

Insurance, like

- Major medical/health insurance
- Dental insurance
- Contact lens insurance
- Cancer insurance
- Medicare, Part A (only voluntary enrollment premiums paid, not any payroll taxes)
- Supplemental Medicare insurance (including Medicare, Part B)
- Hearing aid insurance
- School insurance
- Sports insurance
- Long-term care insurance

Over the counter drugs, like*

- Antacids
- Allergy medicines
- Pain relievers
- Cold medicines
- Hormone replacement

Other expenses, like

- Abortion (if legal)
- Acupuncture treatments
- Alcoholism treatments, including AA
- Artificial limbs and teeth
- Breast reconstruction surgery (following a mastectomy for cancer)
- Birth control pills
- Braille books and magazines
- Capital expenses, like wider entrances, doorways, adding handrails, moving or modifying electrical outlets, etc.
- Chiropractor
- Christian Science practitioner
- Contact lenses
- Co-payments
- Deductibles
- Dental treatments, implants, and braces (but not teeth whitening)
- Drug addiction
- Eyeglasses
- Eye surgery (including laser eye surgery or radial keratotomy)
- Fertility enhancement
- Lead-based paint removal
- Lodging ($50 per person/$100 a night)
- Long-term care (qualified amounts only)
- Medical conferences (for chronic illnesses of you or your family)
- Medical services (physicians, surgeons, specialists, and other medical practitioners)
- Medicines and drugs (prescribed)
- Nursing homes and services
- Psychiatric care
- Psychoanalysis
- Special education
- Sterilization
- Stop-smoking programs
- Therapy
- Transplants
- Transportation
- Trips
- Tuition (schools for learning disabilities, visually impaired, hearing impaired, etc.)
- Vasectomy
- Weight-loss program
- Wigs

Expenses that do not qualify for Section 105 plan reimbursement include

- Cosmetic surgery (those that are unnecessary, like face-lifts, hair transplants, teeth whitening, and liposuction)
- Dance lessons
- Health club dues
- Illegal operations and treatments
- Maternity clothes

---

* For details and explanations of the above expenses, see IRS Publication 502, Medical and Dental Expenses. You can download a copy by going to the IRS website at www.irs.gov.

** An individual taxpayer may not deduct over-the-counter drugs; however, the Section 105 medical plans may reimburse *prescribed* over-the-counter drugs and claim deductions for the reimbursements. See Bonus 2 that follows for more information.

Anyway, the W-2 itself proves nothing. The time sheet proves the work. Make absolutely, positively sure that you have the time-sheet evidence in good order.

Hot issue 2—The insurance policy: The IRS says that if the insurance policy is in the name of the employer-spouse, then the taxpayer-spouse must claim the insurance deductions as a self-employed insurance deduction, and not as an employee welfare benefit for her employee spouse. Obviously, this undesirable classification cuts into your cash benefit.

Tip—Buy in employee's name: If possible and easy, buy the insurance in your employee-spouse's name.

Tip—Buy in your name to save money: If you save money because the policy is in your name, get ready to fight the IRS. But keep in mind that you only have to fight if
1. you get audited, and
2. the IRS brings up the insurance as an issue.

Let's assume that's the case and you are up for the fight. The IRS has no basis for attacking the insurance. It is not in a ruling, a law, or a regulation. It is not part of any legislative history. This is simply the IRS's wish. You can easily argue for your position.

Saving money is a big hammer: You have a good argument when you save money. The fact that you can buy insurance that covers your employee-spouse and his family cheaper because the insurance is in your name carries great weight. Actually, both the courts and the IRS favor the "saving money" issues.

Hot issue 3—Retroactive start date: In Revenue Ruling 2002-58, the IRS ruled that the start date of the plan may not precede the date the plan is established. For example, if the plan is established on December 1, the plan may not start retroactively on January 1 of the same year.

Tip—Start today: Establish the plan as early in the year as possible. In any event, don't procrastinate. Make sure you have your plan in place today.

Two Additional Bonuses with the Section 105 Plan

Bonus 1. Business plan produces 100 percent deductions for long-term care insurance

The employer deducts 100 percent of the premiums for long-term care insurance that it pays on its employees under the same basic rules that al-

Notes

Good News: Ralph Frahm hired his wife Erica and reimbursed her for the health insurance that was in his name. Mrs. Frahm paid the premiums on Mr. Frahm's policy from her personal checkbook. The court ruled that the insurance was deductible as a medical reimbursement under Section 105(b). Ralph E. Frahm v Commr., TC Memo 2007-351.

Continued on page 96

# Sample **Plan Adoption Agreement and Description**
Medical Expense Reimbursement Plan for (name of business or, if no separate business name, your name as shown on your tax return)

This sample plan adoption agreement is for coverage of one-employee only and applies to tax years beginning January 1, 2014 and later. Under 2014 law, with more than one eligible employee, your health reimbursement plan must include group health coverage, but with one eligible employee only, the plan may avoid "group health coverage" and reimburse all qualified medical expenses, including the cost of health insurance purchased by the employee.

1. PURPOSE: The purpose of the plan is complete and full medical care for one eligible employee of (name of business). The plan is designed and intended to qualify as an accident and health plan within the meaning of Section 105 of the Internal Revenue Code of 1986, as amended, and to comply with the requirements of IRS Notice 2013-54 as a qualified Health Reimbursement Account under the Affordable Care Act. The Section 105 plan allows the employee to exclude the medical benefits of this plan from his or her gross income.

2. EFFECTIVE DATE: The effective date of this plan is _____ and it operates on a calendar-year basis hereafter. The plan year is the same as the tax year of this business and, like the records of the business; the records of the plan shall be kept on a calendar-year basis.

3. ELIGIBLE EMPLOYEE: Because this plan does not include group health insurance, it is a one-employee plan. All full- and part-time employees of (name of business) may participate in this plan, but should the plan cover more than one eligible employee, then the plan will be amended to purchase qualified Affordable Care Act "group health coverage" as a component of the plan.

4. BENEFITS: Within 15 days of reimbursement requests, (name of business) shall reimburse the employee for expenses incurred for the medical care of the employee, the employee's spouse, the employee's dependents, and any child of the employee who, as of the end of the taxable year, has not attained age 27. The plan covers only qualified medical expenses incurred by the employee on or after the date of hire.

"Medical care" for the Section 105 plan is defined in Section 213(d), which is the section that authorizes itemized deductions. Thus, the employee may submit for reimbursement any expense incurred that would otherwise qualify as an itemized medical expense deduction on Schedule A of IRS Form 1040. (See IRS Publication 502, *Medical and Dental Expenses*, for a list of qualifying expenses.) In addition, the employee may submit for reimbursement the costs incurred for "prescribed" over-the-counter drugs and medicines used to treat illness or injury.

"Dependents" for Section 105 are defined in Section 152, determined without regard to Subsections (b)(1), (b)(2), and (d)(1)(B). In general, this means the dependents you claim on your tax return. In addition, this means that an individual could be your dependent for the Section 105 plan even though the individual is not your dependent for your Form 1040 because

- the individual is a dependent of another taxpayer—Section 152(b)(1);
- the individual is married and files a joint tax return—Section 152(b)(2); or
- the individual has gross income equal to or above the exemption amount—Section 152(d)(1)(B).

"Child" is defined in Section 152(f)(1) to include the employee's son, daughter, stepson, stepdaughter, eligible foster child, or legally (or placed) adopted child. The term "eligible foster child" means an individual who is placed with the employee by an authorized placement agency or by judgment, decree, or other order of any court of competent jurisdiction.

Any child of divorced parents to whom Section 152(e) applies shall be treated as a dependent of both parents for purposes of Section 105.

This Section 105 medical reimbursement plan may reimburse a medicine or a drug only if

1. the medicine or drug requires a prescription,
2. it is available without a prescription (an over-the-counter medicine or drug) and the individual obtains a prescription, or
3. it is insulin.

The prescription rules apply to medicines and drugs only. They do not apply to

- equipment (such as crutches),
- supplies (such as bandages), and
- diagnostic devices (such as blood sugar test kits).

(Name of business) shall not reimburse any expenses paid by another employer.

(Name of business) may pay the medical expenses directly to the medical provider or by purchasing insurance that pays employees' expenses. In cases where the company pays the expenses, employees shall not seek reimbursement.

Similarly, expenses reimbursed by insurance are not eligible for reimbursement to an employee under this plan.

5. LIMIT ON BENEFITS: The plan ceiling for reimbursements is $ _____. Amounts in excess of the ceiling shall not be reimbursed by the plan. *(Your plan looks like a medical reimbursement plan that a business would have when you establish a ceiling on the benefits. Most businesses do not want to leave themselves open to unlimited liability.)*

6. SUBMISSION OF EXPENSES: The eligible employee must submit claims for reimbursement not less than annually. The employee is encouraged to submit claims more frequently. The employee must submit claims that clearly show that the employee or his or her dependent incurred a valid medical expense. The employee need not have paid the claim for the employer to reimburse such claim, but the evidence must clearly show that the employee is liable for the expenses.

7. ADMINISTRATION: (Name of business) has both the authority and the responsibility to control and manage plan operations and administration. (Name of business) shall keep a copy of this plan document at the office of the business, where employees or participants may inspect and review it during (name of business) regular business hours. Also, should any employee or covered dependent desire a copy of the plan, (name of business) shall provide such copy within a reasonable time of the request.

8. AMENDMENT AND DISCONTINUATION: (Name of business) may amend this document at any time. Any amendment may not retroactively preclude any reimbursement. Similarly, (name of business) may terminate this plan anytime, but any such termination may not retroactively preclude benefits.

9. NOTIFICATION AND ACKNOWLEDGMENT: (Name of business) shall promptly notify all eligible employees that this plan is available and give such employees a copy of the plan for their review. Eligible employees shall acknowledge acceptance or rejection of the plan with a signature, as set forth below.

Acknowledgment by employee
(Circle choice — Accept   Reject)

Employee _____

Printed name _____

Date _____

(Name of business)
For the employer:

By _____

Title _____

Date _____

(As a course owner, you have our permission to copy this plan and use it to help support your medical plan and reimbursements. For a copy of this plan in Microsoft Word, go online to the updates page at www.bradfordandcompany.com/2016.

Notes

Continued from Pg. 93

low the employer deduction for health insurance.[11] Watch how this *business deduction* far exceeds the long-term care deduction for the self-employed or individual taxpayer.

Pitiful deduction: First, the law puts a cap on the self-employed health insurance and personal deductions for long-term care insurance. For example, the taxpayer, age 51 to 60, may deduct only $1,230 in long-term care premiums.[12] If this taxpayer pays $5,000 for long-term care insurance, his self-employed medical insurance deduction gets whacked two times.
- First, he loses $3,770 in deductions to the $1,230 ceiling.
- Second, the $1,230 ceiling deduction goes on the front of the Form 1040, where it reduces only his income tax.

Compare this with a Section 105 plan: Watch how this shakes out for the Schedule C taxpayer in the 25 percent income tax bracket:
- The after-tax cash benefit for the $5,000 as a Section 105 deduction is $2,015 a year (40.3 percent x $5,000).
- The after-tax cash benefit for the $1,230 self-employed medical insurance deduction that shows up on the front of the IRS Form 1040 is only $308 (25 percent x $1,230).

This is impressive! The $2,015 Section 105 plan benefit is 654 percent more valuable than the benefit from the long-term care insurance deduction on the front of IRS Form 1040.

You might get more benefit. This assumes a self-employed insurance deduction for the long-term care insurance, which might not happen. Two rules could destroy the insurance deduction.
- Rule 1: You may not claim the self-employed health insurance deduction for insurance obtained through another employer either by you or your spouse.
- Rule 2: If you get slammed by Rule 1, the long-term insurance cost goes on your Schedule A as an itemized deduction, where it often gets obliterated by the 10 percent floor.

Bonus 2. New health care law continues to allow select over-the-counter drugs

Health care reform enacted on March 23, 2010 revised the definition of what the Section 105 medical plan could reimburse for over-the-counter drugs.[13]

The New Prescription Requirement

For expenses incurred after December 31, 2010, the Section 105 medical reimbursement plan may reimburse a medicine or a drug only if

1. the medicine or drug requires a prescription;
2. is available without a prescription (an over-the-counter medicine or drug) and the individual obtains a prescription; or
3. is insulin.

A "prescription " means a written or electronic order for a medicine or drug that meets the legal requirements of a prescription in the state in which the medical expense is incurred and that is issued by an individual who is legally authorized to issue a prescription in that state.

Other Over-the-Counter Expenses

The new prescription rules apply to medicines and drugs. They do not apply to

- equipment (such as crutches),
- supplies (such as bandages), and
- diagnostic devices (such as blood sugar test kits).

Crutches, bandages, and test kits continue to qualify as Section 105 reimbursable medical care if they otherwise meet the definition of medical care in Section 213(d)(1), which includes expenses for the diagnosis, cure, mitigation, treatment, or prevention of disease, or for the purpose of affecting any structure or function of the body.

Planning note. With or without a prescription, the individual taxpayer may not deduct any over the counter drugs on his or her Form 1040, Schedule A. Thus, the Section 105 plan adds another benefit with the allowance of prescribed over-the-counter drugs, such as allergy medicines.

How the IRS Looks at Total Compensation

In paragraph 8 of its settlement guidelines, the IRS recognizes that total compensation includes cash wages plus the cost of the medical plan. The courts also view total compensation as all remuneration, whether as taxable or nontaxable fringe benefits, deferred or nondeferred compensation, or other means.[14]

Example 1: Say you pay your employee-spouse $1,080 in cash wages and give her a 100 percent medical reimbursement plan that costs you $11,514. Total pay for reasonable compensation purposes is $12,594 ($1,080 plus $11,514). With 500 hours of work, you paid $25.19 an hour for reasonable compensation purposes, but only $1,080 subject to FICA and Medicare taxes.

Example 2: You pay your employee-spouse zero cash wages and cover your spouse with a Section 105 plan that provides him with an $11,514 tax-free medical reimbursement for the year. You paid $11,514 for reasonable compensation purposes, none of which is subject to any payroll taxes.

Tips for Making Your 100 percent Medical Reimbursement Plan Stand Up to the IRS

The IRS requires that you put your medical reimbursement plan in writing.[15] Use the sample plan in this section as a guide. Make sure to personalize it.

A plan that covers only the owner and his or her family is not subject to ERISA. But once you add an outside employee, you trigger both ERISA and discrimination rules that require a written instrument for the medical reimbursement plan.[16]

Prepare your written plan today.

The sample plan in this section of your reference book meets the ERISA requirement for a written "summary plan description." You must write the summary plan description so that the average plan participant can reasonably understand his rights and obligations.[17] Further, you must give every participant (even your employee-spouse) a summary plan document.[18]

Reimburse medical expenses monthly: From your separate business checking account, reimburse employee-submitted expenses monthly. If possible, reimburse your employee-spouse for every medical expense, so you have a clean audit trail for the medical expenses. To make this work, you need:
- A separate business checking account
- Payment of medical expenses and insurance from personal accounts

The reason you want this scenario is that your medical plan is a "reimbursement" plan. You need expenses and someone to reimburse.

Obviously, you could have some payments made directly from the business to the vendors. Further, your spouse may have a medical insurance plan with another employer for which you reimburse him or her based on pay stubs that show amounts withheld to cover the employee's payment for insurance. No problem! Reimburse based on the dollars taken from the paycheck. Keep the pay stub as evidence.

What You Can Do When You Have Other Employees

Discrimination allowed: If you expect to hire other employees after you hire your spouse, you can use the tax law's Section 105 allowable discrimination rules to exclude from the medical reimbursement plan:
- Employees who do not have 3 years of service
- Employees not yet age 25 on the first day of the plan year

Making discrimination work: To make this discrimination work for you, you must apply the discrimination rules *after* you hire your spouse or friend.

Notes

The Afforable Care Act impacted what you need to do with a Section 105 plan if you want to cover employees other than your spouse. See the updates page at www.bradfordandcompany.com/2016 for issues and solutions.

Notes

Endnotes–Section 15

1. IRC Section 162(a)(1).
2. Reg. Section 1.162-10(a).
3. IRC Section 213.
4. IRS Industry Specialized Program (ISP) Settlement Guideline for Health Insurance Deductibility for Self-Employed Individuals (UIL No. 162.35-02) Factual issue, January 25, 2001.
5. Ibid.
6. IRC Section 105(g).
7. IRS Industry Specialized Program (ISP) Settlement Guideline for Health Insurance Deductibility for Self-Employed Individuals (UIL No. 162.35-02) Factual issue, January 25, 2001.
8. Ibid.
9. See Section 12 of IRS Industry Specialized Program (ISP) Settlement Guideline for Health Insurance Deductibility for Self-Employed Individuals (UIL No. 162.35-02) Factual issue, January 25, 2001. The IRS based its position on Revenue Ruling 71-588.
10. IRC Sections 318; 1372. Also, see Revenue Rulings 91-26; 88-76.
11. IRC Sections 7703B(a)(3); 213(d); 106(a); 162(a).
12. Revenue Procedure 2009-50—inflation-adjusted premiums for 2010; IRC Section 213(d)(10).
13. Notice 2010-59.
14. Sanders & Sons, Inc. v Commr., 26 T.C.M. 671 (1967); Rev. Rul. 67-341, 1967-2 C.B. 156; Edwin's Inc. v U.S. 501 F.2d 675 (7th Cir. 1974); Edwin's Inc. v U.S. 501 F.2d 675 (7th Cir. 1974); LaMastro v Commr., 73 T.C. 377 (1979).
15. Reg. Section 1.105-11(b)(1)(i).
16. ERISA Section 3(l), 29 cfr 29, 1002(l).
17. ERISA Section 102; DOL Regs. Section 29 cfr 2520, 102-3.
18. ERISA Section 102; DOL Regs. Section 29 cfr 2520, 102.

Section 16

Court Case Shows How a Wife's Business Covers the Husband with a Section 105 Medical Plan

Thank the court for a case study on how to implement a husband-and-wife Section 105 plan. In this section, we will show you how the Section 105 plan works for the sole proprietor who has only one employee, her husband.

Mrs. Speltz hired Mr. Speltz to work part-time in her day-care business. Mr. Speltz already had a full-time job and a couple of side businesses. Mrs. Speltz paid Mr. Speltz no cash wages. Instead, she set the wage equal to the Section 105 medical plan reimbursement.

Planning tip: With the Section 105 plan in lieu of cash wages, Mrs. Speltz saved the considerable time and trouble involved in a payroll.

In court, the IRS said that Mrs. Speltz, the sole proprietor, could not deduct $7,818 in Section 105 medical reimbursements for the two years at issue before the court because[1]
- the Section 105 plan she put together was improper;
- the Section 105 plan failed on its own terms;
- Mr. Speltz was not a bona fide employee of the business;
- the medical reimbursements were not ordinary and necessary business expenses;
- the medical reimbursements were not reasonable based on the hours worked and the work performed; and
- if all of these arguments failed with the court, then the insurance part of the reimbursement was improper because it was deductible as a self-employed expense on the front of the Form 1040, not as a Schedule C business expense.

Notes

You have to admire the IRS's laundry list of assertions. Most people would have been intimidated. Not Mrs. Speltz. She is a tough lady. She beat the IRS like a rug on every IRS argument, winning her Section 105 medical reimbursement plan deductions in total.

She Put the Plan in Writing

With the help of her tax advisor, Mrs. Speltz used the IRS's Coordinated Issue Paper "Health Insurance Deductibility for Self-Employed Individuals" as a guide to putting together
- an employment contract,
- a salary redirection document, and
- a client data sheet.

The medical plan was embedded in these documents.

IRS regulation 1.105-5(a) states that the medical reimbursement plan need not be in writing, but the participant must know and have knowledge of the plan. In this case, the IRS argued
- that there was no proper plan under Section 105; and
- that, if the court deemed the plan proper, then Mr. Speltz did not have proper notice of the plan.

Realize that the IRS was making this argument in court. When Mrs. Speltz decided on the medical plan, she had a written client data sheet from her tax advisor stating that the medical plan would start in March and that employees (her husband was the only employee) were eligible for reimbursements of up to $6,500 a year for medical expenses and insurance. Mrs. Speltz also had an employment contract, signed by Mr. Speltz, which stated his salary would be in the form of medical reimbursements. He would see no cash.

The court ruled that Mrs. Speltz's proprietorship did indeed have a Section 105 plan and Mr. Speltz certainly had notice of the plan as evidenced by his employment agreement, testimony before the court, and his use of the plan.

Planning tip: A written Section 105 plan would have avoided this trouble. Put your plan in writing. Make sure your spouse acknowledges the contents of the plan by signing the plan document. Then, have your spouse turn in the medical expenses on a monthly basis, as this makes the plan more businesslike. The preceding section contains a sample plan that you can adapt for your business.

Forget the Employment Contract—Require a Time Sheet

Mr. Speltz signed an employment contract that required him to
- complete specific business chores,
- work a minimum of 12.5 hours a week, and
- work a minimum of seven months a year.

The IRS argued that Mr. Speltz did not work a minimum of 12.5 hours each and every week. The court ignored the 12.5-hour minimum because it conflicted with the seven-month requirement. In other words, if the intent was a minimum of 12.5 hours a week, why put in the seven-month requirement? Based on this analysis, the court ruled that Mr. Speltz abided by the terms of his employment contract.

The employment contract gave rise to a second argument by the IRS: the contract required duties that were personal chores, such as grocery shopping. The court agreed and, as part of this proceeding, Mrs. Speltz subtracted the time required for the personal chores from the business time.

Planning tip. Forget the employment contract. This agreement is often a disaster for husband-and-wife employment. In this case, as in many cases, the employment contract created hurdles for the IRS, the court, and the Speltzes. Further, you sign the employment contract today; but times change and businesses change. Changes invariably result in both you and the employee violating the agreement.

Sure, you could update the contract periodically. Will you do that? Maybe, but probably not! Why take a chance? Forget the employment contract. Even when the contract is perfect, it does not amount to much in your arsenal of proof.

Ensuring the Employee–Employer Relationship

The IRS argued that Mr. Speltz was not a bona fide employee. The court disagreed and gave a number of reasons why Mr. Speltz was a bona fide employee:
- Mrs. Speltz controlled and directed Mr. Speltz's work efforts.
- Mr. Speltz worked for the day-care center on a consistent basis, as evidenced by his testimony and the entries in Mrs. Speltz's calendar notations.
- Mr. Speltz's work was legitimate work that contributed to the success of the business.
- Mr. Speltz obtained the six hours of required training needed to work in Mrs. Speltz's day-care business.
- Mr. Speltz did the work.

Notes

Notes

The court noted that many cases like the Speltz case fail the legitimate employee test because the taxpayer fails to prove that the employee provided the services. In this case, the court found the testimony concerning the work credible. The court also liked Mrs. Speltz's notes on the calendar that showed the work done by Mr. Speltz.

Going to court is a pain. Mrs. Speltz was lucky that the court liked her notes showing the work done by Mr. Speltz.

A good time sheet provides far better proof than notes on a calendar. Quite possibly, the existence of a properly kept time sheet would have kept the Speltzes out of court.

A good time sheet
- is signed by the employee,
- is turned in on a weekly basis,
- shows the hours worked on a daily basis, and
- describes the work performed.

Planning tip. Do not create expectations with an employment agreement. Instead, use the time sheet as the proof of valid employment where actual work gets done. Avoid the employment agreement. It simply gives you something to violate.

Keep another thing in mind when it comes to proof. The time sheet is your employee-spouse's written statement that the work was done. Making this statement in writing on a weekly basis meets the timely recording requirement that permeates tax law.

How do you prove that your spouse is not cheating on the time sheet? Your spouse could, for example, simply enter the time and not do the work. How would the IRS know?

First, take our word; the IRS knows. Auditors learn how to identify cheating. The first clue the auditor sees is no corroborative evidence. For example, your spouse says he is helping with the advertising, but not one of the invoices or other advertising documents bears any notes, directions, or annotations by your spouse. This might indicate that your spouse did *not* help with the advertising.

When deciding on your tax evidence, be honest and try to think like an auditor.

The Section 105 Plan Is a Proper Business Expense

At the Speltz trial, the IRS asserted that the medical payments were personal—and not business—expenses. The IRS noted that taxpayers may not deduct personal, family, or living expenses.

The IRS noted for the court that Mr. Speltz picked up the mail and groceries and did other personal chores that Mrs. Speltz counted as business chores.

The court recognized the IRS arguments but found that Mr. Speltz did enough business chores to qualify as an employee.

Next, the court addressed the issue of compensation, which was in the form of medical reimbursement only. Here the court noted that Section 162 allows tax deductions for employee compensation and that such compensation includes payments for sickness, hospitalization, and medical expenses. Based on this review of the law, the court ruled that Mr. Speltz was an employee who was properly compensated for his work effort by reimbursement of medical expenses.

Planning tip: The IRS did not contest that the medical plan could be a business expense. The primary reason that the IRS had for saying that the medical expenses were personal involved the fact that Mr. Speltz did personal chores, and that, by association, made the medical payments personal expenses. Had there been no employment agreement and had Mr. Speltz kept a time sheet where he recorded only business chores, this discussion would not have taken place in court.

Mrs. Speltz Paid Mr. Speltz a Reasonable Amount for His Work

Remember, Mr. Speltz received no cash wages. He was paid solely with medical reimbursements under the Section 105 plan.

The IRS asserted that the amounts paid to Mr. Speltz were unreasonable. The court noted that reasonable compensation is based on facts and circumstances and not on fixed rules or exact standards.

The court divided the medical reimbursement amounts by the hours worked and came up with an equivalent wage of about $6.50 an hour. The court thought this rate comparatively low, considering that Mrs. Speltz would have to pay a third party $13 an hour.

Notes

Then the court did a second computation. This time the court said that if half of the hours logged by Mr. Speltz were not business hours, but were instead devoted to personal chores, then Mr. Speltz's rate of pay would have been about $13 an hour—the amount Mrs. Speltz would have had to pay a third-party worker.

Based on its two computations, the court ruled that the compensation paid by Mrs. Speltz to her husband was reasonable compensation.

Planning note. When you see how much the Section 105 plan is worth per hour, try to think in terms of reasonable pay for the work done. If you are going to err, err on the side of underpaying for the work. But make it a point to document what a reasonable wage for the work would be, and then do your best to make the medical reimbursement match that documented reasonable wage.

Deduct Reimbursed Insurance as a Business Expense for Medical Reimbursement

Mr. Speltz worked as a full-time employee in addition to helping his wife. In his full-time job, he received medical insurance that covered him and his family. He paid about $1,000 a year to his employer for his part of the medical, dental, and cancer insurance premiums.

The IRS asserted that Section 162(l) precluded Mrs. Speltz from deducting the insurance premiums, because this plan was subsidized by her spouse's employer. The "no-employer-subsidy rule" applies to the self-employed individual who desires the self-employed insurance deduction on page 1 of IRS Form 1040. That's not what Mrs. Speltz desired.

She wanted to deduct the medical reimbursement as a Schedule C business expense of her sole proprietorship.

The court noted that Mrs. Speltz was self-employed, but that she was not deducting the premiums as an individual self-employed person. Instead, she was deducting the premiums as an employer reimbursing an employee. Thus, ruled the court, Mrs. Speltz could deduct as a business expense on her Schedule C the insurance premiums taken from her husband's W-2 that she reimbursed her husband as part of her medical reimbursement plan for employees.

The fact that the reimbursement to Mr. Speltz was for a family plan made no difference whatsoever. Mrs. Speltz was reimbursing an employee for allowable employee medical benefits that, under law, allow for a family plan.

Some Final Conclusions

Had Mrs. Speltz lost her Section 105 medical plan deductions, she would have lost her medical deductions altogether. Considering her day-care business and her husband's employment, she did not qualify for the sole-proprietorship deduction on the first page of Form 1040, and more than likely the 10 percent floor would have eaten any medical expenses she put on Schedule A of her Form 1040.

When you consider her self-employment tax, her and her husband's combined federal income tax, and her and her husband's state income tax rates, the Speltzes realized about half of the $7,818 in deductions as cash savings.

We assume that they have continued the Section 105 medical plan for the years since this encounter with the IRS. The medical plan is like an annuity for Mr. and Mrs. Speltz. It pays them cash savings every year that they have this plan in Mrs. Speltz's business.

Mrs. Speltz won her case because she had basic knowledge of the rules and adequate documentation to prove that her husband was an employee. With just a little attention to some details, she could have avoided the trip to court. Don't put yourself in her place. Follow these basics to protect yourself:

1. Put the plan in writing.
2. Require the employee-spouse to keep a time sheet and submit that time sheet to you every week.
3. If you have other employees, consider the cost of covering the other employees.
4. Pay a zero salary if this will turn out to be reasonable, so that medical reimbursement is the only remuneration to your employee-spouse. (This avoids payroll taxes.)
5. Make the medical reimbursements on a recurring basis, perhaps monthly, so you don't forget to make the reimbursements.

Finally, thank Mrs. Speltz for her tenacious pursuit of her medical deductions. Note how the IRS made a plethora of attacks against her medical reimbursement plan. Most people would have backed right down. Not Mrs. Speltz. She deserves accolades.

However, try to avoid the route she took. A time sheet combined with a written Section 105 medical reimbursement plan will help make your plan stand up to the IRS and and help you avoid any trips to court.

Notes

Endnote—Section 16

[1] Peter F. Speltz v Commr., TC Summary Opinion 2006-25.

Section 17

IRS Puts Screws to S Corporation Health Insurance

The S corporation owner always gets the short stick when it comes to health insurance. That stick just got a lot shorter and might even disappear for owners who don't pay attention to this section of the course and take action.

First, let's review why the S corporation is a lousy place for the owner's health deductions. After this review, we'll explain how the S corporation got even worse with this latest news from the IRS. Then we'll list the steps you need to take to fix the problem now.

The Basic Rule

For purposes of fringe benefits, like health insurance, IRC Section 1372(a) treats the S corporation as a partnership and the more than 2 percent shareholders as partners. Revenue Ruling 91-26 holds that accident and health insurance premiums paid by a partnership to a partner as remuneration for services are guaranteed payments under Section 707(c); they are deducted by the partnership and should be included in the recipient-partner's W-2.

IRC Section 162(l)(5) holds that a more than 2 percent shareholder treated as a partner is a self-employed person who may deduct health insurance premiums on the front of IRS form 1040 (creating an above-the-line deduction). (This works only when the S corporation pays the premiums directly to the insurance company or reimburses the employee for the premiums--and then reports these amounts as W-2 compensation to the more than 2 percent owner employee.)

Even When It Works, It's Lousy

Under the rules above, you have the health insurance as income from your S corporation and you can deduct the health insurance on your 1040. Let's see why this health insurance deduction produces generally lousy results:
- The 1040 front-page deduction is not a business deduction; therefore, it does not reduce self-employment taxes.
- The 1040 front-page deduction is for health insurance only; therefore, you claim your prescription drug costs and doctor visit co-pays as

itemized deductions subject to the 10 percent adjusted gross income floor (which generally kills these deductions).

Claiming medical deductions under the rules above produces a poor tax result.

Why Things Just Got Worse

The IRS recently posted a new position that could put your S corporation medical deductions in far worse shape than the lousy shape they're already in. Let's say you are a more than 2 percent S corporation shareholder who cannot find health insurance that you want to buy in the corporate name, so you buy health insurance in your own name. Your tax results change dramatically. With the health insurance in your own name, the IRS says that[1]

- the S corporation does not give you medical insurance;
- since the S corporation is not buying the insurance, it does not give you a fringe benefit;
- without the fringe benefit from the S corporation, you receive no guaranteed payment;
- without the fringe benefit, you are not treated as a partner with respect to the medical insurance;
- if you are not treated as a partner for the purpose of medical insurance, you are not treated as self-employed for your personal purchase of medical coverage; and
- you do not qualify for the front-of-the-form 1040 deduction;
- therefore, you have to deduct the health insurance as an itemized deduction, subject to the 10 percent adjusted gross income limit.

The American Institute of CPAs (AICPA) submitted a proposed revenue ruling that it would like the IRS to issue concerning health insurance for the S corporation owner.[2] This proposal would simply make the IRS's position that we just described official. Thus, you need to plan your S corporaton medical insurance if you want the best deductions.

Planning You Need to Do

Choice 1: Eliminate the S corporation. You achieve a far better result when you can deduct your entire medical costs as business expenses. This is a good time to evaluate the S corporation as your choice of entity. Spend a few minutes with the section of this course that helps you choose the right business entity for you.

Proprietorship. Say you could operate this business as a proprietorship with no employees other than your employee-spouse. In this situation, you could cover the employee-spouse with a Section 105 plan that would, in turn, produce business deductions for all the family medical expenses (insurance and otherwise).

If you have this situation but you need liability protection, you can achieve both proprietorship treatment and liability protection with a single-member LLC. Also, in a community property state, the husband-and-wife LLC can elect single-member LLC status.

C corporation. The C corporation can cover its employees (even if you are the one and only employee) with a medical reimbursement plan and deduct all the medical reimbursements as business deductions.

Choice 2: Create a new plan in the S corporation. If you are happy with the S corporation and would like to continue with the S corporation without sacrificing the Form 1040 deduction for insurance, establish a medical insurance reimbursement plan at the S corporation level. You can make this plan pay the insurance premiums directly or require it to reimburse you and your spouse for premiums if you pay them individually. Your S corporation then includes the medical insurance payments made by the plan in your W-2 as guaranteed payments. This treatment is necessary to claim the insurance on the front of your Form 1040.

Action is necessary. This new IRS position on the health insurance deduction for the S corporation shareholder should galvanize you to act. Don't wait. Monies already spent could be in jeopardy, but action now can protect the money you are going to spend in the future.

Notes

Summary

In summary, if the more than 2 percent owner-employee of an S corporation buys health insurance in his own name,

- he deducts the cost of insurance in that unfavorable personal itemized deduction category on Schedule A of his personal 1040 tax return, *unless*
- the corporation reimburses him via a Section 105 plan reimbursement for the medical insurance, in which case the corporation reports the reimbursement as a self-employment taxable guaranteed payment to the owner. Because of the guaranteed payment, the owner can deduct the cost of the insurance on page 1 of his Form 1040, where it does not suffer any reduction from the 10 percent floor.

Thus, the best the S corporation can offer the owner-employee is a family medical insurance deduction on page 1 of the Form 1040 and personal itemized deductions for out-of-pocket expenses, co-payments, and other non-insurance covered expense.

Both the C corporation and the proprietorship can create business expenses for the cost of all medical insurance and all out-of-pocket and other medical expenses generally considered itemized deductions. Big difference!

Endnotes–Section 17

[1] Notice 2008-1.

[2] 2006 TNT 250-23; proposed revenue ruling from the Tax Executive Committee of the AICPA to the IRS, submitted by Jeffrey Hoops, chair, December 27, 2006.

Section 18

Pocket Self-Employment Taxes by Renting from Your Spouse

If you are single, consider forming an S corporation. Then, listen to the CDs (do this first always) and then read this section with the thought that this S corporation could be your "no-hassle spouse" (we see that smile!), possibly producing the same basic results that the married person gets in this section.

The *IRS Market Segment Specialization Program Training Guide* tells IRS auditors that they need to be aware of the *Cox*[1] case, as it expands deductible spouse rentals to include those reported on joint tax returns. Before the *Cox* case, the IRS disallowed spouse rentals when joint returns were filed. The training manual directs the IRS's field force to know that the court allowed a deduction for rent paid by one spouse to the other, even though they filed a joint tax return.[2]

In *Cox*, the court ruled that Sherman Cox could deduct the business rent he paid for his wife's interest in their jointly owned office building. Thus, Mr. Cox could deduct this rent as a business expense on his Schedule C.

Maxine Cox, his wife, reported the rental income on Schedule E of their jointly filed tax return.

The deduction on Schedule C reduced Mr. Cox's self-employment taxes. Rental income is not subject to the self-employment tax, so Mrs. Cox did not pay any self-employment taxes on the rental income. Presto! The Cox family put money in their pockets by reducing their self-employment taxes.

Save Up to 14.13 Percent

For 2016, the published self-employment tax is 15.3 percent of your Schedule C income of up to $118,500.[3] Above this plateau, your self-employment tax drops to 2.9 percent (the Medicare part).

However, the real self-employment tax is assessed on 92.35 percent of net earnings up to $128,316, which gives you the $118,500 maximum. This means that you can save at the effective rate of 14.13 percent on your first $128,316 of net 2016 self-employment income.

Note the subhead of this section: "Save Up to 14.13 Percent" which is your true rate. The "up to" part is because the savings in your self-employment tax reduce your page 1 deduction for one-half of your self-employment tax. We will show you the net dollars in an example below.

Notes

Short History of the Spouse Rental Deduction

In 1974, the IRS ruled that a Wisconsin man could deduct the rent he paid his wife in that community property state on his separately filed Form 1040.[4] This 1974 ruling updated a 1948 ruling.

In 1981, the IRS issued a private letter ruling to an individual, telling him that he could not deduct the rent he paid his wife because he and his wife did not file separately as did the couple in Wisconsin.[5]

In 1993, the *Cox* case nullified the joint return requirement.

Today, things stand exactly as the IRS's training guide points out to its agents and auditors. If you pay your spouse a bona fide rent for his or her separate ownership of property that you use in your business, you may deduct the rent regardless of how you file your tax return.

Technique Does Not Increase Deductions for Passive Losses

As you are reading this, lightbulbs might be going off at the idea that you can count this spouse rental income as positive passive income. No dice. Lawmakers and the IRS saw you coming.

IRS Regulation 1.469-2(f)(6) recharacterizes rental income from an activity in which you materially participate as non-passive income. This is the self-rental rule. Further, regulations 1.469-5(f)(1) and 1.469-5T(f)(3) attribute your spouse's participation to you.

The result here is simple. You may not use the passive income generated by paying rent to your spouse to increase your passive income and deduct more of your passive losses. Nevertheless, the self-employment savings may be more than enough to warrant serious consideration of this pay-rent-to-your-spouse strategy.

How You Pocket the Cash

Let's say that your net earnings from your Schedule C business are $105,576. Now you pay your spouse $20,000 in rent for your office space. Your spouse has no other source of income. (For purposes of pocketing cash with this strategy, the income of your spouse makes no difference. We mention "no other source of income" for the spouse only because we use that situation in the tax calculation example in the next paragraph.)

Assuming no personal exemptions except for you and your spouse and only the standard deduction, your net after-tax cash from this rent is

$2,476. (The $2,476 is less than the 14.13 percent because this is the net cash in your pocket after everything is considered, including the deduction for one-half of your self-employment tax on page 1 of your Form 1040.) This $2,476 is money in the bank this year and every year that you can use this strategy.

Keep in mind that this savings strategy costs you nothing. You simply make a rent payment to your spouse. This is like moving money from your left hand to your right hand. You just have to do it right.

Think Commercial Lease and IRS Review

If you want the rent to your spouse to stand up to scrutiny from the IRS, you need to think and act as if you are paying the rent to an unrelated third party.[6]

This starts with paying a fair-market rent for the business property or asset. If you don't pay fair rent, you likely will lose the business deductions.[7]

Making consistent, systematic, and timely rent payments to your spouse is very important here. That's what you would do with a commercial lease.

You want to make sure that you have rental money footprints, called an audit trail, from your sole and separate business account to your spouse's sole and separate account. Canceled checks and deposit slips identify and prove the money footprints. Likewise, electronic transfers verify the movement of money.

Besides proving that you paid the money, your audit-proofing strategies should include proof that you and your spouse signed a legal written lease and that the asset (or portion of the asset) you are leasing from your spouse is owned by your spouse. To stand up to IRS scrutiny, the lease must be an enforceable legal instrument.[8]

You can obtain model office and equipment leasing agreements from your local office store or online. You can engage your lawyer to draft a lease for you. Regardless of how you get the lease in place, make sure the terms are similar to those required by a third-party lessor and lessee. If two months' advance rent is normal, your lease should require two months' rent in advance. If a deposit is normal, your lease should require a deposit. You want to have a "normal" lease in writing.

State sales and use taxes might apply if the rental between you and your spouse involves equipment, furniture, or other personal property. If this is the case, your proper treatment of any applicable sales or use taxes helps prove your rental.

Getting Bigger Dollars in the Rental Equation

Short leases call for higher monthly payments and higher profits to your lessor spouse. With the shorter lease, you pay more rent each month. To learn about appropriate rental charges, phone, write, or e-mail commercial establishments that rent the items you and your spouse are considering.

Think of all the assets you need in your business. Think next of who owns what you need. In a community property state, you probably own half. You can rent from your spouse the half owned by your spouse, including your
- office;
- home office;
- cars, trucks, and vans; and
- furniture and equipment.

If you live in a non-community property state, your spouse may own the office building or vehicle in its entirety. This also can be true in a community property state.

Final Thoughts and Summary

The first question on this issue of renting from your spouse is: Will you or your spouse file a Schedule C subject to self-employment taxes? If your answer is "yes," then the rent-from-your-spouse strategy can put self-employment tax money in your pocket. (If your net income is high so that you are paying self-employment taxes only at the Medicare rate, then the savings are probably too little to justify the strategy.)

If you are single and you like this strategy, you might consider the S corporation as your leasing entity. It can provide the same basic benefits as the spouse rental without your having to get married. If you are considering an S corporation, you do need to look at the extra fees and possible extra state taxes associated with the S corporation.

If you are married with business income subject to self-employment taxes, you spend no real money to make this strategy work for you. You simple move the money from your hand to your spouse's hand and allow the government to pay you for doing that.

Endnotes–Section 18

[1] Cox v Commr., T.C. Memo 1993-326.
[2] MSSP Training Guide, Independent Used Car Dealers, Chapter 6, Expense Issues, Rent Expense.
[3] http://www.ssa.gov/OACT/COLA/cbb.html.
[4] Rev. Rul. 75-209.
[5] Private Letter Ruling 8404004.
[6] Logan Lumber Co. v Commr., (CA-5) 365 F.2d 846.
[7] International Color Gravure, Inc., 20 TCM 61, T.C. Memo 1961-15.
[8] Currier Farms, Inc., v Commr., 7 TCM 677.

Section 19

Prepay Your Expenses

A Tried-and-True Planning Tactic Recently Clarified by Regulations

A tried-and-true tax planning tactic over the years has been to pay some of next year's expenses this year so you can get the deductions this year.

The prepayment of expenses has been used less as a planning tactic in the past decade, because lawmakers and the IRS erected a series of hurdles that created considerable confusion. But now, like a brilliant ray of sunshine, the IRS has issued final regulations that show exactly what you can and can't do.

Hurray, hurray for clarity! Clarity in tax law is magnificent!

The rules apply to both accrual- and cash-basis taxpayers. In this section, we will give you the planning tools you need as a cash-basis taxpayer.

If, for some odd reason, you are an accrual-basis taxpayer, you will be happy to know that the rules outlined in this section pretty much pertain to you as well. This is amazing when you think of it, because under the accrual method you recognize the expenses as you incur them rather than as you pay them. But the new regulations provide a 12-month safe harbor rule that applies to both cash- and accrual-basis taxpayers, granting accrual-basis taxpayers the ability to prepay expenses much as cash-basis taxpayers do.

The Safe Harbor 12-Month Rule

In final IRS Reg. 1.263(a)-4(f), the safe harbor 12-month rule states that you may expense (other than where directly prohibited as explained below) amounts paid to create a right or benefit that
- does not extend more than 12 months, or
- does not extend beyond the end of the taxable year following the taxable year in which you made the payment.

Expensing prohibited: When another section of the tax law says that you must give an expenditure a required treatment, that required treatment

Notes

Year 1 prepayment

DEDUCT if only for year 2

AMORTIZE if it touches year 3

prevails. In these cases, you may not use the prepayment tax planning tactic. For example, you may not use the prepayment tactic to deduct
- interest, loans, and other financial interests;[1]
- the costs of self-created intangibles;[2] or
- furniture, equipment, and other capital assets.[3]

Example 1: You are having a great year. Come December 1 of this year, you decide to pay your business insurance or malpractice premium, which carries a cost of $11,000 and covers the period from December 15 this year through December 14 next year. You may deduct the entire $11,000 this year because[4]
- insurance does not have a special code section governing its deduction;
- coverage does not extend more than 12 months; and
- the payment does not give you benefit in the year after next year (i.e., does not extend beyond the end of the taxable year following the year in which you made the payment).

Planning note: If you are a cash-basis taxpayer, take a look at your insurance for the possibility of prepayment so you can achieve bigger deductions this year.[5]

Example 2: Assume the same facts as in Example 1, except that the policy runs from February next year through February of the following year. You may not deduct the prepayment of this premium in December this year because the payment gives you a benefit in the year after next year.[6]

Example 3: You are a cash-basis taxpayer who pays $3,000 a month in rent. On December 31 of this year, you pay 10 months of next year's rent. You may deduct the $30,000 because[7]
- the payment does not cover more than 12 months rent, and
- the payment does not extend your benefit into the year after next year.

Planning note. If you were on the accrual basis, you would not qualify for the prepaid rent deduction because of the "use of property" rule.[8] For prepayment purposes, the cash method makes prepayment easy and uncomplicated.

Over-the-Hump Strategy

Assume that you are in the 48 percent tax bracket this year, but next year you will be in the 20 percent bracket. Pay this year and save an extra 28 percent.

If this happens every two years, you can use the prepayment strategy to create your own private income-averaging method and save the 28 percent every other year.

Tax-Reform Strategy

Politicians have made tax reform a political issue for the past 25 years. Keep an eye on this. If next year's rates will be lower than this year's rates, you pocket the difference by prepaying this year.

Example: You are in the 35-percent bracket this year. Next year the 35-percent bracket becomes a 25-percent bracket. You prepay $47,000 of expenses and pocket $4,700 (10 percent x $47,000).

Not a Repetitive Strategy

Say you are in the 48 percent tax bracket (15.3 percent self-employment tax, 25 percent federal income tax, and 7.7 percent state income tax). Assume further that you prepay $43,000 in expenses. That puts $20,640 in your pocket in tax refunds.

If your income remains the same and you do not want to give back the $20,640, you will have to prepay your expenses every year. Let's say you do that for 25 years.

Let's assume also that during this 25-year period, you put your one-time savings of $20,640 into an investment that grows at 10 percent a year, compounded annually after taxes. The investment grows to $223,628. You take the cash, pay the $20,640 in taxes caused by no prepayment this year, and pocket $202,988 after taxes.

Problem: You had to put out the $43,000 prepayment a year early each year for 25 years, resulting in a loss of $422,892 in compounded value. Therefore, the change in net worth from this strategy is the $202,988 gain minus the $422,892 loss, for a net loss of $219,904.

Thus, use the prepaid-expense strategy to solve a current cash flow problem or pocket more tax money because this years tax rate is more beneficial than next year's tax rate.

Cash Method Makes This a Go-To Strategy

The prepaying strategy discussed in this section applies to cash-basis taxpayers. When you are on the cash method, you can apply the 12-month rule to most transactions.

Notes

The accrual-basis taxpayer also may use the prepayment strategy, but this taxpayer faces more rules than the cash-basis taxpayer; for example, the use-of-property rule discussed above.

The reason for the difference is simple:
- The cash-basis taxpayer generally deducts expenses as payments are made.
- The accrual-basis taxpayer generally deducts expenses as expenses are incurred.

This is a big difference. The IRS prefers the accrual method because it matches income and expenses, which eliminates many planning opportunities. The cash-basis taxpayer does not suffer from the matching requirement.

With the cash method, you generally pay the taxes as you collect the cash; but you get the deductions when you pay the expenses, even if you pay them in advance using the safe harbor 12-month rule.

Endnotes–Section 19

[1] Reg. Sections 1.263(a)-4(f)(3).

[2] Reg. Sections 1.263(a)-4(f)(4).

[3] Reg. Sections 167 and 168.

[4] Reg. Sections 1.263(a)-4(f)(8), Example 2.

[5] Accrual-basis taxpayers may have to request a change in accounting method (automatic for prepaid expenses that qualify under the law).

[6] Reg. Section 1.263(a)-4(f)(8), Example 1.

[7] Reg. Sections 1.263(a)-4(f)(8), Example 10(iii).

[8] Reg. Sections 1.263(a)-4(f)(8), Example 10; 1.461-4(d)(3).

Section 20

Guide to Section 179 Benefits for Your Business Property

Usually, tax law is kind to those who know what they're doing and downright brutal to those who don't. But the rules for Section 179 expensing contain both kindness and brutality, even for those who are up on the law.

When you buy new or used Section 179 property, you have a choice:
- write off the cost of the property over its depreciable life, or
- write off the total cost of the property (or just some of it) immediately.

Which would you rather do—write it off slowly over time or write off the WHOLE thing RIGHT NOW?

Example: You spend $2,000 for a new desk. You have two choices:
1. Depreciate the desk using the seven-year depreciation table.
2. Immediately expense all or part of the $2,000.

Because you can invest your money at a profit and because you live in an inflationary economy in which money becomes less valuable each year, the time-value-of-money rule says you are usually better off expensing rather than depreciating.

Example: You have a choice. You can
- get a tax refund of $7,000 today, or
- get a tax refund of $1,000 each year for the next seven years.

Say you earn a 7 percent after-tax return on investments. An annual investment of $1,000 at 7 percent will grow to $9,260 at the end of seven years. A one-time up-front $7,000 investment will grow to $11,240 in seven years. In this seven-year period, the time value of money gives you an extra $1,980. That's 21 percent more cash in your pocket. It comes as a result of your knowledge of how you benefit with Section 179 expensing.

To build your net worth, do two things:
- First, put your money to work as early as possible.
- Second, earn a good rate of return on your investments.

Notes

Lawmakers may extend the Section 179 deduction for software as they have done almost annually since 2002 and sometimes retroactively to the previous year. Check for updates at the updates page (www.bradfordandcompany.com/2016).

Property That Qualifies for Section 179 Expensing

Most of the furniture and equipment you buy for your business qualifies for Section 179 expensing.

Generally, you may claim Section 179 expensing on both new and used furniture and equipment.[1] Special limits apply to passenger automobiles and sport utility vehicles (SUVs) with gross vehicle weight ratings (GVWRs) in excess of 6,000 pounds.

You may claim Section 179 expensing for computer software placed in service after 2002 and before 2015.[2]

In general, you qualify for Section 179 expensing when you
- purchase the property from a third party[3] *and*
- place the property in service for business use.[4]

Planning tip: You may count built-in desks and counters as personal property eligible for Section 179 expensing. Local law does not govern the federal tax law classification of tangible personal property.[5] Local law often treats fixtures as real property, but federal law treats fixtures as eligible Section 179 property.[6]

The Section 179 Purchase Requirement

To qualify for Section 179 expensing, you must acquire the property by purchase for business use.

Property acquired for personal purposes and then converted to business use does not qualify. Similarly, property acquired by gift or inheritance does not meet the test for Section 179 property.

Property acquired from certain relatives and business entities does not qualify. For example, you do not qualify for Section 179 expensing when you purchase property from your spouse, ancestors, or lineal descendants.[7] Under this rule, property you buy from your brother or sister may qualify for Section 179 expensing,[8] but property you buy from your father or mother does not qualify. Your in-laws look very good under this rule. Regarding business entities, if you purchase property from a corporation in which you have more than 50 percent ownership, that property may not qualify for Section 179 treatment.[9]

Property That Does Not Qualify

Section 179 property typically does not include:[10]
- Property that you, as an individual, lease to others (For an exception to this rule, see the later discussion to this section under the subheading: "Qualifying for Section 179 When You Rent Property to Your Corporation.")
- Property used primarily to furnish lodging or in connection with the furnishing of lodging
- Air-conditioning and heating units
- Property used primarily outside the United States,[11] except property described in Section 168(g)(4) of the Internal Revenue Code

Laying Claim to Your Section 179 Deduction

You elect to take Section 179 expensing by filing Form 4562 with your tax return.[12] You may claim the deduction on the original tax return, even if you file this return late (e.g., this year's return filed two years late).[13]

Also, you may amend your Section 179 claims for tax years after 2002 and before 2015.[14]

Thus, if you took Section 179 expensing and are now sorry that you did, you may revoke your deduction by filing an amended return within the normal three-year amendment period. However, you may only do this once; when you revoke your election, the revocation may not be undone.[15] Likewise, if you failed to take Section 179, you may amend during the regular three-year period for amended returns.

2015 and 2016 Section 179 Dollar Limits

In addition to the earned income limit (discussed below), the following limits can affect your 2015 and 2016 Section 179 expensing:
1. A $25,000 ceiling on aggregate Section 179 expensing for the tax years beginning in 2015 and later[16] (See the note in the right margin.)
2. For the taxable years beginning in 2015 and later, a reduction in the $25,000 ceiling for each dollar of Section 179 property placed in service during the year that exceeds $200,000[17]
3. A $25,000 limit on an SUV with a GVWR over 6,000 pounds[18]

Useless for autos: On a passenger automobile subject to the "luxury limits," section 179 expensing gives zero benefit because the law[19]
- limits the expense amount to what you would otherwise depreciate, and
- eliminates depreciation to the extent you claim Section 179 expensing.

Margin note: Based on recent history, it's very possible that lawmakers will again increase the $25,000 overall limit to $500,000 and leave the $25,000 for SUVs as is.

Do This. Check for updates at the updates page (www.bradfordandcompany.com/2016).

Notes

Applying Section 179 Expensing Limits If You Are Married

If you file a joint return, tax law treats you and your spouse as one taxpayer for purposes of applying the Section 179 limits.

If you and your spouse file separate returns, you must first treat yourselves as one person for the ceilings and limits. Then you and your spouse may elect how you want to handle the allocations in your tax returns. If you do not make a formal election, the law makes a 50/50 allocation.[20]

Example: Say you are married and you place in service $20,000 of qualifying Section 179 property during the year. With elections on separately filed returns, you and your spouse may choose how to allocate the $20,000. You could take all, give all to your spouse, or take $15,000 and give $5,000 to your spouse. If you don't choose, the law will give each of you $10.000.

Planning note: Filing joint returns almost always put more tax dollars in your pocket than filing separate returns. Also, with the joint return, you do not have to make that formal election to allocate Section 179 expenses. Think of it this way: the joint return makes for less paperwork and fewer headaches.

Business Income Limits on Section 179 Expensing

You may not use Section 179 to deduct more than your business income. For purposes of Section 179, your business income is more than you would think. It includes:[21]
- Net income or loss from your active businesses (e.g., Schedule C income, K-1 income from your S corporation or partnership, etc.)
- Net income or loss from your spouse's active businesses
- Gains and losses from sales of your and your spouse's business assets (found on Form 4797 and technically referred to as Section 1231 gains and losses)
- Interest income from the working capital of your and your spouse's trade or business
- W-2 and other earned income, both yours and your spouse's

You have an active business when you meaningfully participate in its management or operations.[22]

Example: Albert, a sole proprietor, owns a salon. He employs Beatrice to operate it. Albert periodically meets with Beatrice to review developments relating to the business. Albert approves the salon's annual budget that Beatrice puts together. Beatrice performs all the necessary operating functions, including hiring beauticians, ordering beauty supplies, and writing checks to pay the bills and the beauticians' salaries. The IRS says that Albert actively participates in this salon.[23]

Albert also is a partner in PRS, a calendar-year partnership, which owns a grocery store. Charlie, a partner in PRS, runs the grocery store and makes all the management and operating decisions. The IRS says that Albert does not actively participate in this grocery store.[24]

Partnerships and S Corporations

With a partnership, the limits apply to both the partnership and the partner, but not exactly as you would expect.[25]

First, the partnership calculates its Section 179 deduction subject to the limits. Then the partnership allocates the Section 179 deduction to the partners, giving them K-1s that show the expensed amounts.

When the partner does her tax return, she just ignores the partnership for purposes of the $200,000 ceiling. She considers only herself for the ceiling.

If the partnership buys $500,000 of equipment and therefore can expense nothing, there is no effect on the partner's individual return. Say she also operates a proprietorship which claims $22,000 in Section 179 expensing on its $80,000 of equipment purchases. No problem. The partner deducts the $22,000 of Section 179 deductions.

The S corporation and its shareholders follow the same rules as does the partnership.

Many Motor Homes Exempt from $25,000 SUV Limit and Could Qualify for ???

No, the ??? is not a typo. It's a problem with lawmakers who keep changing the Section 179 deduction after the fact, recently making a retroactive change in the 2014 limit from $25,000 to $500,000.

Here's where we are at the moment. The $25,000 SUV limit on Section 179 expensing of SUVs does not apply to vehicles with GVWRs over 14,000 pounds.[26] That's not a big deal since the overall Section 179 limit as we write this is also $25,000. But lawmakers could easily increase the 2015 and 2016 overall limits from $25,000 to $500,000.

Planning note: If you plan on buying a business motor home in 2016 and you want Section 179 expensing, check the limits before you buy.

> **Notes**
>
> *Turkeys.* Don't lawmakers know that it's impossible to tax plan for retroactive deductions. You can gamble, but you cannot plan.
>
> To see if changes in Section 179 expensing were enacted, see the updates page at www.bradfordandcompany.com/2016.

How You Use the Motor Home Impacts Section 179 Expensing

When does a motor home qualify for Section 179 expensing?

In *Shirley*,[27] the court addressed this question: "Is the motor home predominately used for lodging and therefore not eligible for Section 179 expensing, or is the motor home used predominately for transportation and therefore eligible for Section 179 expensing?" If the motor home is used for both lodging and transportation, which use is the primary use?

To decide this issue, the court looked at what the motor home took the place of. If the motor home replaced lodging, it was a lodging facility. If the motor home replaced transportation, then it was a transportation facility.

While looking at the lodging, the court had to answer the question, "What is a facility primarily used to furnish lodging?" Voila! Property used like a hotel, motel, inn, or similar establishment is not a property used predominantly to furnish lodging if more than half of the rooms are used by transients. Normally, *transient* applies to accommodations rented for fewer than 30 days.

In the *Shirley* case, most customers rented the motor homes for less than 30 days. Thus, the motor homes were not facilities used predominately for lodging. Further, under its replacement theory, the court noted that the motor home renters would have had to rent motel rooms had they not rented the motor homes.

With its replacement theory, the court had no decision to make. The motor home qualified for Section 179 expensing either as
- a transportation facility or
- personal property used in the motel business.

What is your motor home? Is it a transportation facility, a home, or a hotel? The right answers produce Section 179 expensing deductions.

Planning tip: Transportation use is your best choice. You have a transportation facility if you can prove that you used your motor home for transportation on more days than you used it for lodging.

If you fail the transportation test, you have one other possibility: Is your motor home nothing more than a motel that houses transients? If so, your use fits the *Shirley* case and it makes no difference how much you use the motor home as a hotel or for transportation.

Certain Pickup Trucks Are Not SUVs

The $25,000 SUV limit on Section 179 expensing does not apply to pickup trucks with a cargo area at least six feet long that is open (or designed for use as an open area but enclosed by a cap) and not readily accessible from the passenger compartment.[28] Pickup trucks with GVWRs greater than 6,000 pounds that pass this test are eligible for full expensing up to whatever lawmakers establish as the 2015 and 2016 limits.

Example: Say lawmakers establish a $100,000 limit and that you buy a new or used $35,000 pickup truck with a GVWR of 7,200 pounds and a cargo area seven feet long that is not accessible from the passenger compartment. You may expense the full $35,000 under Section 179. (See the updates page at www.bradfordandcompany.com/2016 to see what lawmakers did with the 2015 and 2016 limits.)

Certain Cargo Vans Are Not SUVs

To qualify for Section 179 expensing in excess of $25,000 (assuming there is an excess in 2015 and or 2016), a van with a GVWR greater than 6,000 pounds must[29]
- fully enclose the driver compartment and load-carrying device,
- not have seating behind the driver's seat, and
- have no body section that protrudes more than 30 inches ahead of the leading edge of the windshield.

If your van does not meet these qualifying tests, it is subject to the $25,000 limit on Section 179 expensing of vans.

How the $25,000 Limit Applies to SUVs and Crossover Vehicles

The law says that your vehicle is a tax-classified SUV subject to the $25,000 limit when your vehicle has a GVWR greater than 6,000 pounds and is[30]
- a four-wheel vehicle (i.e., not a two or three wheeler),
- designed to carry passengers,
- not a vehicle subject to the luxury limit (see below), and
- less than 14,000 pounds GVWR.

The tax classification of SUVs includes crossover vehicles and certain vans, but the SUV classification does not include any vehicle:[31]
- Designed to seat more than nine people behind the driver's seat (think passenger van)
- Designed with an open cargo area of at least six feet that is not accessible directly from the passenger compartment (think pickup truck)

Notes

Notes

- Designed to enclose the driver compartment and load-carrying device, with no seating rearward of the driver's seat and no body section protruding more than 30 inches ahead of the leading edge of the windshield (think van)

Not subject to luxury limit: To qualify for expensing of up to $25,000, your vehicle must NOT be subject to the luxury limits. Vehicles subject to the luxury limits fall into the following two categories:
- Cars with *unloaded* (curb) weight of 6,000 pounds or less[32]
- Trucks with *loaded* weight of 6,000 pounds or less

Technically this loaded weight is called the GVWR which includes[33]
- the weight of the truck,
- the weight of the people who ride in the truck (standard weights, not all the people you could pack in), and
- the weight of the cargo.

Almost no cars are exempt from the luxury limits under this curb-weight test. For example, the really big 2015 Rolls-Royce Phantom Coupe costs about $471,000 and has a curb weight of only 5,795 pounds.[34]

When Vehicles Become Trucks for Tax-Favored SUV Status

For purposes of SUV status, your vehicle is either an automobile or a truck. You want *truck*. The SUV classified as a truck for tax purposes qualifies for up to $25,000 of Section 179 expensing.

For both the luxury auto limits and SUV expensing, lawmakers use the gas-guzzler definitions to define a truck and a car. This is a good thing, since trucks can now be built on either a truck or unibody chassis (unibody had traditionally been only for cars).

The gas-guzzler tax ranges from $1,000 to $7,700 and applies to automobiles that have a combined fuel-economy rating of less then 22.5 miles per gallon.[35] An automobile is any four-wheeled vehicle
- built for use on public highways,
- rated at 6,000 pounds unloaded gross vehicle weight or less,[36] and
- not classified as a light truck.

The Department of Transportation gas-guzzler rules consider any automobile that meets either of the following criteria a light truck:
1. The cargo-carrying area can be expanded by removing the seats using simple tools such as screwdrivers and wrenches, to create a flat, floor-level surface from the front seats to the rear of the SUV.[37]

2. It has either four-wheel drive or a GVWR of more than 6,000 pounds and has at least four of the five following characteristics:[38]
   - Approach angle of not less than 28 degrees
   - Breakover angle of not less than 14 degrees
   - Departure angle of not less than 20 degrees
   - Running clearance of not less than 20 centimeters
   - Front and rear axle clearances of not less than 18 centimeters.

Quick test: Here's a quick test you can use on your SUV to see if it qualifies for section 179 expensing of up to $25,000:
- Is the GVWR 6,000 pounds or more? If yes, continue to next bullet.
- Does this SUV have a combined fuel economy rating of less than 22.5 miles per gallon? If yes, continue to next bullet.
- Does the gas-guzzler tax apply to this SUV? If no, you have an SUV that qualifies for expensing.

Chassis: Your vehicle can be a light truck regardless of chassis type. Thus the crossover vehicles built on unibody frames, such as the Mercedes ML-350, Volkswagen Touareg, and BMW X5, qualify for truck status as does the Ford Expedition built on a truck chassis.

If a vehicle is subject to the gas-guzzler tax, you will find the tax on the window sticker. If the tax is there, you have an automobile, not a qualifying SUV.

Applying the Definitions

Here are some practical applications of the rules for defining when a vehicle is eligible for SUV expensing:

1. This SUV has a curb weight of 5,100 pounds and loaded GVWR weight of 6,500 pounds. For gas-guzzler tax purposes, it averages 19 miles per gallon. The government does not levy the gas-guzzler tax against this SUV. Result: this SUV is a light truck eligible for up to $25,000 of SUV expensing.

2. This crossover vehicle is built on a unibody frame and has a curb weight of 4,700 pounds and a GVWR of 6,050 pounds. The gas-guzzler tax does not apply. Result: this is a light truck eligible for up to $25,000 of SUV Section 179 expensing.

3. Your four-door pickup truck has a bed that extends only four feet behind the cab. It has a curb weight of 4,700 pounds and a GVWR of 6,350 pounds. It is not subject to the gas-guzzler tax despite its 14 miles per gallon for the combined gas-guzzler mileage rule. Result: this is a light truck eligible for up to $25,000 of SUV Section 179 expensing.

4. Your SUV has a curb weight of 6,300 pounds and a GVWR of 9,700 pounds. Although this is not a light truck, it is an SUV eligible for expensing of up to $25,000.

Avoid the Section 179 Gotcha When Renting Equipment to Your Corporation

Avoid the gotcha.

That's a good tax rule to follow in all cases.

When you operate as an S or a C corporation, you generally want to get the money out of the corporation without exposing it to payroll taxes or double taxation. One technique for that is to rent equipment to your corporation.

The Gotcha

As an individual, you can qualify for Section 179 expensing on equipment you rent to your corporation when you meet all three of the following requirements:

1. The lease term, considering options to renew, must be less than 50 percent of the property's class life.[39]
2. Your business deductions in the first 12 months of the lease must exceed 15 percent of the rental income.[40]
3. Your equipment rental activity may not involve holding property simply as an investment for the production of income.[41] In other words, your rental has to rise to the level of an active business to qualify for Section 179 expensing.[42]

The 50 percent and 15 percent rules are hard to meet, but the real gotcha part is that the rental has to rise to the level of a business. In other words, you can't qualify for Section 179 expensing as a passive investor who simply rents the equipment to his or her corporation.

Beating the Gotcha

Actually, none of the three requirements above are all that easy to meet, but there is a way for you to own the property personally and have the corporation get the deduction.

As explained in Section 41, you simply have your S or your C corporation reimburse you for the deduction using the employee reimbursement rules.

With the corporate reimbursement to the owner-employee, you achieve the following:

1. Avoid the big gotcha.
2. Avoid the harsh 50 percent and 15 percent rules.
3. Move the Section 179 deduction to the corporation.
4. Continue to own the asset personally, but now the asset's basis in your hands is reduced by the Section 179 deduction. (No problem—that's what you were trying to accomplish in the first place.)
5. Create a gain or a loss when you sell the Section 179 expensed asset. (Again, no problem—that's what would have happened if you had rented to the corporation.)
6. Avoid claiming the asset as an "employee-business expense" where either (a) the alternative minimum tax (AMT) would destroy that expense deduction in full, or (b) the 2 percent of adjusted gross income floor would cut into your deduction.

Yes, the reimbursement is the magic potion that beats the gotcha. It's nice to beat the gotcha.

Endnotes–Section 20

[1] IRC Sections 179(d)(1)(A)(i); 168; 167.

[2] IRC Section 179(d)(1)(A)(ii).

[3] IRC Sections 179(d)(1)(C); 179(d)(2).

[4] Reg. Section 1.179-1(a).

[5] IRS Publication 946, *How to Depreciate Property* (2011), page 17.

[6] Ibid.

[7] Reg. Section 1.179-4(c)(ii).

[8] Reg. Section 1.179-4(c)(ii), last sentence.

[9] Reg. Section 1.179-4(c)(ii).

[10] IRS Publication 946, *How to Depreciate Property* (2011), page 18.

[11] See IRC Section 168(g)(4) for exceptions.

[12] IRS Publication 946, *How to Depreciate Property* (2011), page 24.

[13] IRC Section 179(c)(1)(B); IRS Publication 946, *How to Depreciate Property* (2011), page 24.

Notes

14. IRC Section 179(c)(2).
15. IRC Section 179(c)(2).
16. IRC Section 179(b)(1)(B).
17. IRC Section 179(b)(2)(B).
18. IRC Section 179(b)(5)(A).
19. Revenue Procedure 2006-18.
20. IRC Section 179(b)(4).
21. IRS Publication 946, *How to Depreciate Property* (2011), page 21.
22. Reg. Section 1.179-2(c)(6).
23. Reg. Section 1.179-2(c)(6)(iii).
24. Ibid.
25. IRS Publication 946, *How to Depreciate Property* (2011), page 23.
26. IRC Section 179(b)(5)(B)(i)(III).
27. Robert D. Shirley v Commr., T.C. Memo. 2004-188.
28. IRC Section 179(b)(5)(B)(ii)(II).
29. IRC Section 179(b)(5)(B)(ii)(III).
30. IRC Section 179(b)(5)(B)(i).
31. IRC Section 179(b)(5)(B)(ii).
32. IRC Section 280F(d)(5) (passenger automobile is rated at 6,000 pounds unloaded gross vehicle weight or less).
33. Ibid (For a truck or van, substitute "gross vehicle weight" for "unloaded gross vehicle weight").
34. http://www.edmunds.com/rolls-toyce/phantom/2015features-specs.html
35. IRC 4064; 4064(c).
36. IRC Section 4064(b)(1)(A).
37. 49CFR523.5(a)(5).
38. 49CRF523.5(b)(2).
39. IRC Section 179(d)(5)(B).
40. Ibid.
41. Reg. Section 1.179-1(i)(1).
42. TD 8455.

Section 21

Section 179 Recapture Problems Lurk in the Shadows

Strategies to Avoid Recapture

Here we explain what happens when you stop using your Section 179 property, trade it, sell it, or give it away. As you will see, you have a couple of different roads to travel where your Section 179 deductions will make you either happy or really sad. This section will help you avoid the pitfalls and pocket the most cash.

Don't Let Recapture Destroy Your Deductions

Overview. If your business use of a Section 179 asset drops to 50 percent or less during the property's designated recovery period, tax law makes you recapture and pay taxes on any advance deductions you achieved with expensing. In other words, the recapture rules can really hammer you. Avoid recapture.

Recapture period. To avoid recapture, you must keep your business use above 50 percent during the "designated" recovery periods. There are two of these:
- For listed property, you will avoid recapture if you keep your business use at more than 50 percent for the depreciation period that applies to the alternative depreciation system (ADS).
- For all other property, you will avoid recapture if you keep your business use at more than 50 percent over the MACRS depreciation period.

IRS Publication 946, How to Depreciate Property, contains a table with all the ADS and MACRS recovery (depreciation) periods. We will discuss the two depreciation periods shortly, but first let's look at what happens when you suffer recapture.

Example: In Year 1, you claimed a $53,000 Section 179 deduction on a qualifying motor home. In Year 3, your business use drops to zero, so you must recompute your Year 1 and Year 2 deductions.

Let's say that this motor home is listed property because your primary use is for transportation.[1] Because it is listed property, you must recompute the

allowable deductions by using the ADS straight-line depreciation rates and lives,[2] which will result in the following:
- A $5,300 depreciation deduction in Year 1 (10 percent of $53,000)
- A $10,600 depreciation deduction in Year 2 (20 percent of $53,000)

With Section 179 expensing, you originally deducted the entire cost, all $53,000 in Year 1. Now, because you let your business use decline to 50 percent or less, you trigger the recapture computation above that produces a total allowable deduction for both Year 1 and Year 2 of only $15,900 ($5,300 plus $10,600).

On this year's tax return (your Year 3 recapture return), you must report $37,100 of taxable recapture income ($53,000 minus $15,900). You report the recapture in Part IV of IRS Form 4797, and it ends its taxable journey on the same tax form where you claimed the original $53,000 deduction.[3] Thus, if you reported the original deduction on Schedule C, the recapture amount ends up on Schedule C.

Don't Convert Section 179 Property to Personal Use during the Recapture Period

The Section 179 recapture rules and the listed property rules operate independently of other depreciation recapture provisions. These two sections of the law require recapture whenever business use drops to 50 percent or less during the recapture period.[4]

When you convert listed property to personal use before the end of the property's ADS class life, you trigger depreciation recapture.[5] Listed property includes the following:[6]
- Passenger automobiles
- Other transportation property
- Computers and peripherals that, although not located in a regular office, you deduct on your taxes (Computers located in your regular office are not listed property.)
- Any property of a type generally used for purposes of entertainment, recreation, or amusement

You calculate listed property recapture by taking the difference between the amount expensed and depreciation (cost recovery) calculated by using
- ADS straight-line rates, and
- ADS class lives.

For Section 179 property that falls outside the listed property category, you calculate the recapture by taking the difference between the amount expensed and depreciation calculated by using
- the fastest allowable depreciation method available (usually MACRS), and
- the shortest allowable class life (usually the MACRS life).

The fastest depreciation over the shortest life gives you the lowest amount of recapture.

Planning tip. AVOID recapture due to a drop in business use to 50 percent or less. Recapture due to the drop in business use is punitive.

Tax law is much kinder to the trade-in or sale of your Section 179 property as discussed below.

Avoid Gifts That Trigger Recapture of Your Section 179 Deductions

In general, a gift of personal property does not trigger income tax for either the donor or the recipient. However, a gift of Section 179 property does trigger the recapture tax for the business owner.[7]

Example: Last year, you claimed a $50,000 Section 179 deduction on a truck. This year, you give the truck to your daughter. Because of this gift, the recapture calculation puts $45,000 in taxable recapture income on this year's return. It puts that income in the same place on the same schedule where you originally claimed it.[8]

Avoid Recapture with a Trade-In

When you trade in a business asset—for example, your car for another car—you are making a like-kind exchange.[9] If you receive no cash or debt relief on the trade, you have no taxable income on the exchange.[10]

Example: Two years ago, you bought a truck that qualified for Section 179 expensing and you wrote off the entire $43,000 business cost. Now you want a different Section 179 qualifying truck. The dealer tells you to give him the old truck plus $12,000. Assuming 100 percent business use, this transaction produces
- no tax on the trade of the old truck, and
- a new basis in the new truck of $12,000.

Notes

This new basis is eligible for Section 179 expensing (and/or depreciation). Note that there is no recapture on this transaction.

A retirement example: Say the facts are the same as in the example above, but a few months after you make the trade for the new truck, you retire. Your new vehicle stands alone. Here are two benefits you will like:
1. You suffer no recapture tax on trade of the original business truck for the new business truck.
2. You suffer no recapture on the new truck, because you are going to convert it to personal use upon your retirement and you will not have claimed any accelerated depreciation or Section 179 expensing.

Planning tip: Avoid trapping yourself: think about your recapture escape before you claim Section 179 expensing.

Avoid Recapture Detriments with a Sale

To the extent of prior depreciation including Section 179 expensing, your sale of furniture, equipment, or vehicles produces ordinary income.[11] You report the income from the sale of your business assets on IRS Form 4797. Income from the sale of the assets you use in your business is not subject to self-employment taxes.

Example: Rhonda has a choice:
- She could sell her fully expensed truck for $35,000 and buy a new truck for $55,000.
- She could trade in her fully expensed truck plus $20,000 for the new truck.

Sale: On the sale of her fully expensed old truck, Rhonda has taxable income of $35,000. She offsets that taxable income by expensing the $55,000 cost of the new truck. This gives Rhonda a net reduction of $20,000 in her ordinary income—the same as she gets by electing to expense the cash should she make a trade. Her big benefit from the sale is that the entire $55,000 she expenses reduces her self-employment income, netting her $7,771 in saved self-employment taxes.[12]

Trade: There is no income tax on the trade. Rhonda expenses the $20,000 boot to make the trade. This gives her a self-employment tax benefit of $2,826.[13]

Benefit: The net reduction in ordinary income of $20,000 is the same in the trade and the sale of the old truck and purchase of the new truck. The self-employment tax benefit in the sale of the old truck and purchase of the new truck is $7,771 compared to $2,826 in a trade in of the old truck on the new truck. Thus, Rhonda gains $4,945 bottom-line after-tax cash by knowing that, in her case where she is subject to the self-employment tax, the sale and purchase beats the trade.

Summary

When the tax law gives you a great break like Section 179 expensing, you need an exit strategy to avoid getting burned. Seldom does the tax law give you a free lunch.

Your best strategy for Section 179 expensing is to keep the asset working in your business until the asset dies. Then you should either sell or trade it.

Don't convert a Section 179 asset to personal use without knowing how much recapture you will suffer. Also, if you are thinking of retiring or otherwise getting out of your business, make sure you know what recapture costs you may be liable for.

In general, if property is not deducted using Section 179 expensing or Section 280A (listed property) MACRS depreciation, you may convert it to personal use without suffering a recapture tax.[14]

Notes

Endnotes–Section 21

1. IRC Section 280F(d)(A)(ii).
2. IRC Sections 280F(b)(2); 280F(d)(1), coordinating with Section 179.
3. IRS Form 4797, Part IV (2010); 2011 Instructions for Form 4797, Part IV, page 10.
4. IRC Sections 179(d)(10); 280F(b)(2); Reg. Section 1.179-1(e)(2).
5. Reg. Section 1.168(i)-4(c).
6. IRC Section 280F(d)(4).
7. IRC Section 1245(b) says that 1245(a) does not apply to gifts. Reg. Section 1.179-(e)(3) says that if IRC Section 1245(a) applies, there is no recapture of the Section 179 deduction. Since gifts do not count as Section 1245(a) transactions, you have recapture.
8. See 3 above.
9. IRC Section 1031.
10. IRC Section 1031(a)(1); Reg. Sections 1.179-1(e)(3); 1.168(i)-6T(d)(3).
11. IRC Section 1245(a).
12. 15.3% self-employment tax times 0.9235 times $55,000 = $7,771.
13. 15.3% self-employment tax times 0.9235 times $20,000 = $2,826.
14. Reg. Section 1.168(i)-4(c

# Section 22

Add to Your Net Worth with Cost Segregation

Good tax planning tells you to accelerate your deductions and defer your income. Cost segregation can add tremendous acceleration to the depreciation deductions you claim on a building. That puts money in your pocket.

Imagine the acceleration in your depreciation deductions if 30 percent of your buildings could be depreciated using 5-year depreciation rather than 27.5- or 39-year depreciation. The 5-year plan is almost eight times faster than the 39-year plan.

This can happen for you right now. It can happen with a building you already own and have owned for some time. It can happen with a building you plan to buy. It can happen with a renovation you are about to undertake.

The purpose of this section is to expose you to "cost segregation," which allows you to segregate a building into two components: personal property and land improvements. When you apply the cost segregation strategy, you realize deductions faster. Considering the time-value of money, you are adding dollars to your net worth.

One study we reviewed describes a $10 million building that segregated into
- $2 million of equipment (20 percent);
- $2 million of land improvements (20 percent);
- $6 million of building (60 percent).

Focus on the percentages: Had this building cost $100,000 rather than $10 million, the percentages could have been the same. You may have an office in your home for which the percentages could be this high. Consider that 20 percent of this building qualified for 5-year rather than 27.5- or 39-year depreciation, while another 20 percent qualified for 15-year depreciation. The end result: a major difference in the timing of deductions. The timing advantage can produce huge dollar benefits for you.

Time-Value of Money

Tax law allows you to depreciate today's buildings, land improvements, and equipment to zero. Thus, the $10 million building described above has the ability to produce $10 million in depreciation.

Cost segregation hurries up your deductions. Assuming that your deductions produce tax benefits, you get the cash benefits earlier and put that cash to work sooner in your other investments. To illustrate, say that you
- earn 6 percent after taxes on your investments;
- are in the 50 percent tax bracket; and
- have $2 million that you could depreciate using either the 5-year modified accelerated cost recovery system (MACRS) or the 39-year straight-line depreciation schedule.

Using a present value of 6 percent to put your tax refunds into today's dollars, you would have
- $852,624 in today's dollars if you used MACRS depreciation, or
- $382,427 in today's dollars if you used 39-year straight-line depreciation.

In this example, you are almost half a million dollars (223 percent) better off with the faster depreciation. This is real money. This is a huge difference. This is what makes cost segregation so valuable.

Will You Qualify for the Big Benefits?

Cost segregation works for you when you will
- benefit from the quicker deductions (i.e., the passive loss rules do not limit your deductions);
- benefit from the time-value of money (i.e., you will keep the building or be in the rental business long enough to benefit); and
- spend less on the cost segregation study than you realize in cash benefits.

To benefit from cost segregation, you must realize the tax benefits of the quicker deductions. You will not realize those benefits if the passive loss rules are limiting your real-estate loss deductions.

In general, the passive loss rules destroy the loss deduction benefits of rental properties. Before considering the cost segregation opportunity, you need to identify the effects of the passive loss rules on you. You might be exempt from the rules or you might be subject. If the rules apply and limit your losses, then creating a bigger loss with cost segregation does you absolutely no good.

Example. Your modified adjusted gross income is $200,000 and you are subject to the passive loss rules. You have no passive income and you have a $35,000 net loss on your rental properties.

Result. Your $35,000 loss is a passive loss, not deductible this year because of the passive loss rules. The loss carries forward to next year, when you will again look to offset it with passive income.

The passive loss rules do not apply to you if you qualify as a real estate professional. Similarly, the passive loss rules do not apply to your business building or home office, assuming you materially participate in the business.

Planning tip. Make qualifying to deduct your passive losses your number one priority in deciding whether you want to consider cost segregation. If you can't deduct your losses now, you will not benefit from the time-value of money, meaning that you will not benefit from cost segregation.

The next consideration is the length of time you will keep the building. The longer you keep the building, the greater the benefit from cost segregation.

How many rental properties you own and how long you plan to own them are other factors to consider. With planning, you can use a Section 1031 exchange not only to defer taxes, but also to carry the segregation benefits from one building to another.

The final factor concerns the cost of the study. Surprisingly, segregation studies can be very reasonable, especially in light of the benefits.

Tax Advantages to Consider

Cost segregation can produce an array of business advantages, including the following:
- **Faster depreciation** (allowing you to put the time-value of money to work for you)
- **Section 179 expensing** on qualifying personal property assets (usually in commercial buildings and home offices)
- **Look-back depreciation** on a building you already own with which you have never used cost segregation[1] (you probably don't want to look back more than five years or so)
- **Bonus depreciation** when your look-back period includes the bonus depreciation years of 2001–2004, and/or 2008-2012[2]
- **A one-time big adjustment** that you might want to use when you have a particular tax problem (you claim all the previous years' depre-

Equipment Found in a Real Property Building

Cost segregation is hot not only with tax advisors and taxpayers, but with the IRS, too. The reason is simple: the building you see is not the building you depreciate.

The IRS Web site contains relevant court cases to help IRS examiners decide whether assets are equipment or buildings.[3] They need the guide because cost segregation takes the building you think you see and breaks it into smaller components, including equipment and building.

For ideas about parts of a building that can be classified as equipment, review the following assets for which the courts have allowed equipment-style depreciation:

- blowers
- cabinets
- carpeting
- chandeliers
- connecting fixtures to appliances
- coolers
- copper drain lines from refrigerators
- décor wall lights
- décor window treatments
- door units in partitions
- electric adapters, relays, and fuses
- electric gutters, plus ends and cuttings
- electrical branch to television equipment
- electrical outlets
- electrical switches (30 amps)
- electrical wiring for intercom equipment
- Eliason doors
- fences
- fluorescent fixtures
- gas lines to cooking elements
- glass/door storefront partitions
- kitchen grease traps
- kitchen hoods and exhaust fans
- kitchen hot water heaters
- kitchen water piping
- kitchen water traps
- lattice millwork
- lighting (emergency)
- moisture-proof lamps
- partitions (ceiling height)
- partitions (glazed)
- spotlights and flood lamps
- storage sheds
- telephone jacks
- vinyl wall covering
- water lines to cooking tables

ciation in one lump sum in the year of adjustment, using IRS Form 3115[4])
- **Asset replacement identification** for faster write-offs (As a side benefit, say you identify the cost of a roof in the study, then replace the roof in a later year. Now, you can write off the remaining cost of the original roof and start the depreciation on the replacement. Without cost identification, you would not be in a position to write off the undepreciated cost of the old roof.)
- **Lower transfer taxes** because you separated the cost of the personal property from that of the real property
- **Lower property taxes** (depending on the taxes that apply to personal property and those that apply to real property)
- **No user fee payable to the IRS** to make this accounting change[5] (Most people who make an accounting change have to pay the IRS a user fee of $2,500, although with gross income of less than $250,000, the fee is only $625.)
- **Immediate write-off** for the cost of the segregation study as a business (rental) expense in the year the study is done[6]

Tax Disadvantages to Consider

The first disadvantage: the depreciation recapture tax on personal property can be greater than the recapture tax on real property.

To the extent of gain, the depreciation claimed on personal property is recaptured as ordinary income at rates up to 35 percent. The gain attributable to depreciation of real property is taxed at a maximum rate of 25 percent. You might be looking at this difference when you sell.

Of course, the longer you wait before you sell, the less impact the depreciation recapture taxes will have. Further, you may not be in the 35 percent rate bracket at the time you make the sale.

Planning tip. If you are subject to the alternative minimum tax (AMT), use 150 percent declining balance depreciation on the personal property to avoid the 200 percent declining balance preference for AMT purposes.[7]

Again, you don't want to use cost segregation if faster depreciation will not give you tax benefits because you suffer under the passive loss rules.

Engaging a Professional

To obtain the advantages of a cost segregation study, you must engage qualified professionals. This is a wise expenditure when it puts real cash in your pockets.

Notes

In most cases, CPAs and engineers team up to provide cost segregation services. The American Society of Cost Segregation Professionals is a good place to look for a professional, although you should first check with your tax advisor for his or her recommendation.

The cost segregation professional puts together all the paperwork you need to prove the segregation. In general, the package you receive will be backed by
- audit work papers,
- experience, and
- credentials.

If you use a professional and submit the paperwork to the IRS properly, you will suffer no increased risk of an IRS audit because of the cost segregation study. In fact, a properly submitted cost segregation study might actually lower your risk of an audit, because you're showing the IRS that you know the rules and have done your due diligence to comply.

Timing Your Look-Back Cost Segregation Study

When you do your look-back cost segregation study, you submit the cost segregation depreciation changes under the rules for an automatic change in accounting, which allow you to do this for free and without IRS approval (the approval is automatic). But the IRS does not allow automatic approval whenever you get the urge. You get automatic approval once; after that, you have to wait five years or go through the IRS approval process.[8]

Recommendation. Do the cost segregation on all your properties at once. If you are going to change the depreciation in your business office, rental property, and home office, do so in a single submission.

An Unusual Opportunity

You might consider a cost segregation study when you receive an inheritance. Say, for example, that your spouse dies and the property becomes yours with a stepped-up basis. You can use cost segregation on this new stepped-up basis to allocate basis to equipment and land improvements.

You might mention to your heirs that cost segregation of the property can be a big benefit when they inherit the property after you die.

Summary

Cost segregation deserves your attention. It can create benefits with buildings you already own and buildings you will buy.

The benefits are easy to quantify. Cost segregation is one of the few investments you can make that absolutely guarantees your rate of return. In fact, you know just about everything that will happen when you give the go-ahead for a cost segregation study.

Before doing the study, make sure you are on top of the passive loss rules. If the passive loss rules deny your annual real-estate losses, a cost segregation study will do you no good.

Also, consider the AMT in choosing the depreciation method for your cost-segregated personal property.

Once you have all this in order, do the cost segregation study. Smile. You are putting the time-value of money to work for you.

Notes

Notes

Endnotes–Section 22

1. Reg. Section 1.446-1T(e)(5)(iii).
2. IRC Section 168(k).
3. Cost Segregation ATG - Chapter 6.4 Relevant Court Cases; www.irs.gov/businesses/article/0,,id=134671,00.html.
4. Rev. Proc. 2002-19, Section 2.02(2).
5. Rev. Proc. 2002-9, Section 6.02(7).
6. Write off the cost of the study as a 162 expense as recommended in "Cost Segregation Applied," by Jay A Soled, JD, and Charles E. Falk, CPA, JD, *Journal of Accountancy,* August 2004.
7. IRC Section 56(a)(1)(A)(ii). AMT adjustment applies only to 200 percent declining balance depreciation. Taxpayer may choose 150 percent under IRC Section 168(b)(2)(C) and avoid the AMT problem.
8. Rev. Proc. 2006-34; Rev. Proc. 2006-12, Section 5.04 modifying Rev. Proc. 2002-9, Section 4.02(6).

Section 23

Antiques Can Make Smart Assets for Your Business

Let's say that you have narrowed the purchase of your business desk to either an antique or a regular desk. Each desk sells for $5,000. Which desk gives you the best business result? Is the difference worth thinking about?

First, some relatively recent events have pretty much turned the antique desk into just another asset, eligible for Section 179 expensing and depreciation that produces the same business deduction results as a regular desk. However, the similarity in this equation ends with deductions.

There can be a huge difference in financial results at the time of sale. For example, in 10 years,
- the antique desk could increase in value to $15,000, whereas
- the regular desk could decline in value to $500.

To see the true financial results, you need to look at the after-tax numbers. Let's say you are in the 35 percent income tax bracket and the 15 percent capital gain bracket at the time of sale. On the $15,000 proceeds from the sale of the antique desk, your federal taxes would be
- $1,500 on the $10,000 capital gain part of the profits ($15,000 selling price minus $5,000 original basis times 15 percent);
- $1,750 on the $5,000 of depreciation recapture ($5,000 depreciated in full, taxed at the ordinary income tax rate of 35 percent).

After taxes, you pocket $11,750 on this sale of your antique desk ($15,000 minus $1,500 minus $1,750)

On the sale of your regular desk, you pocket only $325 after taxes ($500 sales proceeds minus $175 in recapture taxes).

The antique desk gives you 36 times more cash ($11,750 compared with $325). Imagine an entire office full of antiques!

Ton of Logic

If you can buy an antique car, clock, rug, desk, cabinet, bookcase, paperweight, conference table, chair, umbrella stand, coatrack, library table, or other asset that will function just as well as a new purchase, take the antique that might increase in value. It simply adds to your net worth.

Notes

Notes

How many of the business assets you bought and used in your business have gone up in value? For most businesspeople, the answer to this question is "none" or "very few." In fact, antiques are seldom even on the table, so to speak.

But now that you know their potential, give antiques a serious look. With antiques, you can get the best of all worlds:
- Beautiful assets you use in your business
- Assets you can depreciate and Section 179 expense against your business income
- Assets that can increase in value

The Court Cases

In the *Liddle*[1] and *Simon*[2] cases, the appeals courts agreed with the majority opinions of the Tax Court: that these two professional musicians who used antique and collector violins in their business as musicians for the Philadelphia Orchestra could depreciate the antique and collector violins as business assets.

The musical instruments in these cases were almost 300 years old when they were purchased for about $30,000. After use in business for less than 10 years and depreciated to zero by the musicians, the instruments were worth about $60,000. The courts noted that before the Economic Recovery Tax Act of 1981 (ERTA) changed the depreciation rules, antiques could not be depreciated, no matter how often they were used in business.

According to the Tax Court, the Second Circuit Court of Appeals, and the Third Circuit Court of Appeals, you and these musicians may now depreciate and Section 179 expense antiques. ERTA eliminated the useful-life rules and put in their place statutory depreciation periods. That change means that you now qualify for tax-favored expensing and depreciation when you
  1. physically use the antiques in the normal course of business; and
  2. subject the antiques to wear and tear as you do any other assets.

The IRS Position

The IRS did not agree with the results in the *Liddle* and *Simon* cases and issued a formal nonacquiescence in 1996, stating that it would attack taxpayers seeking antique depreciation in the other seven circuits.[3] This was 11 years ago. The IRS has not attacked yet.

Your Position

As we discuss below, we think it unlikely that the IRS will attack any depreciation on an antique physically used in your business.

The IRS is *not* going to attack antique depreciation if you live in Vermont, Connecticut, New York, New Jersey, Pennsylvania, Delaware, or the Virgin Islands. Why? These are the areas covered by the Second and Third Circuit Courts of Appeals where Liddle and Simon had their Tax Court wins affirmed at the appellate levels.

Further, beginning shortly after ERTA, lawmakers improved taxpayer rights. Now the courts can order the payment of attorney fees when the IRS brings a case that is "not substantially justified." The IRS, in its *Publication 556*, explains "not substantially justified" as follows:[4]

The position of the United States is presumed not to be substantially justified if the IRS:
- *Did not follow its applicable published guidance (such as regulations, revenue rulings, notices, announcements, and private letter rulings and determination letters issued to the taxpayer)...*
- *Has lost in courts of appeal for other circuits on substantially similar issues*

If you live in a jurisdiction outside the Second or Third Circuits, you are not likely to face an IRS attack on your antique depreciation for two reasons:
1. The IRS has already lost in other courts of appeal—the Second and Third Circuit Courts. (Thus, bringing a case along the lines of *Liddle* and *Simon* and losing would clearly be "not substantially justified" and could require the IRS to pay lawyer fees.)
2. The IRS has not made any new challenges since it issued its nonacquiescence in 1996.

Your Tax Preparer's Position

Your tax preparer can rely on *Liddle* and *Simon* for his position that you have better than a one-in-three or 50-50 chance of sustaining the antique depreciation deduction.

Artwork Doesn't Make the Deduction Grade

To claim deductions for depreciation or 179 expensing of tangible property, the asset must[5]
1. be of a type that is subject to wear and tear, and
2. be used in the taxpayer's business.

Notes

The antique violins in *Liddle* and *Simon* were deductible because they suffered wear and tear from physical use in the business.

In deciding that the antiques were deductible, the court followed *Noyce* and distinguished the holding in *Clinger*, where Ms. Clinger, a professional portrait painter, bought an oil painting for her business.[6] However, Ms. Clinger merely displayed the painting on the wall.

Unlike the violins, the painting on the wall did not endure ordinary wear and tear from physical use in the business. Therefore, the court ruled that the painting was not deductible.

Businessperson Beats Antique Dealer

When you can use an antique in your business, you pocket more cash than the antique dealer would pocket. The dealer deducts the cost of the antique as a cost of sale when he makes the sale. He then pays taxes on the profits. Those profits are subject to both self-employment and ordinary income taxes.

As a businessperson, you have the following advantages over the antique dealer:
- You can deduct your cost of the antique at the time of purchase, using Section 179 expensing (the dealer has to treat the antique as inventory, and he gets no deduction for the antique's cost until the sale takes place—maybe a year or so after purchasing it).
- The profit in excess of your purchase price is a Section 1231 gain (because the asset is used in your business). Assuming no offset with Section 1231 losses, your Section 1231 gains on the sale of antiques used in the business for over a year are treated as tax-favored capital gains

Retroactive Deductions

You may already own antiques that you are using in your business and that you have not deducted because you were following the old rules. You can claim the benefits from the overlooked depreciation this year by retroactively claiming what you missed, using IRS Form 3115.

Example. Eight years ago, Sam Aspen bought an antique clock to dress up the entryway to his office. At that time, he and his tax preparer decided that they would not depreciate the clock, because they were afraid of attack by the IRS, as they lived outside the Second and Third Circuits.

Today, realizing that he can deduct this antique clock, Aspen files IRS Form 3115. This puts eight years' worth of clock depreciation on Aspen's tax return for this year.

Summary

You have to love the two musicians who took on the IRS to win depreciation deductions on their antique musical instruments. There must be something about the Philadelphia Orchestra. Over the years, musicians from this orchestra have won a variety of court cases on business issues ranging from the home-office deduction to violin depreciation.

If you were to buy antiques for your business today, you could expense up to $133,000 of qualifying costs. Thus, the "business antique" can produce immediate deductions.

When you sell, say, 11 years from now, you pay tax-favored capital gain taxes on any appreciation above your original basis (generally, your purchase price). True, you have to pay recapture taxes on the depreciation claimed, but that's a minor inconvenience when you compare the gain to that from the usual business asset, which is just about worthless when you sell it.

The conclusion is easy: you have more after-tax cash when you choose antiques as working business assets.

Notes

Endnotes–Section 23

1. Brian P. Liddle v Commr., No. 94 7733, 76 AFTR2d &95 5327, 3d Cir, September 8, 1995, aff'g 103 T.C. 285, 94 TNT 165 8 (1994).

2. Richard L. Simon v Commr., No. 94 4237; 76 AFTR2d &95 5496; 95 2, 2nd Cir., October 13, 1995, aff'g 103 T.C. 247, 94 TNT 165 7 (1994).

3. AOD 1996 009, July 15, 1996.

4. IRS Pub. 556, Examination of Returns, Appeal Rights, and Claims for Refund (Rev. May 2008), p. 10.

5. Noyce v. Commr., 97 T.C. 670 (T.C. 1991).

6. Clinger v. Commr., T.C. Memo 1990-459 (T.C. 1990).

Section 24

Should You Use IRS Mileage Rates or Actual Expenses?

As we go to press, the IRS has not yet released its 2016 standard mileage rates. It's likely that the 2016 business mileage rate will approximate the 2015 standard mileage rate of 57.5 cents a mile.[1]

In this section, we are going to answer the following questions, among others:
- Should you use the standard mileage rate to deduct the cost of your vehicle?
- Do you qualify to use the standard mileage rate?
- What happens when you sell or otherwise dispose of a vehicle on which you claimed the standard mileage rate?

Notes

Go to the updates page at www.bradfordandcompany.com/2016 to see if the IRS has released the rate for 2016 and what that rate is.

Should You Use the Standard Mileage Rate?

You have a choice: You may use either the
- standard mileage rate, or
- actual expenses.

The standard mileage rate is in lieu of all operating expenses and depreciation or lease payments. When chosing the standard mileage rate as your deduction method, you deduct in addition to the standard rate
- parking,
- tolls,
- personal property taxes,
- interest, and
- loss on sale of the mileage-rate vehicle (assuming you don't trade).

To determine which is better—and how much better it is—you need to compare the standard rate with your actual expenses. To ensure that you get this comparison right,
- compare expenses for the full period you plan to keep the vehicle (say, three or five years) and
- compare expected gains and losses on the future sale of this vehicle.

Make the comparisons with after-tax cash: Vehicle expenses reduce business income, and that reduces your self-employment taxes. Gains and

Continued on page 155

153

Pick the Method (IRS or Actual) That Gives the Biggest Deductions

Overview: To find which method is best, do as we have done below: compare projected actual expenses with IRS rates from the time you buy until the time you expect to sell, including any projected gain or loss on sale.

Facts: You buy a car with a business cost to you of $37,000, expecting to drive it 60,000 miles during the next five years, and then selling it for $7,000 in the middle of January of Year 6. You anticipate that the mileage rate will average 56.5 cents a mile and that embedded depreciation will be 23 cents a mile.

Step 1. Compare actual expenses with IRS mileage rates			
Actual expense method		**IRS mileage rate**	
Depreciation (See below)	$15,998	Miles driven	60,000
Operating expenses	32,000	IRS rate per mile	0.565
Total deductions	47,998	Total deductions	$33,900
Tax rate	47.3%	Tax rate	47.3%
Cash savings	$22,703	Cash savings	$16,035
Step 2. Compare cash savings when car is sold			
Actual expense method		**IRS mileage rate**	
Cost of car	$37,000	Cost of car	$37,000
Less depreciation	-15,998	Less depreciation	-13,800*
Adjusted basis	21,002	Adjusted basis	23,200
Less sales proceeds	-7,000	Less sales proceeds	-7,000
Loss (gain)	14,002	Loss (gain)	16,200
Tax rate**	32.0%	Tax rate**	32.0%
Cash savings	$4,481	Cash savings	$5,184
Step 3. Compare total cash savings			
Actual expense method		**IRS mileage rate**	
From deductions	$22,703	From deductions	$16,035
From loss on sale	4,481	From loss on sale	5,184
Total cash savings	$27,184	Total cash savings	$21,219
Extra cash (after taxes) with actual method		**$5,965**	

Operating expenses include:
- Maintenance (including car washes)
- Repairs
- Tires
- Gas and oil
- Insurance
- License fees
- Registration fees

In addition to the IRS rate, you also deduct:
- Interest on vehicle loans (assuming you are not an employee)
- State and local personal property taxes on the vehicle
- Parking
- Tolls

Note: In the comparison on the left, we made sure that we compared apples with apples—none of these additional expenses were used in either the IRS or actual computations.

* 60,000 miles x 23 cents per mile estimated depreciation embedded in the estimated IRS rates of 56.5 cents-a-mile equals $13,800.

** Sale of a vehicle does not trigger any self-employment taxes or savings. Thus, use only your income tax rate for taxes on the sale of your vehicle.

*** Tax law limits annual depreciation deductions on automobiles with approximate costs exceeding about $16,000.

Estimated Luxury Limited Depreciation

Method	Computed	Limit
Yr. 1 20% MACRS	$7,400	$3,160
Yr. 2 32% MACRS	11,840	5,100
Yr. 3 19.2% MACRS	7,104	3,050
Yr. 4 11.52% MACRS	4,262	1,875
Yr. 5 11.52% MACRS	4,262	1,875
Yr. 6 Half Yr. in Yr. of Sale	1,066	938
Totals	$35,934	$15,998

Note: You may not use the the standard mileage rate to deduct a motorcycle.[2]

Continued from page 153

losses go on the sale of business asset form (IRS Form 4797) and do not affect self-employment taxes.

Example: Shirley Jones, a married woman, pays federal income taxes at a rate of 35 percent on her and her husband's taxable income. She also pays self-employment taxes of 15.3 percent on her net self-employment income of $90,000.
1. When calculating her after-tax cash savings using either the standard mileage rate or the actual expense method, Shirley uses 50.3 percent as her tax rate for the four years she expects to own the vehicle.
2. When calculating her after-tax cash gain or loss from selling her business vehicle at the end of four years, Shirley uses the 35 percent rate.

Look at These Five Planning Tips to Help You Get the Most Out of Your Vehicle Expenses

Planning tip 1: Unlike employees who may not deduct interest, self-employed taxpayers may deduct interest on their car loans, regardless of whether they use the standard mileage rate or the actual expense method for deducting their vehicle costs.[3]

Planning tip 2: If you use a home equity loan to pay for some or all of your business vehicle, the law treats treat the business part of the loan as a business loan; therefore, you deduct the interest as a business expense.

Planning tip 3: In addition to the IRS mileage rate, you may deduct, as business deductions, any state and local personal property taxes you pay on your standard-mileage-rate vehicle.[4]

Planning tip 4: Lawmakers recently made the sales tax deduction in lieu of the state income tax deduction a permanent part of the law.[5] Divide your vehicle into its business and personal components. Add the sales tax that applies to the business component to your depreciable business basis. If you choose to deduct sales taxes in lieu of state income taxes, you may deduct the sales tax that applies to the personal portion of your vehicle. This is an easy decision if you live in a state with no income tax.

Planning tip 5: Pay attention to your gain or loss on the sale of your standard-mileage-rate vehicle. First, you need to recognize that the mileage rate includes depreciation. Therefore, you have adjusted basis. That means you have a gain or loss on sale. Usually, this is a loss, which is to your benefit.

Notes

The net self-employment tax is actually 14.13% because only 92.35% is taxable. The 35% is understated because some itemized deductions are phased out. When comparing tax returns, we found phase-outs offsetting the 92.35%; accordingly, we stayed with the gross amounts in this section of the course.

Do You Qualify to Use the Standard Mileage Rate on Your Vehicle?

You may not use the standard mileage rate if you
- operate your business as a corporation and claim the vehicle as a corporate expense;[6]
- use five or more vehicles at the same time in your business;[7]
- claim a depreciation deduction on the vehicle using any method other than straight line (such as MACRS or bonus depreciation);[8]
- claim Section 179 expensing on any part of the vehicle;[9] or
- claim actual expenses on a leased vehicle.[10]

The new rules allow you to use the standard mileage rate on up to four vehicles at the same time.[11] The old rule put the limit at two vehicles.

Example: You have four vehicles in your household. You, your employee-spouse, your employee-daughter, and your personal assistant are sometimes all on the road at the same time, driving your four vehicles. Under the new rule, you may claim the standard mileage rate on all four vehicles.

Alternatively, you could claim the standard mileage rate on one of the vehicles and use the actual expense method on the other three vehicles.

As you can see, qualifying for the standard mileage rate is not difficult. The bigger question is: Does the standard mileage rate put more money in your pocket than the actual expense method? Do the easy arithmetic described above to determine the better method.

What Happens When You Sell or Otherwise Dispose of a Vehicle on Which You Claimed the Standard Mileage Rate?

You depreciate your vehicle when you use the standard mileage method. The rate of depreciation is as follows:

Year(s)	Cents per Mile
2015	24.0
2014	22.0
2013	23.0
2012	23.0
2011	22.0
2010	23.0

2009	21.0
2008	21.0
2007	19.0
2005–2006	17.0
2003–2004	16.0
2001–2002	15.0
2000	14.0
1994–1999	12.0
1992–1993	11.5
1989–1991	11.0
1988	10.5
1987	10.0
1986	9.0
1983–1985	8.0
1982	7.5
1980–1981	7.0

For tax years after 1989, the depreciation rates apply to all business miles. For tax years before 1990, the depreciation rates apply to the first 15,000 miles.

Example 1: You bought a vehicle for $22,000 in 1987 and drove it 20,000 miles that year. You calculate your adjusted basis by subtracting depreciation of 10 cents a mile on the 15,000-mile ceiling, not on the 20,000 miles you drove that year. Thus, your adjusted basis for gain or loss is $20,500 after you subtract depreciation of $1,500 ($0.10 x 15,000 miles).

Example 2: You bought a vehicle for $35,000 in 2008 and drove it 20,000 miles a year in 2008 and 2009. You deducted your car expenses using the standard mileage rates. Included in the standard mileage rates is depreciation of 21 cents a mile. Multiply the 21 cents by 40,000 miles and you get $8,400 of depreciation. Thus, your adjusted basis at the end of 2009 is $26,600 ($35,000 minus $8,400).

Do you use the standard mileage rate? If so, you will have a gain or loss when you sell. How much is your gain or loss? You should know! If it is a loss, think of this loss as money in the bank. You can deduct the loss and reap the tax benefits when you sell your car to a third party.

Planning tip triggered by vehicle trades: Did you do these two things with your business vehicle?
1. Did you trade your old business vehicle for your replacement business vehicle (say, a car for a car)?
2. Did you use IRS mileage rates?

Notes

If you answered "yes" to both questions, your basis in the replacement vehicle consists of both vehicles. You might have a large deduction when you sell this vehicle.

Example: Say you have been in business for 10 years; during that time, you have had four cars. You paid $30,000 for the first car; with each of the three subsequent trade-ins, you paid $15,000, for a grand total of $75,000 invested in cars during your 10-year business life.

During this 10-year period, you drove your vehicles an average of 17,000 miles a year. Further, to keep our numbers simple, let's assume that the average rate of depreciation in your standard mileage rate deductions is 15 cents a mile, for a total of $25,500 over the 10 years.

This gives you an adjusted basis of $49,500 on the car you currently drive ($75,000 minus $25,500). This basis is higher than the $30,000 sticker price for the car. How does that happen? Trades! Trades roll over your old basis to the new car. That's what allows you to think of all the cars at once in one easy-to-grasp arithmetic view.

If you can sell this standard mileage rate vehicle for $15,000, you have a deductible loss of $34,500 ($15,000 minus $49,500), producing a nice piece of change just for knowing what you are doing.

Luxury Auto Limits

When you use the actual expense method to deduct your vehicle, you can rub against the luxury auto limits that apply to depreciation deductions. Revenue Procedure 2015-19 contains tables detailing the limits on depreciation that apply to passenger automobiles, including trucks and vans, first placed in service in 2015. The IRS will release the 2016 tables during spring 2015.

Will lawmakers enact bonus depreciation for 2015 and 2016? Check the updates page at www.bradfordandcompany.com/2016.

Passenger auto limits: The limits for passenger automobiles first placed in service in 2015 are as follows:[12]

Tax Year	New	Used
1st Tax Year	$3,160	$3,160
2nd Tax Year	5,100	5,100
3rd Tax Year	3,050	3,050
Each Succeeding Year	1,875	1,875

The limits condemn a new car for which you choose bonus depreciation to a maximum of $23,060 in depreciation during the first five years of ownership. The practice of restricting depreciation on cars goes back to 1984, when Congress defined and limited deductions on so-called luxury cars.

Planning note: The luxury limits often mean that you have a deductible tax loss when you sell your business car to a third party.

Question: If you sold your business car today, would you have a gain or a loss? How much?

Note: When you sell a car that you deducted using the IRS mileage rate, you also have a taxable gain or deductible loss.

Limits on light trucks and vans: For purposes of the luxury limits, the term "trucks and vans" refers to passenger vehicles classified as trucks, including minivans and sport utility vehicles (SUVs). This group is classified as "light" because it fails the more than 6,000 pound GVWR test; therefore, luxury limits apply. The depreciation limits for *light* trucks and vans first placed in service during 2015 are as follows:[13]

Tax Year	New	Used
1st Tax Year	$3,460	$3,460
2nd Tax Year	5,500	5,500
3rd Tax Year	3,350	3,350
Each Succeeding Year	1,975	1,975

Will lawmakers enact bonus depreciation for 2015 and 2016? Check the updates page at www.bradfordandcompany.com/2016.

This table condemns the light truck or van to a maximum of $16,260 in depreciation during the first five years of ownership. In other words, Congress thinks that a new light truck, van, crossover vehicle, or SUV costing $16,260 is a luxury vehicle.

As we go to press, the 2015 and 2016 Section 179 limits are $25,000. Lawmakers may increase the $25,000 Section 179 limit to $500,000. Check the updates page at www.bradfordandcompany.com/2016.

Remember, trucks, vans, and SUVs with gross vehicle weights of 6,001 pounds or more avoid the luxury limits. The 2015 and 2016 first-year limits on these vehicles are as follows:
- For qualifying SUVs, up to $25,000 in Section 179 expensing, plus 50 percent bonus depreciation, and up to 20 percent MACRS depreciation.
- For qualifying heavy pick up trucks and vans, up to $25,000 in Section 179 expensing, plus 50 percent bonus depreciation, and up to 20 percent MACRS depreciation.

Summary

To determine whether the standard mileage rate of 56.5 cents a mile is right for you, compare it with your actual expenses (operating expenses plus either depreciation or lease payments). This takes only a few minutes and can produce some true savings. Using the right method could easily enable you to pocket thousands in after-tax cash.

If you will save money with the standard mileage method, make sure that you qualify for the deduction.

If you used standard mileage rates, be sure to calculate gain or loss on sale. Not only is this the law, but the results are usually to your benefit.

Don't procrastinate—make the gain or loss on sale calculation now.

If you have traded in business cars, consider all the cars in the string of trades. A trade (technically a Section 1031 exchange) rolls over the basis of your vehicle to the new vehicle, which can produce some magnificent deductions when you sell the new vehicle to a third party.

Endnotes–Section 24

[1] IRS Notice 2014-79.

[2] Revenue Procedure 2010-51, Section 3.01 makes it clear that this procedure applies to automobiles, vans, pickups, and panel trucks. It does not apply to motorcycles.

[3] Revenue Procedure 2010.51.

[4] Ibid.

[5] IRC Section 164(b)(5).

[6] Revenue Procedure 2010-51, Sections 7.07 and 7.08 states that the standard mileage rate is an optional rate for employees and self-employed individuals.

[7] Revenue Procedure 2010-51, Section 4.05(1).

[8] Revenue Procedure 2010-51, Section 4.05(3).

[9] Ibid.

[10] Revenue Procedure 2010-51, Section 4.02.

[11] Revenue Procedure 2010-51, Section 4.05(1).

[12] Revenue Procedure 2015-19.

[13] Ibid.

Section 25

Avoid Taxes with Section 1031 Exchanges of Vehicles

All Exchanges Work, Including the Delayed and Reverse Starker Exchanges

How would you like to sell your old business vehicle without paying any taxes on the gain? That's exactly what you can do with a properly designed 1031 exchange. In this case, you first engage an exchange intermediary (sometimes called an exchange facilitator) for the proper paperwork and timing on the sale and replacement vehicles.

You also can do a two-party 1031 tax-deferred exchange by going to the dealer and trading your old vehicle for a like-kind replacement. You do not need an intermediary or a facilitator to make this happen.

More business people are paying more taxes on their vehicle sales. Why? They took advantage of Section 179 expensing and bonus depreciation when it was available. Now, when it's time to sell, the basis is low (maybe even zero) and the taxes are high. Hence, the need for the 1031 vehicle strategies we give you in this section.

This section shows you how to stop paying taxes on the sale of your vehicles. In the first part of the section, we will show you how to identify the tax problem or benefit with your vehicles. In the second part, we show you how to apply the immediate, delayed, and reverse 1031 exchanges to your vehicles.

You Have Gain or Loss

If you own your business vehicle, you have a reportable tax gain or tax loss when you sell that vehicle, regardless of how you deducted it. To plan wisely, you need to know if you have a gain or loss. Why?
- Gains create taxes, which you can avoid with 1031 exchanges.
- Losses create cash from reduced taxes, which you can realize by selling your vehicle to a third party.

Notes

Tax law gives you only two ways to deduct vehicles:
1. The IRS standard mileage rate method
2. The actual expense method

Regardless of the deduction method you use—mileage rate or actual expense—the vehicle sale produces a taxable gain or a deductible loss.

Example 1: Wilson uses the IRS standard mileage rate to deduct his car. In 2010, he drove 30,000 business miles and used 50 cents a mile as his deduction. Inside the 50 cents is depreciation of 23 cents a mile.[1] Thus, by claiming the 50 cent mileage rate, Wilson depreciated his car $6,900 in 2010, and he will have a gain or loss when he sells the car.

Example 2: Nelson used Section 179 to expense the entire business cost of his qualifying SUV. If Nelson sells the SUV, he will pay taxes on his gain (at ordinary rates to the extent of his expensing benefit).

Six Easy Steps to Find Your Vehicle's Gain or Loss

Remember, if you own the business car, you have a gain or loss when you sell it. If you want to make a wise decision on your vehicle, you need to know your gain or loss before you take action.

Step 1. Beginning Basis

Example 1: Sampson bought a $30,000 car, paying $5,000 down and financing $25,000. Her beginning basis is $30,000, the amount paid.

Example 2: Nash bought a personal car for $30,000. She converts the personal car to business use when it has a retail *Blue Book* value of $23,000. Nash uses the lower of the original cost or the market value at the date of conversion to find her beginning basis of $23,000.[2]

Example 3: Mason converted her personal vehicle to business use when it had a market value of $30,000. She later traded this vehicle and $15,000 for vehicle number 2. Later, she traded vehicle number 2 plus $15,000 for vehicle number 3, then traded number 3 plus $15,000 for vehicle number 4, which she currently drives. Her original cash basis is $30,000, plus $15,000, plus $15,000, plus $15,000, for a total of $75,000.

Step 2. Split Basis between Business and Personal

To find your business basis, consider only the miles driven since you started using the vehicle for business. Mason, from Example 3 above, drove her four vehicles a total of 250,000 miles, of which 200,000, or 80 percent, were for business. Thus, her business basis is $60,000 (80 percent x $75,000) and her personal basis is $15,000.

Business: On the business part, you deduct losses and pay taxes on the gains.

Personal: On the personal part, you may NOT deduct the losses, but you pay taxes on the gains.

Step 3. Split Sale Proceeds between Business and Personal

Let's go back to Mason's fourth vehicle, the one she now drives. Say she could sell that vehicle for $20,000. In Step 2, Mason had business use of 80 percent; therefore, she has business sale proceeds of $16,000 (80 percent of $20,000) and personal sale proceeds of $4,000 (20 percent of $20,000).

Step 4. Find Adjusted Basis

At the time of sale, you are selling two assets: a business vehicle and a personal vehicle. We will look at the business and personal aspects separately, starting with the business aspect.

The final number you need to find for the business gain or loss is depreciation (including any amounts expensed using Section 179). You can find this number in your tax returns if you used the actual expense method.

If you used the IRS method, the depreciation is embedded in the mileage rate. Either way—actual expense or IRS mileage rate—you claimed depreciation benefits in your tax returns.

As with all assets, you calculate gain or loss by comparing net sales proceeds with your adjusted basis. Typically, your adjusted basis is
- beginning basis,
- plus improvements,
- minus depreciation.

Mason claimed $23,000 in business depreciation on her four vehicles. Again, remember that regardless of how Mason deducted her vehicles—IRS mileage rate or actual expense method—she claimed depreciation in her tax returns. Let's find Mason's adjusted basis in her vehicle.

Her original business basis is $60,000 (see Step 1). She made no improvements to her vehicles. Her business depreciation (and Section 179) deductions totaled $23,000. Accordingly, Mason's adjusted basis is $37,000 ($60,000 minus $23,000).

Notes

Step 5. Calculate Business Gain or Loss

Here is how Mason calculates her business loss on the sale of her car for $20,000:

Business proceeds (Step 3)	$ 16,000
Adjusted basis (Step 4)	-37,000
Business loss	$-21,000

When you will have a loss, you want to sell the vehicle to a third party so you may deduct the loss.

Planning tip 1: Do not sell the vehicle to a relative or to a corporation of which you own 50 percent or more. In most cases, this will cancel your loss and neither you nor your relative will get any benefit from the loss deduction.[3]

Planning tip 2: If you have a gain, use the Section 1031 exchange to avoid taxes on the gain.

Step 6. Calculate Personal Gain or Loss

Generally, vehicles go down in value, so your odds of having a taxable gain on the personal part are slim. But in those rare instances when vehicles appreciate in value, you could have a gain on your personal part. Here is how Mason calculates her personal part:

Personal proceeds (Step 3)	$ 4,000
Personal basis (Step 2)	-15,000
Nondeductible loss	$-11,000

Section 179 Expensing and Bonus Depreciation in Previous Years Make Taxable Vehicle Gains

During the past seven years, tax law has created big deductions for Section 179 expensing and, in certain years, added first-year bonus depreciation. If you took advantage of these breaks, you are likely to have a taxable gain on the sale of your vehicle.

Nelson, for example, expensed the entire $25,000 cost of his SUV. Thus, his adjusted basis is zero. If he sells this SUV for $14,000, he will have a gain of $14,000, taxable as ordinary income. If Nelson's combined federal and state tax rate is 40 percent, he will pay $5,600 tax on the sale. But with a Section 1031 exchange, Nelson defers this $5,600 tax to the replacement vehicle, where, depending on how well he plans, the tax may or may not pose a problem in some future year.

Applying Four Types of Section 1031 Exchanges to Vehicles

In general, you may use the following four types of exchanges with your vehicles:
1. Two-party exchange
2. Simultaneous exchange
3. Delayed exchange
4. Reverse exchange

The IRS now considers the following vehicles as like-kind for purposes of a Section 1031 tax-deferred exchange:[4]
- Cars
- Crossover vehicles
- Sport utility vehicles (SUVs)
- Minivans
- Cargo vans
- Light, general-purpose trucks for use over the road and having actual unloaded weight of less than 13,000 pounds

The official definition of "unloaded vehicle weight" according to Department of Transportation regulations is "the weight of a vehicle with maximum capacity of all fluids necessary for operation of the vehicle, but without cargo, occupants, or accessories that are ordinarily removed from the vehicle when they are not in use."[5]

Under this definition of "like-kind," you can exchange a Ford F-450 truck (this is a really big truck) for a little car such as a Ford Focus.

1. Two-Party Exchange

When you trade in your old vehicle for a replacement vehicle, you are engaging in a two-party tax-deferred exchange. Most often, you do this with the dealer, arriving in your old vehicle and leaving in the new one.

2. Simultaneous Exchange

Technically, in the simultaneous exchange, you use a qualified intermediary to facilitate the exchange. When the exchange is simultaneous, you arrive with your vehicle title and leave with the title to the replacement vehicle.

3. Delayed Exchange

Do you like to sell your vehicles personally? If so, the delayed exchange is for you. Many people refer to the delayed exchange as the "Starker exchange," after the Supreme Court case in which Starker prevailed.

Step 1: Before doing the delayed exchange, you should find a qualified intermediary who will facilitate your exchange and ensure that you meet the tax-deferral rules. In Google, we entered "1031 exchange intermediary cars trucks fees" and got 950 hits, including many with fees under $500 for the entire exchange.

Since the exchange of a vehicle is far simpler than the exchange of real estate, you might find or negotiate lower fees. Obviously, the fee will affect your desire to do the exchange.

Let's say you find a fee of $450 and you can sell your vehicle for $5,000 more than a dealer will give you. Obviously, you want to do the exchange, which means you sell the vehicle using an intermediary, pay the intermediary $450, and pocket the extra $4,550. The delayed exchange allows you to do this.

Planning note: You do not physically pocket the money, as cash receipts and debt reduction trigger taxes in a 1031 exchange. You realize the cash in the form of paying less for the replacement vehicle (so, really, you do have $4,550 more cash in your pocket).

Step 2: Here is an amazing thing: In the delayed exchange, you actually market the vehicle in your normal manner. When you find the buyer, you use the forms and exchange accommodation language that make the intermediary a "substitute seller." Thus your first step is to find the intermediary, so your second step will be easy.

Step 3: You have 45 days to identify the replacement vehicle.[6] You will probably do this much quicker, or your feet will do a lot of walking.

Step 4: You must own the replacement property within the parameters of the 180-day rule, which means the earlier of [7]
- 180 days after transfer of the property given up, or
- the due date (with extensions) of your tax return.

In practice, you will have the intermediary buy your new vehicle almost immediately, maybe even before you get rid of the old vehicle, in which case you will use the reverse exchange.

Brief review: In the delayed exchange, the use of the intermediary allows you to
- sell your old car to a third party,
- buy a new car, and
- defer the taxes.

Is this easy, or what? Absolutely! Tax knowledge is powerful; in this case, letting you do what you wanted to do in the first place and allowing you to defer the taxes into the future (with planning, perhaps forever).

4. Reverse Exchange

The reverse exchange is exactly that: the delayed exchange in reverse.[8] Here, as with the delayed exchange, put your intermediary in place before you do anything.

With the reverse exchange of a vehicle, you buy your new vehicle first (so you don't have to walk). Actually, your intermediary buys it. Then you sell your old vehicle, just as you planned, with the intermediary as substitute seller.

The IRS gives your intermediary a new name in the reverse exchange, calling the facilitator an "exchange accommodation titleholder."

A Closer Look at the Intermediary

The IRS has embedded the intermediary (exchange accommodation titleholder) in its 1031 exchange rules, making it far easier than ever before to do a 1031 exchange. You simply use the intermediary as a substitute buyer and substitute seller of your property. In effect, the IRS allows you to make the intermediary the facilitator of the exchange.

Summary

If you will have a big gain on the sale of your business vehicle, you should defer that tax and keep the money in your pocket, working for you. Think of it this way: if your tax is $10,000 on a sale, you can use the 1031 exchange to keep the whole $10,000 in your pocket (where you can see it, use it, and enjoy it).

The 1031 exchange is the cure for the taxes on the sale of your old vehicle. With planning, the taxes on the old vehicle could disappear forever, but that's beyond the scope of this section. For now, let's just use the 1031 exchange to move those taxes to the next vehicle.

Notes

Your choices for the exchange involve either an intermediary or another person, probably a vehicle dealer. You make this choice by counting your money. You need to consider the cost of the intermediary and then answer these questions: How much cash will you part with to get the replacement vehicle after you pay the fees to the intermediary? Next, how does this compare with what it would cost you to get the new vehicle if you simply did the exchange with the dealer?

Once you engage an intermediary, you can do a simultaneous exchange, a delayed exchange, or a reverse exchange.

Finally, remember that you only do the exchange to save money on your taxes. If the sale of your car would produce a loss, you do not trade it or do an exchange with an intermediary. Instead, you sell the vehicle to a third party and deduct your loss.

If the sale of your vehicle would produce a taxable gain, you use the 1031 exchange to avoid taxes on the gain.

Endnotes–Section 25

[1] Revenue Procedure 2009-54, Section 5.05.

[2] IRC Section 179; Reg. Section 1.167(g)-1; *Heiner v Tindle*, 276 U.S. 582, 586 (1928), rev'g 18 F.2d 452, 453 (3d Cir. 1927), rev'g 17 F.2d 522, 524. (W.D. Pa. 1926).

[3] IRC Section 267; For the relative to get any benefit from the loss deduction, the relative must sell the vehicle for more than the relative paid you for it (an unlikely event).

[4] Private Letter Ruling 200912004.

[5] 49 CFR 571.3.

[6] IRC Section 1031(a)(3)(A).

[7] IRC Section 1031(a)(3)(B).

[8] Revenue Procedure 2000-37 sets forth safe harbors and rules for reverse exchanges. Also, see Revenue Procedure 2004-51 for modifications to 2000-37

Section 26

What to Do When the Sale of Your Business Vehicle Would Produce a Loss Deduction

No loss deductions on sales to relatives: Tax law prohibits tax-loss deductions on sales to related parties.[1]

Example: You sell your car to your brother for its $10,000 fair market value and that produces a $5,000 loss. You may not deduct the loss.

Related party loss deduction—probably none: When the related party sells the property to a third party, he, she, or it may deduct the loss, but only to the extent that a third-party sale produces a profit.[2]

Example 1: Your brother sells the car for $10,000. He has no gain or loss. Worse, your $10,000 loss is lost forever.

Example 2: Your brother sells the car for $11,000. He gets to offset the gain by using $1,000 of your $5,000 lost loss. You still get nothing.

Who are your relatives? For purposes of this tax law, your relatives are your:[3]
- Husband or wife
- Mom and dad
- Grandmother and grandfather
- Sons and daughters
- Grandsons and granddaughters
- Brothers and sisters
- Corporations and other entities, when you and your relatives own 50 percent or more of them

Planning tip: In-laws and cousins are not "tax relatives." You can sell to them. Remember, you may not deduct a loss on a sale to a relative. So do not sell loss assets to relatives.

Caution: Never make a gift of a loss-deduction car. Reason: The loss gets lost, as explained below.

Value of a car for gift tax purposes: Tax law assesses gift tax on fair market value at the date of the gift.[4] Your market value on the gift of a car is the price that the public pays an auto dealer for the car (generally, retail

Notes

blue-book value).[5] Market value is not the price you could fetch by selling the car yourself.[6]

Basis of a car gift: Your income tax basis is different from your gift tax value. To find gain or loss on sale for income tax purposes, tax law makes the donee look to the donor's basis.[7] Thus, when you make a gift of your car:
- Fair market value decides the gift tax, and
- Basis leads to gain or loss, and that decides the income tax.

Big ouch—loss on sale: To find loss on sale, tax law makes the donee seller go to the date of gift and use as basis the lower of:[8]
- Donor's basis
- Fair market value

Obviously, this rule reduces the benefits of losses on resale of property acquired by gift.

An ugly example: Sam Wilson kept his business car in mint condition so he could give it to his teenage son. This was Sam's third business car. He traded in car 1 on car 2 and then traded in car 2 on car 3. At the time Sam wants to give his car to his son, Sam's car has:
- A business basis of $45,000
- A business selling price of $5,000
- A business loss of $40,000

Sam gives the car to his son. The son sells the car for $5,000. The $40,000 loss gets lost.

Money strategy: Never make gifts of property that you can sell at a loss. Instead, sell the property and deduct the loss.

Example: Sam sells the car, deducts his $40,000 loss and pockets $20,000 in tax benefits. Now he can buy his son four cars.

Endnotes–Section 26

1. IRC Section 267.
2. IRC Section 267(d).
3. IRC Section 267(b)(2).
4. IRC Section 2512.
5. Reg. Section 25.2512-1.
6. Reg. Section 25.2512-1.
7. IRC Section 1015.
8. IRC Section 1015(a).

Section 27

To Buy or Lease Your Next Business Vehicle

Overview: You need to consider:
- Out-of-pocket costs
- Cash available
- Tax law rules
- Time value of money

Gut check: Also, you need a "gut check." Do you look forward to walking into a car dealership and walking out with a good deal? Do you anguish at the thought of negotiating with the car dealer? Whether you buy or lease, negotiate or not, this section of the course will help you find the best deal.

It is a jungle out there: Before we get into details, you need to know that
- sometimes leasing is better than buying.
- sometimes leasing charges are so outrageous that the lessors warrant jail for car theft.[1] In Florida, some leasing companies take the trade-in vehicle and give the customer zero in return—stealing the traded car from the unwary customer[2]
- Sometimes companies lease cars at great deals to ensure loyalty and get customers back into the showrooms.

On the other hand, there are many horror stories from buyers who got fleeced.

Best way to compare: The formula on the next page gives you the best way to compare the rent-or-buy results. You will need a financial calculator to make the present-value computations.

Did you lease or purchase? Is your car lease a true lease or is it a purchase for tax purposes? If you acquire title or equity, you treat your car lease payments as purchase payments for tax purposes.[3] Generally, for tax purposes, you bought the leased car if any one of the following is true:[4]
- Your rent payments build equity.
- You get title to the car after you make payments.
- The amount paid to use the car for a short period approximates the amount you would pay to own the car.
- You have the option of buying the car at a nominal price after the lease.

Notes

Calculation: Buy or Lease

PRECISE COMPUTATION USING PRESENT VALUE

PRESENT VALUE (PV) IF YOU BUY	
Cash paid at purchase (this is "today's dollars")	Add
PV of total monthly payments for car	Add
PV of tax savings from depreciation and interest—Year 1	Subtract
PV of tax savings from depreciation and interest—Year 2	Subtract
PV of tax savings from depreciation and interest—Year 3	Subtract
PV of expected cash from sale of car	Subtract
PV of tax savings if car sold at a loss	Subtract
PV of tax due if car sold at a gain	Add
Net cash paid for car in today's dollars (PV)	Total of above

PRESENT VALUE (PV) IF YOU LEASE	
Cash paid at date car is leased	Add
PV of total monthly lease payments	Add
PV tax savings—rent deduction less inclusion—Year 1	Subtract
PV tax savings—rent deduction less inclusion—Year 2	Subtract
PV tax savings—rent deduction less inclusion—Year 3	Subtract
PV of guaranteed payment at end of lease, if any	Add
Net cash to lease car in today's dollars (PV)	Total of above

Compare

Notes: You can calculate present values with your business calculator. You get "inclusion" amounts from *IRS Publication 463, Travel, Entertainment, Gift, and Car Expenses*. To obtain a copy of this publication, call 1-800-TAX-FORM or go to www.irs.gov.

Simple Arithmetic Calculation (using quick-and-easy numbers):

1. Total all payments to buy the car and subtract residual value
2. Total all payments to lease the car

Compare

Compare with the same periods of time—three-year purchase compared to a three-year lease. Residual value comes from the lease—it's the amount you pay to buy the car at the end of the lease.

True lease: For tax purposes, you have a true lease even if you can buy the car at lease end for its "clean" value, the value published in the National Auto Research Black Book.[5] In other words, if you pay fair market value to buy the car at lease end, your lease can be a true lease. You also have a true lease for tax purposes if you have the option of buying the car at its projected end-of-lease residual value.[6] You negotiate and set this value when you sign the lease. Because you set the buyout price at fair value when you sign the lease, you call this lease a closed-end lease.

Open-ended lease: In an open-ended lease, you do not know your total liability until you turn in the car. If actual residual value exceeds the estimate, you pay the difference. On the other hand, if the estimate exceeds the actual residual, you get a refund. In the open-ended lease, the leasing company passes the residual value risk to you.

Tax law gives special treatment to open-ended leases of cars for business purposes.[7] To figure out if the open-ended lease is a true lease or a sale, tax law says that you do not consider the car's residual value.[8] You get to exclude residual value from the tax lease or buy rules only when:[9]
- You lease a car, truck, or trailer.
- You certify in writing to the leasing company, under penalties of perjury, that you will use the car more than 50 percent for business.
- The leasing company states clearly in writing that it told you that you are not the owner of the leased property for tax purposes.
- The leasing company lacks knowledge that your certification is false.
- The leasing company has a tax-law defined liability in the car it is leasing to you.

Again, when you meet the above rules, you may exclude residual value when figuring whether a lease is a true lease or conditional sale. You subject all other elements of the lease terms to the same lease-versus-buy tests.

Leases of luxury cars: You deduct the rent you pay on a car lease in proportion to your business use. If you lease a car worth more than the luxury limits, you must add to your business income a dollar amount specified by IRS tables. The IRS uses the "add back" to level the deductions of a lease to those of a purchase. You find IRS "add back" tables in *IRS Publication 463, Travel, Entertainment, Gift, and Car Expenses*. An example auto table appears on the next page. The IRS publishes different tables for leases of trucks, vans and electric cars.

Lease Inclusion Amounts for Passenger Autos

Fair Market Value		Tax Year During the Lease				5th & later
Over	Not Over	1st	2nd	3rd	4th	
$18,500	$19,000	3	8	11	13	16
19,000	19,500	4	9	13	15	18
19,500	20,000	4	10	15	17	20
20,000	20,500	5	11	16	19	23
20,500	21,000	5	12	18	21	25
21,000	21,500	6	13	19	24	26
21,500	22,000	6	14	21	26	29
22,000	23,000	7	16	23	29	32
23,000	24,000	8	18	27	32	37
24,000	25,000	9	20	30	36	42
25,000	26,000	10	23	33	40	46
26,000	27,000	11	25	36	44	51
27,000	28,000	12	27	40	48	55
28,000	29,000	13	29	43	52	60
29,000	30,000	14	31	47	55	65
30,000	31,000	15	34	49	60	69
31,000	32,000	16	36	53	63	73
32,000	33,000	17	38	56	68	77
33,000	34,000	18	40	60	71	82
34,000	35,000	19	42	63	75	87
35,000	36,000	20	45	66	79	91
36,000	37,000	21	47	69	83	96
37,000	38,000	22	49	73	87	100
38,000	39,000	23	51	76	91	105
39,000	40,000	24	53	80	94	110
40,000	41,000	25	56	82	99	114
41,000	42,000	26	58	86	102	119
42,000	43,000	27	60	89	107	123
43,000	44,000	28	62	93	110	128
44,000	45,000	29	64	96	114	133
45,000	46,000	30	67	98	119	137
46,000	47,000	31	69	102	122	141
47,000	48,000	32	71	105	127	145
48,000	49,000	33	73	109	130	150
49,000	50,000	34	76	111	134	155
50,000	51,000	35	78	115	138	159
51,000	52,000	36	80	118	142	164
52,000	53,000	37	82	122	146	168
53,000	54,000	38	84	125	150	173
54,000	55,000	39	87	128	153	178
55,000	56,000	40	89	131	158	182
56,000	57,000	41	91	135	161	187
57,000	58,000	42	93	138	166	191
58,000	59,000	43	95	142	169	196
59,000	60,000	44	98	144	174	200
60,000	62,000	46	101	149	179	207
62,000	64,000	48	105	156	187	216
64,000	66,000	50	109	163	195	225
66,000	68,000	52	114	169	203	234
68,000	70,000	54	118	176	211	243
70,000	72,000	56	123	182	218	253
72,000	74,000	58	127	189	226	262
74,000	76,000	60	132	195	234	270
76,000	78,000	62	136	202	242	279
78,000	80,000	64	140	209	250	288
80,000	85,000	67	148	220	264	304
85,000	90,000	72	159	237	283	327
90,000	95,000	77	170	253	303	350
95,000	100,000	82	181	269	323	372
100,000	110,000	90	198	293	352	406
110,000	120,000	100	220	326	391	452
120,000	130,000	110	242	359	430	497
130,000	140,000	120	264	392	469	543
140,000	150,000	130	286	424	509	588
150,000	160,000	140	308	457	548	633
160,000	170,000	150	330	490	587	679
170,000	180,000	160	352	523	626	724
180,000	190,000	170	374	555	666	769
190,000	200,000	180	396	588	705	815
200,000	210,000	190	418	621	744	860
210,000	220,000	200	440	654	784	904
220,000	230,000	210	462	687	823	950
230,000	240,000	220	484	719	863	995
240,000	And up	230	506	752	902	1,040

The table above is from a prior year and it's for example purposes only. For your leased vehicle, refer to the lease inclusion table for the year you placed your vehicle in service.

Example: Say you leased a $40,500 car for $500 a month over 36 months. Your first-year add-back amount is $25 (see the table on the left). Thus, you deduct $6,000 and add back $25 for a net lease deduction of $5,975. You add back $56 next year and $82 the year after. (If business use is 80 percent, you multiply all amounts by 80 percent.)

Down Payments Usually Make for Deductible Advance Rents

Technical point: With the exception of the safe harbor for prepaying rent as discussed in the "Prepay Your Expenses" section of this course, you generally may not deduct rent paid in advance.

The down payment you make when you enter into a vehicle lease would usually fail the safe harbor in the "Prepay Your Expenses" section. Thus, on your vehicle lease, you generally write the down payment off in equal amounts as rent over the life of the lease.[10]

Why missed: Many taxpayers report only lease payments in the organizers they complete for their accountants or in the interview section of a tax preparation program, like Turbo Tax.

Example: You lease a new car for $2,400 down and $400 a month for two years. Your rent totals $12,000 [$2,400 down plus $9,600 ($400 rent x 24 months)]. You deduct $500 a month for each month of business use. If business use is 85 percent, you multiply the rent times the 85 percent business-use percentage.

Trade-In of Personal Vehicle on a Lease Gives You Deductible Advance Rents

Technical note: The trade of a car on a lease is not a tax-deferred exchange because you did not trade like-kind property.[11]

Treat the value of the trade-in as prepaid rent: As a cash basis taxpayer, you can deduct certain prepaid rent as explained in the "Prepay Your Expenses" section of this course. It is highly unlikely that the value of your trade-in is going to qualify for the prepaid rent safe harbor deduction. In general, your trade-in is going to count as rent during each month of your lease.[12]

Why missed: As with the down payment discussed above, you often report only the monthly rents and miss the rent deduction available because of the trade-in.

Notes

Example: You trade your existing personal car on a new car lease. The dealer gives you a cash credit of $12,000 for your existing car and charges rent of $300 a month for two years. Your rent over the 24 months will total $19,200 ($12,000 down payment from the trade-in value plus 24 times $300). You deduct your new car lease at the rental rate of $800 a month ($19,200 divided by 24 months).

Planning tip: Make sure you tell your tax preparer that you traded your old personally-owned car on the new leased car. Many taxpayers only tell about the new lease payment, and that puts the preparer in the dark. Put your preparer in the light. Tell him or her exactly what you did!

Trade-In of the Business Vehicle You Own on a Lease Generates Both Advance Rent Deductions and Tax Gain or Loss

Technical reminder: Remember, the trade-in of a car on a lease is not a tax-deferred exchange because you did not trade like-kind property.[13] Thus, think of the trade as a cash transaction in which:
- You sell the car traded in for cash equal to its fair market value
- You make a cash down payment on the lease equal to the cash received for the traded-in car

Trade personal car: If you traded your personal car on the lease of your new business car, you sold the personal car for its fair market value. You probably have no taxable gain or deductible loss because you probably sold the car for less than you paid for it. The government does not allow deductions for personal losses.[14] However, the government taxes personal gains.

Trade business car: If you trade your existing business car on the lease of a replacement business car, you treat the trade as a sale. You must compute gain or loss on sale.

Planning tip 1: With today's restrictions on luxury car depreciation, most business car sales produce deductible losses.

Planning tip 2: Have you been in business for many years? Have you always traded the old business cars for new business cars? Did your trades take place every two, three, or four years? Did you drive nice cars? Your basis easily could be $40,000 to $70,000 on a car with a fair market value of $15,000. You could have a $25,000 to $55,000 tax-deductible loss on the trade of the car for a leased car.

Planning tip 3: Did your trade for the leased car occur during the past three years? Did you fail to claim the loss deduction? If so, you may obtain a refund by amending your return.

Summary tip: When you trade your existing business car for a leased car, you are not trading. You are selling the existing car and making a deposit on the new car lease. That trade can produce a:
- Desirable tax-deductible loss on disposition of the old car
- Desirable write-offs of the trade-in value (advance rent deposit) over the life of the lease

Flowchart on the Trade-In of a Vehicle on a Lease

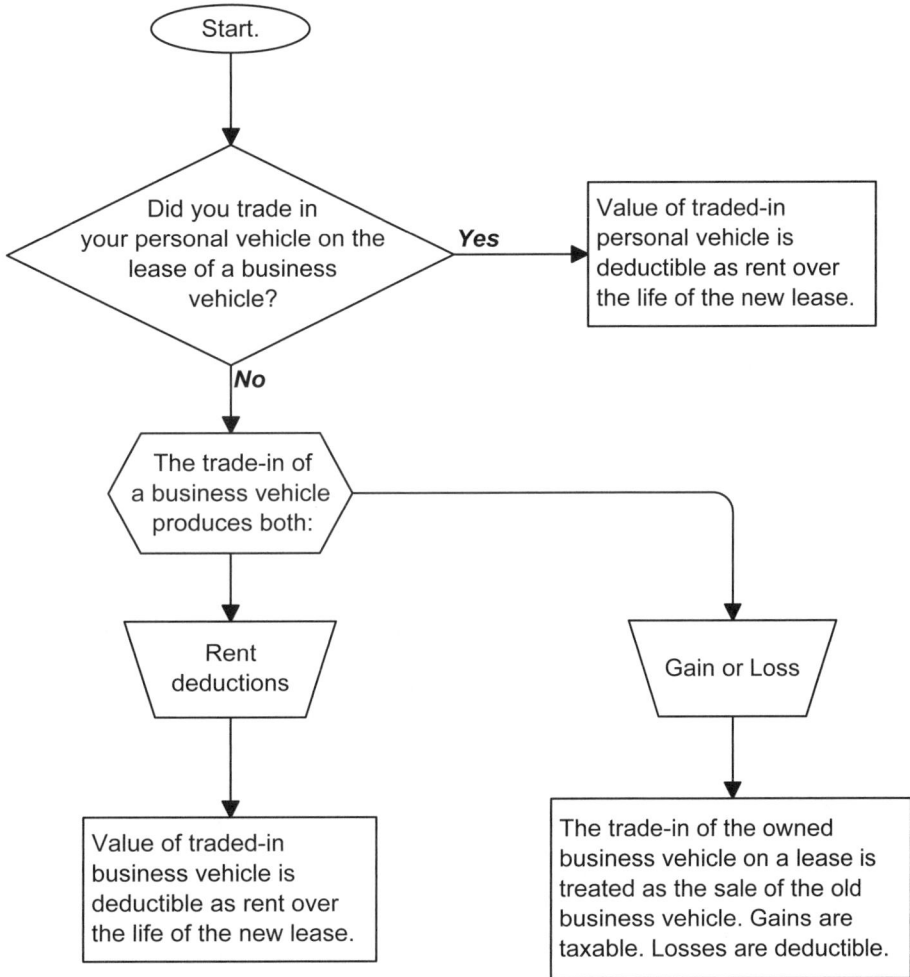

Notes

Endnotes–Section 27

1. The Ins, Outs of Leasing, Michael Clements, USA Today, April 18, 1994, p. 1B.
2. Ibid.
3. Rev. Rul. 55-540..
4. Ibid.
5. Plr 9313001.
6. Ibid.
7. IRC Section 7701(h).
8. IRC Section 7701(h)(3)(A).
9. IRC Section 7701(h)(2).
10. IRS Reg. Section 1.263(a)-4(f) contains the prepayment rules that appear to conflict with *IRS Pub. 463, Travel, Entertainment, Gift, and Car Expenses (2011),* p. 25, where the IRS states that advance rents must be amortized. As you learn in the prepaid expense section of this course, you may prepay rent under the prepaid rules and deduct the prepayment immediately. Regulations are an official publication of the IRS and have far greater authority than does an IRS publication. Also, in the case of a down payment, most down payments would violate the prepayment rules by making a rent payment that benefits a year after the next tax year (i.e., the rent you prepay in year 1 cannot pay a year 3 rent).
11. IRC Section 1031.
12. See endnote 10 above.
13. IRC Section 1031.
14. IRC Section 165

Section 28

Building More Business Miles with Audit-Proof Records

Know Your Business Miles

Official method: The more business miles, the greater your business-use percentage and the greater your deductions. Tax law uses mileage to find your business-percent use of cars.[1]

Commute: You have a personal trip (called a commute) when you drive from home to one or more "regular places of business."[2] Thus, you take an ugly personal trip from your home to your downtown office. Tax law calls it a commute. It's personal and nondeductible.

Escapes from commuting rules: The IRS lets you escape the commuting rules and deduct trips from home to business locations when:[3]
- You drive to a "temporary work location" on the way to your "regular work location"
- You drive from your "home office" to work someplace (for this rule to apply, you must deduct the home office as a principal office, not as a meet-and-greet place or separate structure)
- You have no office at home and none downtown, and you drive to a work location outside the metropolitan area where you live and normally work

Regular work locations defined: Your "regular" work locations are those where you work or perform services regularly. "Regular" does not mean you have to work there each week or on a set schedule.[4] A doctor may travel from his or her home to several regular work stops, such as:[5]
- Offices
- Clinics
- Hospitals

Temporary stops defined: The IRS defines a "temporary stop" as any location where you perform services on an irregular or short-term basis (location that you visit for one year or less).[6]

When a Mile Is a Business Mile

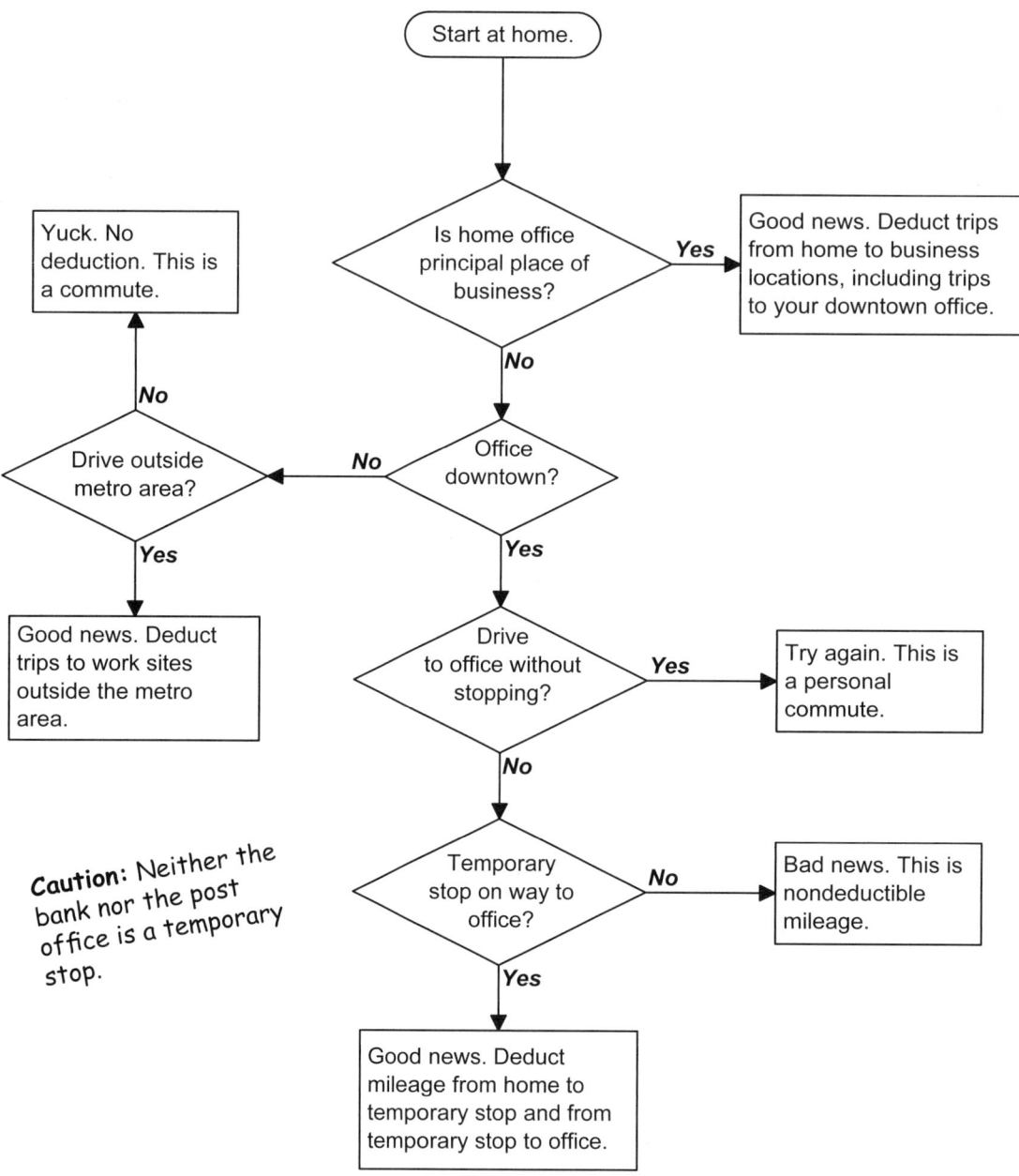

This flowchart applies to a single business. If you have multiple businesses or you are a W-2 employee and working your business part-time, look at IRS Publication 463 for the business-mile rules.

Example 1: You have a personal commute (nondeductible) when you drive from home to your office downtown.[7]

Example 2: Your trip from home to a temporary business stop (to see a prospect) produces business mileage.[8] Then your trip from the temporary stop to your office produces business mileage.[9]

Eliminate commuting with temporary stops.

Example 3: You have business mileage when you drive 200 miles from your home to attend a training course in another city.[10]

Example 4: You claim a deduction for an office in your home on the basis that your home office is your principal office. All trips from home to all business locations produce business miles.[11]

Example 5: You do not qualify for the home office deduction, and you have no office outside the home. Your trip from home to see a prospect and return is a personal, nondeductible commute.

Eliminate commuting with an administrative office in your home. Tax law treats administrative offices as principal offices. (See the home office discussion for details.)

Technical point 1: The person with no principal office in the home and no office outside the home counts as personal commuting mileage the trip from:
- Home to first business contact, and
- Last business contact to home.

Technical point 2: The "office-less" person may not deduct those first and last business stops, but may deduct mileage going from business stop one to business stop two, etc.[12]

Don't be without an office.

Two business locations: You count miles driven between two business locations as business mileage.[13] Thus, trips between two job locations outside the home produce deductible mileage. Similarly, once you make your first business stop and then make a number of other business stops, your business mileage keeps growing. Say, for example, you drive from:
- Home to temporary stop
- Temporary stop to office
- Office to client
- Client to office

You have 100 percent business mileage.

Value: If knowing the mileage rules increases your car deductions by 20 percent, how much does that put in your pocket? That depends on the car you drive and the expenses you incur. With $10,000 in deductions, that puts an extra $2,000 on your return, every year you are in business. Or to put this another way, the car information is worth a lot of money.

Notes

Protect Your Mileage by Knowing These Seven Mileage Myths

Overview: Do not get trapped by mileage myths. Avoid myths! Review the following myths frequently to make sure your mileage is on track for unquestioned deductibility.

Mileage myth 1—My car is a moving billboard. The "moving billboard" (advertising display on the car) does not convert personal miles to business miles.[14]

Mileage myth 2—My car is a portable telephone booth. Making business calls from your "mobile telephone booth" (car phone) does not convert personal miles to business miles.[15]

Mileage myth 3—My car is a moving conference room. Collecting business associates for a discussion in your "migratory meeting room" (car seats) does not convert personal miles to business miles.[16]

Mileage myth 4—I reserve a special vehicle only for hunting and fishing trips. Driving your car to entertainment activities makes your car an entertainment facility, and that mileage is not deductible (if such mileage is more than incidental).[17]

Mileage myth 5—My car is a "production of income" vehicle. Production of income mileage is not business mileage. You may deduct such mileage, but it does not count as business mileage for purposes of the more-than-50 percent-business-use rule discussed later.[18]

Mileage myth 6—I stop at the post office to eliminate my commute. A stop at the post office on the way to the downtown office is not a stop at a temporary location. To be temporary, you must perform services at the stop.

Mileage myth 7—My trips are outside the metropolitan area. Do not count on driving outside your metropolitan area to a business stop. The metropolitan area covers the city, its suburbs, and some distance beyond.[19] In Walker, the IRS and the court agreed that the metropolitan area for this logger covered the entire Black Hills National Forest.[20] The court noted that the forest seems large, but it covers less than 54 percent of the Chicago metropolitan area.

Using Two Vehicles Is an Easy Way to Increase Your Tax Deductions

Old advice: In the past, your advisors told you to drive one car for business and the other car for personal purposes. The new mileage records rules make that advice obsolete. Today, you should drive two cars for business when that increases your deductions.

Technical point: Will the IRS allow use of more than one car for business? Yes! The IRS official method for computing business car use is business miles divided by total miles.[21] In fact, the IRS recognizes in its Form 2106 that taxpayers may drive two or more separate cars for business during a tax year. Actually, if you drive more than two cars, the IRS has you attach a continuation sheet to your tax return.

Calculate benefits: To see if you can benefit, and by how much, make the computation that appears below. In this example, the taxpayer gains a minimum of $7,677 in "found" deductions with the two-car strategy. The added deductions come from depreciation and/or loss on sale. If the taxpayer uses the actual expense method to calculate car deductions, he may gain more deductions than depreciation.

	Before		After	
	Car 1	Car 2	Car 1	Car 2
Business miles	28,000	-0-	14,000	14,000
Total miles	30,000	8,000	19,000	19,000
Business %	93.30%	0.00%	73.70%	73.70%
Cost of cars	$23,000	$21,000	$23,000	$21,000
Estimated sales proceeds	$2,000	$5,000	$3,500	$3,500
Loss in value	$21,000	$16,000	$19,500	$17,500
Tax deductions	$19,593	$0.00	$14,372	$12,898
Totals	$19,593		$27,270	
Advantage	$7,677 or 39.2% more with two cars			

Notes

This is a quick-and-easy calculation that tells you what's best for you every time.

The calculation is over your use of the car. That's where the estimated sales proceeds come into play.

Diary Entry to Support Vehicle Use
The Perfect Entry (you do not need to be perfect, but you must be adequate)

To do's		
2		
3		
4		
5		
6		
7		

Appointments		car miles	bi pc
7:00	Principal to satellite office	30	b
8:00			
9:00			
10:00			
11:00			
12:00	Office Depot	11	b
1:00	J. J.'s Mail Service	22	b
2:00	Lyons 1575 18th St	12	b
3:00			
4:00	Nelson - 29 Park Place	25	b
5:00	Grocery store	0	p
6:00			
7:00	To Principal office	7	b
8:00			
9:00			
10:00			

Business (b)	107	Total miles this day	107
Investment (i)		Circle car driven this day	1 (2) 3
Personal (p)	0	End Odometer	10307
Commuting (c)		Beg Odometer	10200
Total miles	107	Total miles	107

TODAY'S ACTION
Action: Review monthly goals before making your to-do list!
Result: Your list will reflect the important things you need "to do" to realize your goals.

Copyright 1998 by W. Murray Bradford, CPA

Tax Diary System **1**

Circle month of year and day of week

Jan Feb Mar Apr May Jun   Sun Mon Tue Wed
Jul Aug Sep Oct Nov Dec   Thu Fri Sat

_____
_____
_____
_____
_____
_____
_____
_____
_____

CARS
For each vehicle, enter all (100% of) monies spent for gas and oil, tires, insurance, car washes, repairs, and other out-of-pocket expenses.

Car 1 exp	
Car 2 exp	
Car 3 exp	
Parking/tolls	

TRAVEL
Where (city)
Why (business reason)

Air/rail/boat	
Rental car/bus/taxi	
Lodging	
Tips, laundry, other	
Total trv day (no meals)	

MEALS/ENTERTAINMENT/ETC
Who
Where
Why

Trv brkfst	
Trv lunch	
Trv dinner	
Snacks/drinks	
Ent meals	
Associated ent	
Total trv meals & ent	
Presentation exp	
Special sporting events (100%)	

MISCELLANEOUS
For Business Gifts
To whom
Why

Supplies	
Postage	
Business gifts	
Other _____	
Other _____	
Other _____	

Build Audit-Proof Support of Your Mileage the Easy Way

Proof required: You must prove your business car's:[22]
- Mileage
- Cost or other basis
- Actual expenses (if you use the actual-expense method)

How to accumulate proof: You should:
- Record your entries in an account book, diary, log, statement of expense, trip sheet, or similar record.
- Support your entries with receipts and other corroborating documents.[23]

You must make entries in your log book at or near the time you incur the expenses or use the car.[24]

Weekly log: You may keep your log weekly. A weekly log meets the "at or near the time of the expense or use" rule.[25]

Receipt rule: You do not need to record receipt information in your log if:[26]
- You have the receipts
- Your log and receipts complement each other
- You keep orderly records

As a practical matter, you avoid loss of deductions when you record receipt information on the same pages with mileage information. It presents a much better picture to the IRS auditor and shows that you know how to keep good records.

Recording mileage: Your adequate record must prove business use. Detail varies. If you use your car to make 12 business stops in one day, you may or may not record each stop. If you contacted 12 different prospects, your appointment book should contain the 12 names. If you sell real estate and take your prospect to look at 12 homes, your diary entry might contain the prospect's name and mileage to "look at 12 homes." The IRS allows a single entry to account for a round trip or a series of uninterrupted business stops.[27]

Ninety-day sample: The IRS allows you to keep a 90-day log for a typical portion of the year to prove business use for the whole year.[28] To use the 90-day test, you must have collateral support for the rest of the year. For example, your appointment book can confirm that your business use during the 275-day nontest period is comparable to the 90-day test period. With the 90-day sample and similar pattern for the non-90-day use, you prove your business use for the year.

Notes

One-week-a-month sample: If your business use varies by season and the 90-day test would not work for you, you should consider the one-week-a-month test. Under this test, you pick one week a month—say the second week of each month—and you keep your log during that week. You may use the weeks to prove your business mileage, assuming your appointment book and other corroborative evidence prove that the weeks typify your driving patterns.[29]

Receipts needed: You must prove amounts spent for gas and oil, repairs and maintenance, etc. You do not need receipts if the expense is less than $75.[30] However, we recommend that you obtain receipts whenever practical. Remember, receipts corroborate other entries, such as the ones in your diary.

Receipts alone are not enough: You need more than receipts to prove business miles. Langer tried to use only receipts to justify his car deduction. The IRS said, "No!" Langer did not keep track of his miles or record the days or locations of his business trips. The gas receipts did not show the time, place, or business purposes for his trips. The court ruled that Langer's receipts were not adequate records. The receipts alone provided no way to figure business-use percentage.[31]

Canceled checks: A canceled check alone does not prove business cost.[32] You prove business cost when you support your canceled check with other evidence, such as a receipt, to show that you wrote the check for a business purpose.[33]

Proof of cost: You prove the cost of your car with your purchase receipts. You should have a copy of the dealer's invoice to prove how much you paid for the car. You should have a canceled check to prove that you spent your money for your car.

Proof of basis: Basis is much more complex. To prove your basis, you need to keep:
- Receipts and purchase records for all car purchases and trades
- Old tax returns, because they prove depreciation
- Old mileage logs, because they prove business-use percentages
- A copy of the blue book page that shows your car's initial tax value

If you converted a personal car to business use, you must be able to calculate your car's adjusted basis. You need it to report gain or loss on sale of the car,[34] even if you use the IRS standard mileage rate.[35]

Trades: When you trade your old business car for a replacement, you need purchase documents that prove monies spent for both the old and new cars. For recent trades of business cars, you should file IRS Form 8824 to report the trades to the IRS.

Checklist: Good car records ensure your business-car deductions. Make it a habit to keep good car records. You have good records when you have:
- Invoices and receipts to support your payments
- Canceled checks to physically prove that you paid your bills
- Appointment books and records
- Mileage logs
- Old tax returns

If you charged gas and oil to a credit card, keep the invoices and receipts as support for the entries on the credit card statement.

Final thought: Think like an IRS auditor. Keep records that prove your case.

Notes

To visualize how the audit-proofing process works, see the online video: www.tax789.com/2015video

Endnotes–Section 28

1. Temp. Reg. Section 1.274-5T(b)(6)(I)(B).
2. IRC Section 262; Rev. Rul. 90-23, I.R.B. 1990-11.
3. Rev. Rul. 94-47; 1994-29 I.R.B. 1.
4. Rev. Rul. 90-23, 1990-1 C.B. 29.
5. Rev. Rul. 90-23, 1990-11 I.R.B. 4.
6. Rev. Rul. 99-7 supercedes Rev. Rul. 90-23 on "matter of weeks or days" and now defines "temporary" as employment in a single location that you realistically expect to last (and it does in fact last) one year or less.
7. *IRS Pub. 463, Travel, Entertainment, Gift, and Car Expenses (2011)*, p. 14.
8. Rev. Rul. 94-47; 1994-29 I.R.B. 1.
9. *IRS Pub. 463, Travel, Entertainment, Gift, and Car Expenses (2011)*, p. 14.
10. Ibid.
11. Ibid.
12. Ibid.

Notes

13. Rev. Rul. 55-109, 1955-1 C.B. 261.

14. Conference Report on Tax Reform Act of 1984, Federal Register, p H 6651, June 22, 1984. IRS Pub. 17, Your Federal Income Tax (2009), Page 186.

15. Conference Report on Tax Reform Act of 1984, Federal Register, p H 6651, June 22, 1984.

16. Conference Report on Tax Reform Act of 1984, Federal Register, p H 6651, June 22, 1984.

17. Reg. Section 1.274-2(e)(3)(iii)(b).

18. IRC Section 280F((d)(6).

19. Rev. Rul. 190, 1953-2 C.B. 303.

20. Walker v Commr., 101 T.C. 537 (1993).

21. Temp. Reg. Section 1.274-5T(b)(6)(I)(B).

22. *IRS Pub. 463, Travel, Entertainment, Gift, and Car Expenses (2011)*, p. 26-28.

23. Ibid.

24. Ibid.

25. Ibid.

26. Ibid.

27. Ibid.

28. Reg. Section 1.274-5T(c)(3)(ii)(C), Example 1.

29. Reg. Section 1.274-5T(c)(3)(ii)(C), Example 2.

30. Notice 95-50, 1995-42, I.R.B. 1; IR-95-96.

31. Langer v Commr., 8th Cir Dec 2, 1992, 93-1 USTC ¶50,008, aff'g T.C. Memo. 1990-268.

32. *IRS Pub. 463, Travel, Entertainment, Gift, and Car Expenses (2011)*, p. 27.

33. Ibid.

34. IRC Section 1016.

35. Rev. Proc. 2008-72 Section 5.05; IRC Section 1016

Section 29

Tax Breaks When You Total Your Vehicle

Tax law calls the wreckage and totaling of your vehicle both an involuntary conversion and a casualty. Apt descriptions!

If you use your vehicle for both business and personal purposes, you need to split it between its business and personal components in applying the tax rules. This section assumes that the insurance company declared your vehicle totaled.

Your first task is to identify the amount of your gain or loss. Since the vehicle is totaled, the insurance company will keep the vehicle and give you a check. Finding the gain or loss is easy. Simply subtract the basis of your vehicle from the insurance proceeds as follows:

Insurance proceeds	$ 17,883
Basis of vehicle	(5,371)
Gain	$ 12,512

In the absence of a trade, basis is original cost plus improvements minus depreciation. With your vehicle, you likely made no improvements. If so, your basis is simply your cost minus depreciation.

Planning tip. Depreciation exists in both the IRS mileage rates and the actual expense method. Thus, regardless of how you have deducted your vehicle, you have a depreciated basis (called "adjusted basis" in the tax law).

In a trade, basis is determined under the rules for a Section 1031 exchange.

Deduct the Loss Now

If the calculation shows that you have a loss on the wreck, you want to deduct that loss right now. That's easy. Divide the loss between business and personal. Report the business loss as a business casualty loss. Report the personal loss as a personal casualty loss. (Business casualty losses are better than personal casualty losses.)

Example. Say that during the past three years, you have driven your vehicle a total of 6,000 personal miles and 54,000 business miles. You divide the insurance proceeds according to this ratio, with 90 percent to business proceeds and 10 percent to personal.

Notes

Defer the Gain

The calculation above shows a business gain of $12,512. Most gains on vehicles come about as a result of the depreciation and expensing deductions you claimed on the vehicle. When the gain is the result of your vehicle deductions, you pay ordinary income taxes on the gain.

We assume that you would like to put off the payment of taxes on this income as long as possible. And you can do just that!

You have the option to choose deferral of this gain by replacing the vehicle with like-kind property. The law gives you a two-year window for the replacement, beginning the day of the wreck and ending two years later.[1] In private letter ruling 200912004, the IRS ruled that cars, pickups, SUVs, crossover vehicles, minivans, cargo vans, and similar vehicles are like kind.

To defer all the gain, you need to invest the entire insurance proceeds in the new vehicle. If you invest less, gain to the extent of your failure to reinvest is taxable.[2]

Disclose the Deferral on Your Tax Return

To defer the gain, attach a statement to your tax return that discloses[3]
- the date and details of the wreck;
- the insurance reimbursement;
- how the gain is calculated;
- the replacement property;
- the amount of the gain postponed;
- the adjusted basis on the replacement vehicle (as reduced by the deferral of gain); and
- how much of the gain, if any, is taxable.

Why You Can Smile

Wrecking your vehicle is never a pleasant experience, but you have to admit that knowing you can defer taxes on the insurance proceeds is money-saving information. Further, this is a straightforward process when you know the basics, as you now do.

Endnotes–Section 29

[1] IRC Section 1033(a)(2).

[2] IRC Section 1033(a)(2)(A).

[3] *IRS Pub. 547, Casualties, Disasters, and Thefts (2011)*, ps. 12, 13.

Section 30

Commission Rebate Deductions Allowed

Robert Corrigan worked as a stockbroker for Smith Barney. In two years, Corrigan earned $1,403,005 in commissions and rebated $424,926 to one of his clients, JLB Capital. He contended that the rebates were necessary to induce purchases of certain syndicated stock.

The court noted that it is not unusual for brokerage firms that offer syndicated stock to accept reduced commissions, because commissions for syndicated stock transactions are generally larger than those for other stock transactions. On the front of his Form 1040, Corrigan reported his gross W-2 commissions, deducted the rebates against those commissions, and reported his net commissions.

At trial, the IRS brought up several issues regarding the rebates, including these:
- The rebates, if deductible, would be deductible only as an employee business expense and not as an offset against income as Corrigan had claimed on his tax return.
- The rebates may violate California securities law.
- The rebates may result in disciplinary action or suspension by the New York Stock Exchange.
- The rebates are not deductible by Corrigan because the commissions were paid to Smith Barney.

The court ruled as follows:[1]
- Corrigan may not deduct the rebates as an offset to his commissions.
- Corrigan qualifies to deduct the rebates as employee business expenses.
- The rebates are ordinary and necessary business expenses under the law.
- Tax law does not make the rebates "illegal" as set forth in Section 162(c)(2).
- The IRS failed not only to assert, but also to prove as required by law, that the rebates are illegal payments barred from deduction.

Planning note 1: Corrigan's status as an employee puts his rebate deductions in jeopardy. As instructed by the court, he deducts the rebates as "employee business expenses" in the miscellaneous deduction category,

Notes

where they are not deductible under the Alternative Minimum Tax (AMT).

Planning note 2: The AMT will cost Corrigan about $50,000 for his rebates. Had Corrigan been an independent contractor rather than an employee, his AMT would have been zero.

Definition of illegal payments: Section 162(c)(2) states that you may not deduct any payment that constitutes an illegal bribe, illegal kickback, or other illegal payment under any law of the United States, or under any law of a state (but only if such state law is generally enforced), where such payment would subject you to criminal penalty or loss of license or privilege to engage in the business. Kickbacks include payments for referrals. Unlike most sections of the tax law, where you carry the burden of proof, here the IRS bears the burden to prove that the payments are illegal and not deductible.

Endnote–Section 30

[1] Robert E. Corrigan v Commr., TC Memo 2005-119.

Section 31

Save Big Tax Dollars—Hire Your Dependent Children

Overview: The IRS acknowledges that a proprietor's child over the age of 6 may be a bona fide employee.[1] Tax law says that wages paid by parents to children under age 18 are exempt from payroll taxes.[2] Do you operate your business as
- an independent contractor?
- a sole proprietor?
- an employee?

If you answer "yes" to any of the three, you have a tax-planning opportunity with your children who are over age 6 and under age 18.

Caution: You do not get any payroll tax breaks if your child is hired by
- your corporation, or
- your partnership (unless each partner is a parent of the child).

However, you and your child still benefit to the extent your tax bracket exceeds the payroll tax cost. Thus, if your combined federal and state tax bracket is 50 percent and the payroll tax on the child's wage is 20 percent, your family saves 30 percent on money paid to the child.

Maximum benefits: The biggest benefits go to individuals who file Schedule C and can employ their dependent children.

The law: Tax law allows a deduction for your ordinary and necessary business expenses, including wages paid to others for personal services rendered to your business.[3] You may deduct compensation only when it is[4]
- reasonable in amount,
- based on services actually rendered, and
- actually paid.

Wages to children: The IRS says that you may deduct wages paid to your dependent child when the facts show that your child[5]
- did the work as a bona fide employee in the operation of your business, and
- received reasonable compensation for the work effort.

Hiring Your Dependent Child

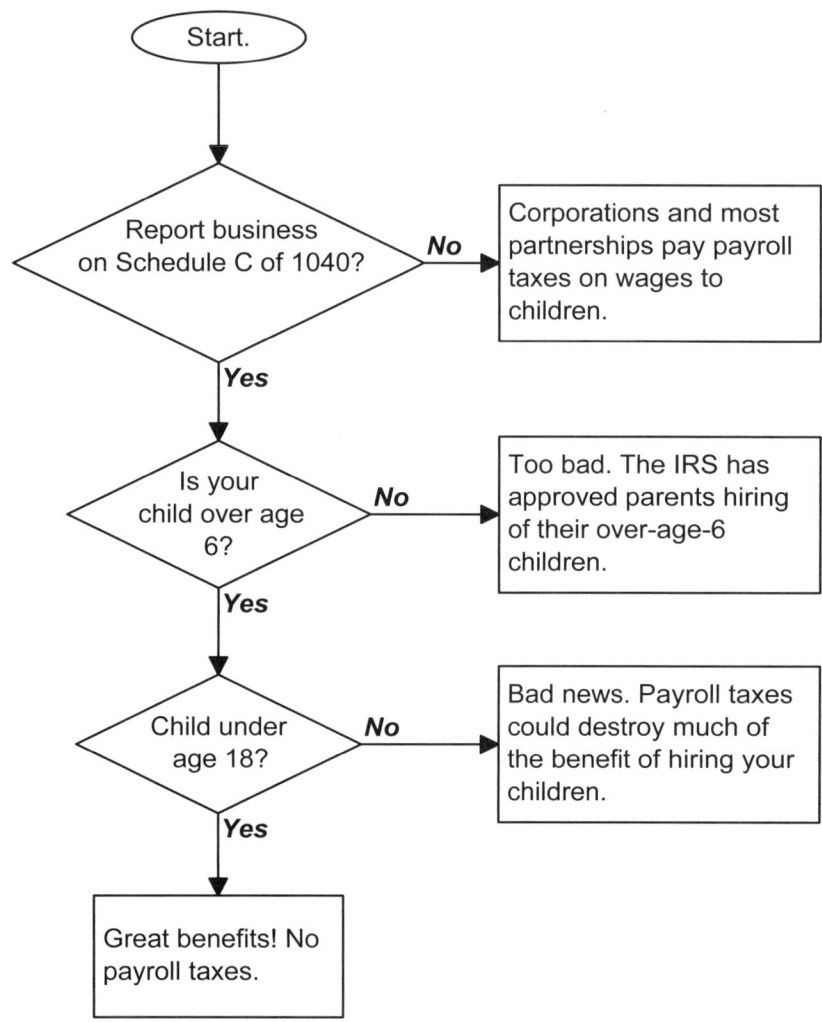

The IRS noted that a parent may employ his child just as he can employ someone else's child. The IRS made it clear that it would not be rational to penalize the taxpayer who employs his dependent child.[6]

Extra scrutiny: The courts note that payments by a parent to a dependent child require careful scrutiny.[7] Because of the family relationship, the court needs to take a close look to make sure there is both a bona fide employer–employee relationship and performance of services for the business.[8]

One court noted that transactions among family members must clear the tax law hurdle that does not allow deductions for personal, living, or family expense.[9] Another court noted that tax law[10]
- taxes income to the person who earns it, and
- disregards devices to divert or assign income from the person who earns it to another.

Caution: Your child's employment must be bona fide. Moreover, you must be able to prove it.

Benefits: You benefit when you pay your child who is under age 18 because:
- You get a tax deduction for wages you pay the child. This tax deduction reduces both your income and self-employment taxes.
- Both you and your child are exempt from payroll taxes.[11]
- Your child pays zero income tax on his or her 2016 earnings up to the standard deduction amount of $6,300 projected.[12]
- Your child can make a deductible contribution of up to $5,500 to an IRA.[13]
- Your child may take funds from his or her IRA to pay for college without incurring the 10 percent penalty tax.[14]
- Your child pays tax of only 10 percent on 2016 taxable income of less than $9,275 projected.[15]

Example 1: You earn $90,000 net (after expenses), report it on Schedule C of your tax return, and live in a state that has no income tax. You employ your two under-age-18 children, paying them each $5,000 a year. You deduct $10,000 and save almost $4,000 on your combined self-employment and income taxes. Your children pay zero tax. Thus, the family savings are almost $4,000.[16]

Child's money: The children may use their wages for whatever they want. It is their money. They can even pay part of their own support without impairing the parent's deduction for the wages.[17]

Notes

At the time we went to press, the IRS had not released the 2016 tax tables or standard deductions. We obtained projected amounts from the RIA Federal Taxes Weekly Alert, Vol. 61, No. 39.

Notes

Value of food and lodging: The value of meals and lodging may not be considered wages by the parents, because parents are legally liable for support and maintenance of their minor children.[18] Thus, where food and lodging furnished to a third-party employee might be a deduction, it is not a deduction when furnished to your minor children, no matter how bona fide the business relationship.

Example 2: After expenses, you net $101,000 in your Schedule C business and your spouse earns $350,000 on a W-2. You pay your 16-year-old child $20,000 for his work in your business during the year. Your child claims the full $5,500 IRA deduction because he plans to use the IRA money for college during those years when his tax bracket is going to be zero.

You and your son live in a state with no income tax. Your son reports his wages of $20,000 and claims the standard deduction and a deduction for his IRA contribution. His net income tax is $820 on his $20,000 of wages. Because of your $20,000 deduction for wages to your son, you and your spouse save $10,746 in taxes (39.6 percent in federal taxes and 14.13 percent in net self-employment taxes—15.3 percent x 0.9235). Your family saves $9,926 in taxes.

Money for college: If your son uses the money for college, it is as if you got an $9,926 tax break for your child's college tuition. That is a great benefit, and in addition, you get to work with someone you know and love.

Advantages: By hiring your children, you get more individual and family benefits than you would by hiring an outsider. There are four major advantages:
1. You do not pay Social Security taxes on the wages you pay to a dependent who is under age 18.[19]
2. You do not pay unemployment taxes on the wages you pay your under-age-21 child.[20]
3. Your child does not pay taxes on the first $6,300 of wages earned and then pays tax at only 10 percent on the first $9,275 of taxable income.[21]
4. The family money supply grows in direct proportion to the net taxes saved.

In effect, you can look at the tax savings as a form of tuition tax credit.

Good "shoebox" needed: The IRS does not pay its auditors to believe that your children are actually working for you. In fact, the IRS tells its auditors to look harder at transactions between you and your dependent children. It expects you to have proof! It expects its auditors to ask you for the proof.

Proof is easy: Here are six easy steps to excellent proof:
- Get an employer ID.
- Require time sheets.
- Document the reasonable wage.
- Pay by check.
- Complete the payroll paperwork.
- Apply common sense.

Notes

TIME SHEET		
Name: *Your Child*		
Date	Description of Work Completed	Hours
7/10/08	Web site design	2
7/11/08	Web site design	2
7/12/08	Web site design	5
	Total Hours Worked	9
	Rate of Pay per Hour	38
	Gross Pay from This Time Sheet	342

Get an employer ID: If your kids work for you, you must first set yourself up as an employer. That starts with your employer identication number (EIN). You may obtain your EIN

- online at www.irs.gov,
- by calling the IRS at (800) 829-4933, or
- by completing IRS Form SS-4.

Require a time sheet: You should collect completed time sheets on a daily or weekly basis. You should require your children and other part-time employees to complete time sheets according to your schedule. (Often, with kids under 10 years old, it is best to get daily time sheets and pay the kids daily to keep them motivated.)

Notes

In any event, you should require a time sheet to prove that your child did the work and to show how long it took. Review the time sheet example on the previous page, and use it as a guide for designing your own. Note how it documents the date, task, and time spent working.

The IRS will disallow your wage deduction if you do not prove that the children did the work. Vernon E. Martens hired his two sons and two daughters, but he lost about 80 percent of his deductions because he did not require time sheets.[22]

Document the reasonable wage: Next, you have to prove that the wage you pay your dependent child is not too high. You need proof that the wage is equal to what you would pay a third party to do the work.

Example: You pay your son $15.50 an hour to do your monthly promotional mailing. He produces 60 units an hour. You tried your neighbor and paid her $16.00 an hour, but she produced only 47 units an hour. You tried a $22.75-an-hour worker from a temporary employment agency, but he produced only 43 units an hour.

You need to document the wages paid to your neighbor and the fee paid to the temporary help agency. You should record the units produced and perhaps have the neighbor and temporary-help person sign statements of production.

Remember, you must have proof: The IRS considers written statements at or near the time you pay your neighbor far more important than statements made later, when both you and your neighbor have less chance of accurate recall.

When your neighbor signs the time sheet, make sure the description includes the number of items mailed. When you combine the time sheet with your summary, you have very convincing evidence.

You can build reasonable support for the wage you pay your minor child if you build a written answer to the question: Why am I paying my child this amount? Once you put your answer in writing, file it with your tax records.

Pay by check: Always pay wages by payroll check. You create a business image when you pay your child like you pay other employees. Also, you need to establish a clear audit trail from your business checkbook to your child's savings or money market account.

New Regulations on Employing Your Children

The Department of Labor recently issued new regulations on employing your children. You can find the new rules at the department's interactive web site: www.dol.gov/elaws.

Your 15-year-old or younger child may work for you, the parent, for any number of hours at any time of day. However, you may not employ your child in mining, manufacturing, or occupations declared hazardous (enumerated on the web site).

When you hire your children to work in your business, it is probably not so you can work them to death. It's likely that your goal is to pay them all you can so they will have money for college but still have time to learn and develop while they're in grade school and high school. Try to find work tasks that pay a lot so your children can earn money for college but still have plenty of time to be children.

Complete the Payroll Paperwork

You must complete the dreaded payroll paperwork. If your child will be your first and only employee, you will find the payroll paperwork a major and disgusting hurdle in the hire-your-child strategy. Do not fret! You could:
- Hire your child to take care of the paperwork, or
- Hire a payroll service like ADP, Paychex, or Payroll One Solutions.

To find a payroll service, ask your accountant or look in the Yellow Pages under "Payroll Services." Also, consider the Internet, where QuickBooks has an online payroll service that costs about $25 a month. Costco recently had a QuickBooks payroll special at $12.95 a month.

If you hire your child as the employee in charge of payroll, you have more business chores that your child can complete.

If you choose the payroll service, you will have an extra $155 to $700 in expenses for the year, but the service will take care of the payroll paperwork, including
- automatically taking any tax money due out of your bank account and sending it to the IRS; and
- automatically preparing each IRS form, such as the W-2, and filing it with the proper taxing authorities.

Remember, your wage payments to your under age 18 children are free of payroll taxes, but could be subject to withholding.

Federal payroll forms that you will need include the following:
- IRS Form W-4: Your child will use this form to tell you how many exemptions and allowances he or she claims.

Notes

- IRS Form W-2: If you paid your child $600 or more in wages, you must provide your child with a copy of IRS Form W-2. You file IRS Form W-3 and copies of the W-2s with the Social Security Administration.
- IRS Form 941: If you pay periodically, you file this form each quarter. If your child is your only employee, you enter zero as the amount subject to Social Security tax. If you pay wages once a year, you file Form 941 on a "seasonal" basis—once a year.
- IRS Form 940: The wages you pay your under-age-21 child are exempt from unemployment taxes. Even so, you must file IRS Form 940. If your child is your only employee, you enter the amounts paid to your child as both (1) gross pay and (2) exempt pay, making a net pay of zero subject to federal unemployment tax.

Apply common sense: Besides the payroll paperwork, you need to use common sense. How young can your child be and still do the work? According to the IRS, any child over age 6 can be a bona fide employee.[23] For peace of mind, you may want to use the IRS-approved age of over 6 years old as the minimum age for your hire.

One final thought: When you pay your child, the money is your child's money. If your child is a minor, you may be the custodian, but remember to exercise your fiduciary responsibilities and protect your child's money for the child's benefit.

Endnotes–Section 31

[1] Eller v Commr., 77 TC 934; Acq. 1984-2 CB 1.

[2] IRC Sections 3121(b)(3)(A); 3306(c)(5).

[3] IRC Section 162(a).

[4] Reg. Section 1.162-7(a).

[5] Rev. Rul. 73-393.

[6] Rev. Rul. 73-393.

[7] Gerald W. Jordan v Commr., T.C. Memo. 1991-50.

[8] Denman v Commr., 48 T.C. 439, 450 (196).

[9] Abdelhamid Hamdi v Commr., T.C. Memo. 1993-38.

[10] Lucas v Ear, 281 U.S. 111 (1930).

[11] IRC Sections 3121(b)(3)(A); 3306(c)(5).

[12] IRC Section 1(c); RIA *Federal Taxes Weekly Alert*, Vol. 61, No. 39.

[13] IRC Section 219(b)(5)(A); IR 2013-86.

[14] IRC Section 72(t)(2)(E).

[15] RIA *Federal Taxes Weekly Alert*, Vol. 61, No. 39.

[16] Self-employment tax savings are 14.13% (15.3% x 0.9235) and federal tax savings are 25%.

[17] Rev. Rul. 73-393.

[18] Ibid.

[19] IRC Section 3121(b)(3).

[20] IRC Section 3306(c)(5).

[21] IRC Section 1(c); Rev. Proc. 2011-52.

[22] Vernon E. Martens v Commr., No. 90-3104, May 91 (4th Cir).

[23] Eller v Commr., 77 TC 934; Acq. 1984-2 CB 1

Section 32

Solo 401(k) Could Be the Perfect Retirement Plan

In spite of recent headlines about the housing market, a revealing statistic shows that in the United States people have most of their net worth in their homes. The home captures wealth in spite of people.

This makes sense. Unlike bank accounts, stock portfolios, or most other places you can store your funds, you cannot quickly withdraw money from your home. So, while your other accounts ebb and flow, depending on immediate needs, your home captures wealth and imprisons it for the long term. Thinking long term is a good thing.

If you have no employees and you or you and your spouse are the owners of a business, new rules make the solo 401(k) another highly desirable capture mechanism for the following reasons:
- You get an individual tax deduction for the money you put into the plan.
- Your business gets a tax deduction for the money it puts into the plan.
- The money in the plan grows tax-deferred.
- Strict rules limit when you can touch (tamper with) it.

This adds up to a capture mechanism with great long-term benefits.

If you have employees, you need to consider them in your plan design; but if you don't, you need consider only yourself.

That's what this section does. It considers only you. It shows you how to put away up to and likely a little more than $59,000 for retirement with
- zero administrative cost, and
- very little tax hassle.

The $59,000 is the 2015 amount and it's indexed for inflation. Expect the 2016 amount to stay the same or increase slightly. Check www.bradfordandcompany.com/2016 for the final 2016 indexed amount.

If you, or you and your spouse, own the business, you can have a solo 401(k) whether your business is incorporated or unincorporated. This includes businesses you operate as C corporations, S corporations, single-member LLCs, husband and wife LLCs, partnerships, and proprietorships.

Notes

If you have employees, this section gives a great overview of strategies. Finish this section. Then, speak with your advisor about a "target" plan that will produce the results you want.

Your 401(k) plan may exclude employees who have not completed a year of service (generally 1,000 hours of service). IRC Sections 401(a)(1)(A)(ii) and 410(a)(3)(A).

Notes

The limits on the right are the 2015 limits which will be indexed for inflation in 2016. Since inflation is low, the increases, if any, will be minor. To see the 2016 limits when released, go to www.bradfordandcompany.com/2016.

The Dow Jones Industrial average increased at an average compound rate of 9.16 percent from January 1, 1982 ($882) to October 20, 2015 ($17,222). Add about 3 percent for dividends and you have about 12 percent as the average annual compound rate of return. That average annual 12 percent return would make for a GREAT retirement plan.

Socking the Money Away

The biggest deal in today's solo 401(k) is that the new law allows you to sock away and deduct far more money than in the past. Prior law had big restrictions on how much you could put into a solo 401(k) that made it a far less desirable plan. Today, the enhanced ceilings on the solo 401(k) allow

- the **employee** deduction for a contribution of 100 percent of your first $18,000 in earnings[1] ($24,000 if you are age 50 or over[2]), plus
- the **employer** deduction for a contribution of 20 percent of your self-employment income[3] (or 25 percent of compensation if you operate as a corporation[4]).

Example: You are 53 years old and your self-employment income is $90,000.

1. With your **employee** contribution, you may put away and deduct $24,000.
2. With your **employer** contribution, you may put away and deduct $18,000—that's 20 percent of your $90,000 of self-employment income.

Thus, at age 53 with earnings of $90,000, you can sock away and deduct $42,000.

Limits. The law imposes an overall ceiling on the combined employer and employee 2015 401(k) deductions and contributions of

- $53,000 if you are under age 50, and
- $59,000 if you are age 50 or over.

That's a tidy chunk. It's possible that the 2015 $53,000 will increase by a small amount for 2016 when it's indexed for inflation.

Tax deferral. Two big deals with the 401(k) retirement plan are the tax deductions for the monies put into the plan and the tax-deferred growth of the money inside the plan. Growing money at 8 percent or 12 percent is far superior to growing money at 5 percent or 7 percent. Tax deferral allows growth at the higher number.

Start early, earn a lot. You put away $40,000 for 21 years. Your tax-deferred compounding accumulation at 8 percent is $2.18 million.[5] That's a hefty amount. But if you could earn 9 percent, you would have an extra $300,000, for a total of $2.48 million. Add four more years and you'd have $3.69 million. So start your plan now; keep it for a long time; and get a good rate of return.

Unlike the simplified employee pension (SEP) where you contribute at the rate of 25 percent of earnings,[6] the 401(k) allows you to sock away 100 percent of the first $17,500 in earnings ($23,000, if you are 50 or older).

Example: Bill's wife, Andrea, makes big bucks and has a retirement plan at her company. Bill is just starting his self-employment, but he managed to squeak out $11,000 of proprietorship income. Bill may contribute the entire $11,000 to his 401(k) plan.

The Flexibility Advantage

The solo 401(k) has the great advantage of not requiring annual contributions—you decide each year how much you want to contribute. You are not locked into a fixed amount, and you can skip years whenever you like.

Further, you may contribute less than the tax law allows. If cash is tight and you don't want to make the 20 percent self-employment contribution, you can contribute 11 percent, 3 percent, or nothing at all. The choice is yours.

The total flexibility of the solo 401(k) is one of its many attractive features.

Set Up Your Plan Now

Since you must have your 401(k) in place by the end of the year, you might as well start this very day. In addition, you should make your employee contribution of up to $17,500 ($23,000 if you are 50 or older) before the end of your business year.[7]

Don't procrastinate. If you wait, your money does not start working. You want your money working in a tax-favored environment at the earliest possible moment.

No-Fee Setup

Charles Schwab and Fidelity do not charge account service fees for solo or individual 401(k) accounts.

Of the many brokerage accounts we examined, we found fees that vary widely, from zero at firms like Charles Schwab to as much as $1,500 a year. That's a big difference. Make sure you do a little research here.

Notes

Filing the Form 5500 EZ

When your 401(k) plan balance exceeds $250,000, you must file IRS Form 5500-EZ.[8] Although the form is straightforward, you probably should have your tax preparer complete it for you. Some plan administrators provide a service whereby they do the 5500-EZs for a fee.

Do not make the mistake of not filing this form. Because you are not required to file the form until your plan balance exceeds $250,000, it is easy to miss the deadline, especially in the first year you have to file it. Depending on your plan contributions and the earnings in your plan, you won't have to file this tax form for at least the first two years. Make a note of the deadline so you don't miss it.

The penalty for failing to file Form 5500-EZ is $25 a day.[9] That doesn't sound like a lot until you consider that in just one year the $25 daily penalty grows to a whopping $9,125. Further, the penalty is not deductible.

In what must have been a weak moment, lawmakers put a $15,000 maximum lid on the $25-a-day penalty.

Avoid the penalty. Make sure you have the filing deadline for this form on your calendar. You have until the last day of the seventh calendar month after the end of the plan year to file the return. For the plan year ending December 31, 2016, you have until July 31, 2017. That's plenty of time for this easy-to-file return.

Rollovers

When you establish your 401(k) account, you may roll over your existing pensions, IRAs, or other tax-deferred retirement accounts into the new 401(k).[10]

Similarly, when you decide to close down your 401(k), you can put together a rollover to your IRA.[11]

When you're doing a rollover, follow this general keep-out-of-trouble rule: Use a trustee-to-trustee rollover. The trustee-to-trustee rollover (e.g., from a Schwab to a Fidelity account)

- keeps the money out of your hands,
- avoids the tax withholding rules,
- ensures that all monies are properly transferred, and
- uses the services of professionals to help you avoid mistakes.

The Borrowing Booby Trap

Because you are the sole participant in the plan, the law treats you as a key employee.[12] Your key-employee status makes your 401(k) plan top-heavy, and that precludes deductions for interest paid on a 401(k) loan.

You will see ads explaining that one of the many great attributes of the solo 401(k) is the fact that you can borrow up to the lesser of $50,000 or 50 percent of the balance. The ads explain that many people roll their existing pensions and IRAs over to a 401(k) and, because they can borrow from it, have less fear of going into business for themselves.

This is absolute baloney. First, the ability to borrow from your 401(k) is probably the last reason on earth that you are going into business for yourself. Second, your key-employee status makes borrowing from your 401(k) a mistake, because you cannot deduct the interest.

Here is how borrowing from your solo 401(k) works, step by step, and why you make a sad mistake when you borrow:

- You borrow money from the 401(k)—you now have the cash.
- You must repay the principal and interest on a business 401(k) loan within five years.[13]—you don't have the cash for very long.
- Because you are a key employee, you may not claim a tax deduction for the interest you pay on the 401(k) loan.[14]
- When your 401(k) distributes to you the interest on which you claimed no deduction, you have taxable income.

You are booby-trapped here. You get no deduction for the interest that you pay to the 401(k), but you pay taxes on that interest as you collect retirement money from your 401(k).

Planning tip. If you need cash for your business, have your business obtain the cash from a source other than your 401(k). That way your business may deduct the interest.

Example. You are a sole proprietor in the 31 percent tax bracket. You borrow money at 8 percent interest from an outside source—not your 401(k)—for use in the proprietorship. Because you may deduct the interest, your after-tax cost of this money is only 5.52 percent. Deductions reduce your cost of money and help build your net worth.

Notes

Steps to Set Up Your Solo 401(k) Plan

Remember, when you have a solo 401(k) plan in either your proprietorship or corporation, you are two entities for plan purposes: You are both the employee and the employer. Keep your two entities in mind and follow the steps below to put your solo 401(k) plan in place.

1. Decide where to put the money. You want a high rate of investment return; low rates can render the retirement benefits of your 401(k) useless.

2. Put your plan in place now. The law requires that your 401(k) plan be in place before the end of your business year (that's probably December 31).

3. Deposit your employee contribution of up to $17,500 ($23,000 if you are age 50 or older) today. There are two reasons to make the deposit today. First, you must make your employee contribution by the end of your personal tax year (probably December 31). Second, the sooner you put the money into the 401(k), the longer it compounds and grows tax-deferred.

4. Deposit your employer contribution of 20 percent if you operate as a proprietorship or 25 percent if you operate as a corporation. Do it now. Today. Don't wait. (The law gives you the ability to later correct excess contributions.)

5. File IRS Form 5500-EZ when your 401(k) assets at the end of a plan year exceed $250,000.

Summary

The solo 401(k) plan is catching on. Although the solo 401(k) has been in this new, enhanced mode for only a few years, you can find many offerings and investment opportunities on the Web. To search, try these short phrases in quotes: "solo 401(k)" and "individual 401(k)."

Don't limit your search to the Web. Speak with your financial and tax advisors. Because your advisors have many clients with 401(k) questions, they are familiar with the plan and can help you implement various solutions that you might find most interesting.

To make the plan produce a strong result, you need a strong rate of investment return. One big advantage to the 401(k) is tax-deferred compounding. The higher the compounding rate, the more you have in your retirement plan.

Put your plan in place today. The solo 401(k) is a very good place to capture your money and keep it growing until you need it.

Notes

Notes

Endnotes–Section 32

1. IRC Section 402(g)(1)(B); IR 2014-99.
2. IRC Section 414(v)(2)(i); IR 2014-99.
3. IRC Sections 415(c)(3)(B); 404(a)(8). These sections produce the 20 percent rate because the law requires the taxpayer to reduce the 25 percent employer contribution by the amount of the employee deduction (25 percent) if you are operating as a proprietorship.
4. IRC Section 404(a)(3)(A)(i)(I).
5. Assumes the first $40,000 is invested at the beginning of the year (an annuity due calculation).
6. SEP contributions are limited to 25 percent of compensation. See IRS Pub. 560, *Retirement Plans for Small Business* (2013), p. 6.
7. IRS Pub. 560, *Retirement Plans for Small Business* (2014), p. 15, states that you may make your individual employee contribution to a 401(k) for the current year after the end of the current year if you meet some special rules and if the plan so allows. The boilerplate solo and individual 401(k) brokerage plans we reviewed required the employee to make the employee contribution before the end of the year. Therefore, the plan's refusal to accept the employee contribution after the end of the year makes the end of the year the deadline.
8. Instructions for Form 5500-EZ (2014), p. 2.
9. Ibid, p. 3.
10. IRC Sections 402(c)(1) and 408(d)(3).
11. IRC Section 408(d).
12. IRC Section 216(i).
13. IRC Section 72(p)(2)(B).
14. IRC Section 72(p)(3).

Section 33
Tips for Building Audit-Proof Support

Proof embedded in this course: You probably noted while reading various sections of this book the good records recommended within the sections. This section is an overview that complements the other proof discussions.

Appointment book is focal point: Build your documentation system around your appointment book. Note in the chart below how your appointments create a line of reasoning to your activities and expenditures.

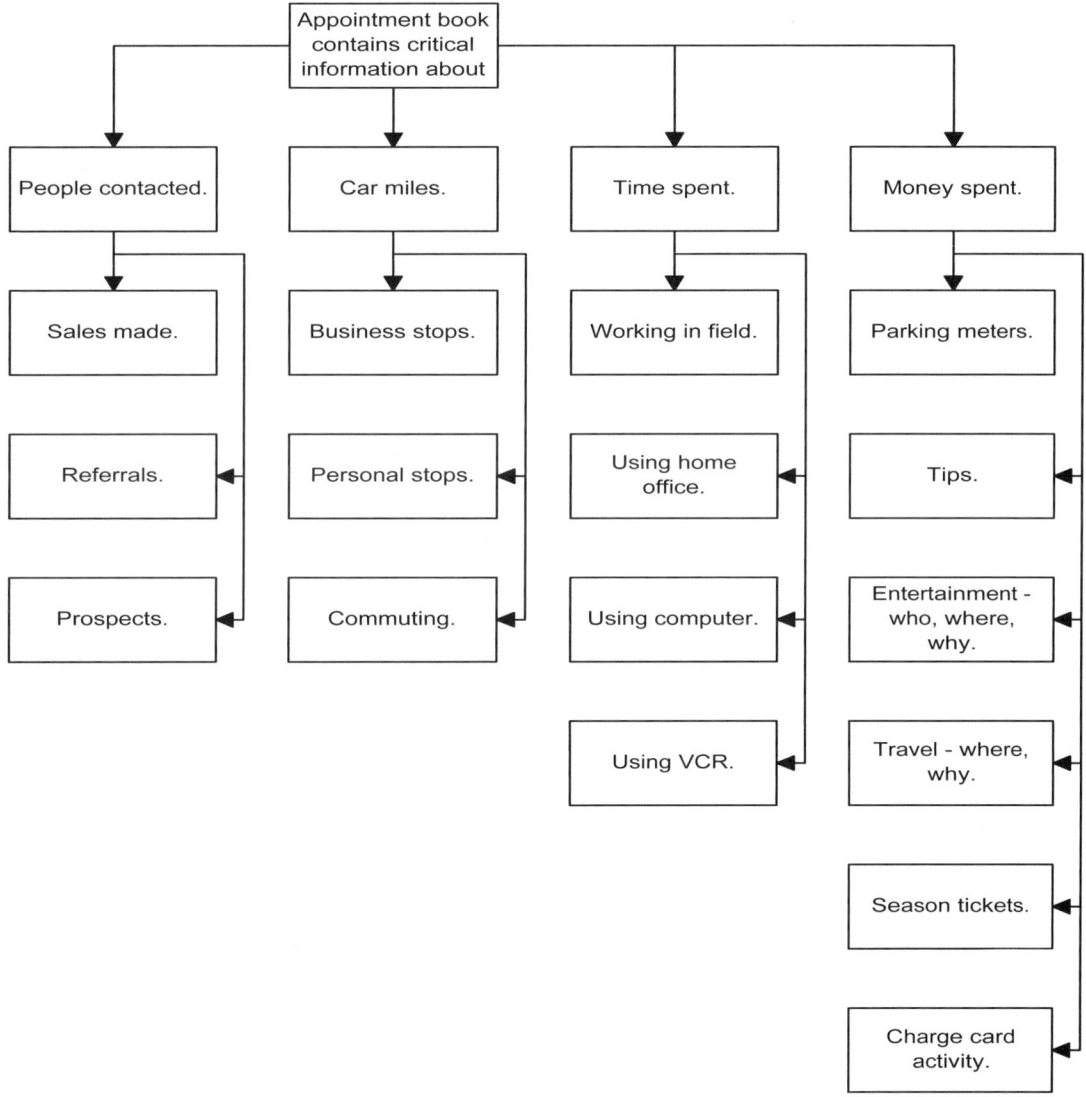

Notes

Keep a Happy "Shoebox"

Shoebox: The shoebox is simply your storage place for receipts and other documentary evidence. It may be a file cabinet, box, or even a real shoebox. If you fail to keep adequate receipts, you lose deductions.[1]

Happy shoebox: Keep your shoebox happy by giving it receipts, canceled checks, invoices, charge slips, correspondence, log books, photographs, and other corroborative evidence. Remember: Pack rats pay less tax.

Make Your Diary Love Your Shoebox

Diary: For all practical purposes, tax law requires you to keep a diary (your appointment book enhanced) to prove ordinary and necessary business activity.[2]

Diary and shoebox need to agree: A good diary/shoebox system requires that you support entries in a diary with receipts and other corroborative evidence. Sanford, a taxpayer, lost his deductions for travel expenses that were $75 or more because he did not have receipts in his shoebox.[3] (Note: The old $25 threshold increased to $75 effective October 1, 1995.)[4] You must gather evidence such as receipts to deduct lodging and expenses of $75 or more while out of town.[5]

Tricks for Your Checkbook

Canceled check: A canceled check is not adequate documentation because it does not show the items making up the expenditure.[6] You should have receipts, invoices, or other written evidence to prove expenses paid by check. The IRS tells its auditors to examine canceled checks with invoices to find the nature of expenditures and verify actual costs.[7]

Three-part voucher checks: To ensure adequate support for business expenditures, use three-part voucher checks.
- Part 1: Original goes to the vendor and ends up at your bank. Your bank should either return it to you or digitize it as part of your bank statement. Make sure you have either the canceled checks or digitized copies in your files at the office.
- Part 2: Attach copy 1 to the receipt, invoice, or other documentation that supports the payment and file alphabetically or by check number.
- Part 3: Numerical file copy. (In the days of computers, this seems redundant, but it makes a good impression in an IRS audit and it takes only a minute to do.

When to Make the Record

Timely recording: Tax law states that written evidence is far superior to oral evidence. The probative value of written evidence is greater the closer in time the recording is to the expenditure. Tax law does not require a contemporaneous log. It says that a log of an expenditure's elements, supported by sufficient documentary evidence, has a high degree of credibility—more credibility than that found in a statement prepared later, when generally there is a lack of accurate recall.[8]

Proving timely recording: Use a credit card to record your entertainment and travel expenses. On the top copy of the credit card receipt, note the business purpose and other pertinent documentation. You produce one of two possible corroborative pieces of evidence with this method:
- A carbon copy that supports the original entry.
- An original that contains handwriting and ink that starts aging that day. With today's science, experts can approximate the date of entry.

What the IRS Expects

Records examiners expect to find: The IRS notes that taxpayers in personal services businesses have some or all of the following accounting and financial records:[9]
- Appointment book
- Customer or client card file
- Daily log or receipts book
- Disbursements book, such as a checkbook
- Running account of expenses paid
- Duplicate deposit slips, bank statements, and canceled checks

Think like a good auditor: Tax evidence tells:
- How many people are sleeping in your room (lodging receipts show occupancy—single and double).
- Side trips you took (airline tickets show stops on the way to and from a business destination).
- Child's use of business car (signatures on gasoline credit-card charge receipts can suggest use by family members other than the business taxpayer).
- Overstated auto mileage (repair bills establish mileage driven during the year).

Notes

To visualize how the audit-proofing process works, see the online video: www.tax789.com/2015video

Notes

Endnotes–Section 33

1. Sanford v Commr., 50 TC 823 (1968), aff'd 412 F.2d 201 (2d Cir. 1969).
2. IRC Sections 162; 274.
3. Sanford v Commr., 50 TC 823 (1968), aff'd 412 F.2d 201 (2d Cir. 1969).
4. IR-95-56.
5. IR-95-56; Reg. Section 1.274-5(c)(2)(iii).
6. Woolley v Commr., T.C. Memo 1986-418.
7. IRS Market Segment Specialization Program Paper, Attorneys, Training 3149-102, TPDS 83183A; June 1, 1994.
8. Reg. Section 1.274-5T(c)(1).
9. IRS Market Segment Specialization Program Paper, Attorneys, Training 3149-102, TPDS 83183A; June 1, 1994.

Section 34

Choosing the Right Business Entity Can Be Critical to Your Business Health

New Stimulus Law Adds Flavors to Choices

Being in business means facing two vultures:
- The legal system that puts your hard-earned assets at risk.
- The tax man who wants his share of your earnings.

Say the delivery man slips and falls on a banana peel left on the doorstep of your business location—which might be inside your home. Your personal assets could be at risk when he decides to sue for his disabling back injury.

How do you protect your personal assets? Well, you could operate your business as an entity that limits your liability to the assets of your business.

The entity choices include S and C corporations and limited liability companies (LLCs). Each of these entities forms a protective legal wall around your personal assets. Since most business-related liabilities can't penetrate that wall, your personal assets should be safe from the delivery man's assault on your wealth.

On the other hand, if you continue operating your business as a sole proprietorship or as a husband-wife partnership, you expose your personal assets to all business-related liabilities.

Once you conclude that you need a liability-limiting entity, the next step is to choose the appropriate kind. Now you have to consider the second vulture. This is where the tax angles become important, because each entity involves different tax rules. You want the entity that delivers the best tax results for you.

Also, because your business and personal circumstances change with time (marriage, children, employees), you need to revisit your choice of entity periodically to ensure maximum benefits.

Selected Winners and Losers for Entity Choices

Description	Single-Member LLCs & Schedule C Taxpayers	C Corporation	S Corporation
Tax on income	Individual level	Corporate level. This is what causes the double-taxation problem	Flows through to the individual level
Net operating loss (NOL)	Flows to individual and offsets other income. If there is still an NOL after the offsets, carryback 2 and forward 20 years	No flow-through, but corp. can carryback 2 and forward 20 years. Use Section 1244 stock to write off initial investment in case of corporate failure	To the extent of basis, the losses flow to the individual and offsets other income. If there is still an NOL after the offsets, carryback 2 and forward 20 years
Paperwork	Easiest! Schedule C is easy. For liability, LLC requires annual filings and separate accounting	Separate corporate and personal tax returns; separate checkbooks and accounting; corporate minutes, annual filings	Separate corporate and personal tax returns; separate checkbooks and accounting; corporate minutes, annual filings
Section 179 expensing	Individual level	Corporate level	Individual level
Payroll taxes on hiring your under-age-18 child	None	All payroll taxes apply	All payroll taxes apply
Section 105 medical reimbursement plan	Available by hiring and covering the spouse with family coverage	Available and easy	Not available to more than 2-percent owners and spouses
FICA and Medicare taxes	Full payment (self-employment taxes)	Full payment	Planning can substantially reduce FICA and medicare taxes
Cost of disability insurance on owner	No deduction; no tax on benefits	Deductible; benefits are taxed to the individual	No deduction; no tax on benefits
Income splitting	None with Schedule C; excellent with multi-member LLC	Poor	Excellent
Death	Assets marked up to fair market value for heirs	Corporation continues, value of shares marked up to fair value	Corporation continues, value of shares marked up to fair value
Liability	Unlimited for the Schedule C taxpayer. Limited to member's capital contribution for an LLC	In most cases, limited to the assets of the corporation	In most cases, limited to the assets of the corporation

Before we start kicking these vultures around, you need one more bit of global knowledge about liabilities. In general, no liability-limiting entity can protect your personal assets from your
- professional errors and omissions, or
- tortious acts. (Tortious acts are things like reckless operation of an auto resulting in injuries or property damage to others.)

To protect your assets from exposure to professional and tort liabilities, you must conduct your business and personal life with due diligence and buy adequate insurance coverage. No surprises here!

Next, you need to consider adding a second layer of protection by establishing a liability-limiting entity to shield your personal assets from business-related liabilities that might arise from things totally beyond your control, like
- bad things done by an employee, or
- the dreaded banana on your business doorstep.

The series of sections that follow will help you defend yourself against both the legal and tax vultures by
- explaining the advantages and disadvantages of each entity,
- showing you an ironclad way to get to the best bottom line for you, and
- putting a smile on your face as you see the dollar savings.

The next section of this book deals with the single-member LLC, followed by one-owner S corporations, then one-owner C corporations, and finally considerations for the husband and wife.

On the left you see a chart of selected winners and losers for the entities. As you can see, many things can happen when you choose a business entity. Some good! Some bad! How do you know what's best?

There is one and only one way to know what's best for you. Put pencil to paper and compare the forms of business and your after-tax cash. In general, we recommend that you and your tax advisor do this together. Further, you want this in writing for two major reasons:
1. An opinion in writing from your tax advisors carries great weight.
2. A written analysis is done with far more care than a casual off-the-cuff comment, which may not consider all the consequences.

Tax advisors enjoy opinion assignments. It gives them more chargeable time and it takes advantage of their training, which is the most enjoyable work.

Notes

Notes

You should clearly understand your written document. Suppose you asked your tax advisor to compare your current proprietorship to an S corporaton. If he or she gave you the comparison that you see in the chart below, you would have a very good understanding of why your current proprietorship is best for you.

Before looking at this chart, keep in mind that this is just a sample. Your answer could easily be the opposite of this result. Your result depends on your situation.

What's best? Proprietorship or S corporation

The following chart tells you exactly how much you benefit and why. You want this in writing. Then, you have proof (just in case the strategy is wrong). When advisors put things in writing, you can bet they did it carefully, and odds are that they did it right.

Start: the way you are—proprietorship	Proprietor
Net income from proprietor's tax return	$150,000
Less federal income taxes paid	-33,000
Less Social Security and Medicare taxes paid	-16,000
Net cash to spend with proprietorship	$101,000
Compare: the way you could be—S corp.	**S corp.**
Net cash to spend with proprietorship	$101,000
Cash saved on Social Security and Medicare taxes with a $75,000 salary and $75,000 in distributions	5,000
Cash lost because the corporation triggers payroll taxes on the hiring of your two children	-6,000
Estimated present value of annual after-tax cash loss on retirement benefits due to contribution at the S corporation level being limited to salary income (versus net income at the proprietorship level)	-4,000
Cash cost (after taxes) for extra tax return, annual filings with the state, and lawyer's fees	-1,000
After-tax cash lost with S corp. medical plan versus the benefits of the 105 plan at the proprietorship level	-2,000
Additional state taxes on S corporation entity (these are in addition to the state taxes on your pass-through income)	-2,250
Net cash to spend with S corporation	$90,750
After-tax cash advantage to proprietorship (or LLC)	**$10,250**

Section 35

Single-Member Limited Liability Companies (LLCs) Are Simple to Operate

All states now allow single-member (one-owner) limited liability companies. Owners of LLCs are referred to as *members*. The single-member LLC provides
- liability protection, and
- maximum simplicity for tax purposes.

The single-member LLC offers corporate-style liability protection. This generally means that only assets owned by the single-member LLC are exposed to liabilities related to the LLC's business activities. So, if you put no assets in the LLC, you have no real exposure. Further, with the LLC, your personal assets are generally off limits. Good!

Single-member LLCs also deliver favorable federal income tax results. First, IRS regulations say that you ignore a single-member LLC for federal tax purposes.[1] For example, say you set up a new single-member LLC to conduct what was previously your sole proprietorship business. As far as the IRS is concerned, nothing has changed; the IRS ignores the existence of your single-member LLC. So your business is still considered a sole proprietorship for federal tax purposes. Therefore, you continue
- reporting your business income and expenses on Schedule C,
- computing your self-employment tax on Schedule SE, and
- making quarterly estimated tax payments as usual.

Now say you establish a new single-member LLC to take over your existing rental real estate operation. Once again, for federal tax purposes, the single-member LLC existence is ignored. You continue reporting the rental real estate income and expenses on Schedule E, and you keep making quarterly estimated tax payments just as before.

As you can see, extreme simplicity is the major tax advantage of single-member LLC status.

Notes

Tax Breaks

The single-member LLC allows you to capture the tax breaks below that accrue to Schedule C businesses:
- Creating a Section 105 plan strategy by hiring your spouse and enabling business deductions for family medical expenses
- Deducting interest paid on car loans
- Incurring no extra cost for a second tax return
- Experiencing no unexpected tax problems when you conduct transactions between yourself and your business (like taking money out of the single-member LLC's business checking account, or transferring ownership of an asset between you and the single-member LLC).

Yes, keeping things simple is good!

Single-Member LLC Caveats

Of course, nothing is perfect—including the single-member LLC. Here are the two significant downside considerations.

First, when you use a single-member LLC to operate a trade or business, the member—meaning you—must pay the federal self-employment tax in the same fashion as a sole proprietor. Basically, you must multiply your bottom-line Schedule C net income by .9235 and pay 15.3 percent self-employment taxes on earnings up to $113,700.

The self-employment tax rate on income above $113,700 is 2.90 percent (this is for Medicare only). There's no upper limit on the amount taxed at that 2.90 percent rate. Finally, you get no deduction for self-employment tax purposes for contributions to your tax-deferred retirement plan account because this deduction does not go on your Schedule C; instead, it goes on the front of your Form 1040.[2]

You actually pay 14.13% on a maximum of $123,119 (.9235 of which is $113,700).

For example, if your Schedule C net income is $100,000, you pay self-employment taxes of $14,130.[3] That's a lot of money!

And this is not a one-time thing; your tax partner takes this money from you year after year.

With a different choice of entity, and the will to put up with some heavy paperwork, you can seriously reduce the Social Security and Medicare tax hits with the S and C corporation options explained later.

Another caution: some states mistreat the single-member LLC and tax it not as a proprietorship, but as a corporation. Most jurisdictions follow the beneficial federal guidelines and ignore single-member LLCs for state tax purposes. In those states, you do not file a separate state return for your single-member LLC.

However, a few states tax the single-member LLC like a corporation. For example, Texas imposes the corporate tax on a single-member LLC. This is pretty bad. Texas does not assess the income tax on the sole proprietor, so the corporate classification in Texas is a definite downside. Thus, it is important to know how your state addresses LLCs.

Summary on Single-Member LLCs

With the single-member LLC arrangement, you get the liability protection you need with maximum federal tax simplicity (state tax simplicity too, in most jurisdictions). This is a great combination! However, you may pay a price in the form of higher Social Security and Medicare taxes. If you can live with that, we heartily recommend the single-member LLC option.

On the other hand, if you are willing to incur more paperwork to pay less Social Security and Medicare taxes, you should consider the S and C corporation options.

Notes

Endnotes–Section 35

[1] Reg. Section 301.7703-3(a) and (b).

[2] Seymour Gale v U.S., 91-2 USTC 50356 (DC IL 1991). Your contribution is deductible for federal income tax purposes on page 1 of Form 1040.

[3] $100,000 x 0.9235 = income for self-employment taxes of $92,350 x 15.3% tax rate equals 14,

Section 36

The One-Person S Corporation

In the preceding section, you learned how the single-member LLC could protect you from legal liability and keep your tax life simple. In the right circumstances, the single-member LLC is a better tax reduction choice than the S corporation or the C corporation.

This section shows you when the S corporation is the best legal choice for your business.

First, since the trigger for changing your form of business from a proprietorship is liability protection, you will be happy to learn that the solely owned S corporation does job one and protects you against business-related liabilities.

With an S corporation, you also qualify for *pass-through taxation* for federal income tax purposes. Under this taxpayer-friendly concept, the law does not assess entity-level federal income taxes on the S corporation itself. Instead, all the corporation's income, deductions, and tax credit items are passed through to you, the shareholder, on a Schedule K-1. Then you report the Schedule K-1 tax items on your Form 1040, and pay the resulting federal income tax at your personal level.

In contrast, if you run your business as a C corporation, you potentially run into the double-taxation problem. Why? First, corporate income is taxed at the corporate level. Then, when the C corporation sends the cash to you as dividends, you pay taxes on the dividend income.

You avoid the threat of double taxation with an S corporation, because the S corporation acts like a big funnel that catches all of the income and expenses and passes through the net income and other condensed items to your Schedule K-1.

Beware of Restrictions and Disadvantages

To qualify for S corporation status and the pass-through taxation benefit, your company must meet strict criteria. Specifically, it must:[1]
- be a domestic corporation or a limited liability company, electing S corporation status,
- have 100 or fewer shareholders,
- have no shareholders other than U.S. citizen individuals, resident alien individuals, estates, certain types of trusts, and certain types of tax-exempt entities, and
- have only one class of stock.

Notes

If your corporation violates any of these criteria, the C corporation tax rules apply (which means that the threat of double taxation lurks in the background).[2]

Thankfully, a single-owner or husband-and-wife owned business generally does not have to worry about violating the rules on being a qualified S corporation. But before you make the decision to operate as an S corporation, consider the disadvantages and advantages that follow.

Disadvantage 1: Even though an S corporation generally pays no corporate-level federal income taxes, you still must file a corporate return each year on Form 1120S. And you must issue yourself a Schedule K-1 each year. The Schedule K-1 includes all the pass-through tax information from your S corporation's business activities (amount of taxable income, deductions, tax credits, and so forth). You must take this information into account when you prepare your personal Form 1040. Depending on where you live, your state may require you to file a state return for your S corporation too, and there could even be a corporate-level state tax bill.

This whole S corporation drill can get very complicated. You should use a competent tax pro to keep things straight. In contrast, choosing to run your business as a single-member LLC keeps things much simpler and keeps your tax-filing obligations to a minimum.

Disadvantage 2: With an S corporation, you'll also face extra tax-related paperwork each time you take money (or any other asset) out of the corporation. Here's why. You must treat each withdrawal as
- salary or bonus paid to you in your capacity as a corporate employee,
- a dividend paid to you in your capacity as a corporate shareholder, or
- proceeds from a loan made by the corporation to you.

If you treat the withdrawal as salary or bonus money, you'll have to deal with employment taxes, employment tax forms, and W-2s. If you treat the withdrawal as a loan, you'll need a written loan document to keep the IRS off your back. No fun!

In contrast, if you choose to run your shop as a single-member LLC, transactions between you and your business generally won't result in extra tax-related paperwork.

Disadvantage 3: An S corporation may not transfer appreciated assets (current value greater than tax basis) to you without triggering a taxable gain that passes through to your Form 1040 and triggers tax at your personal level.[3] With a single-member LLC, you do not have this problem. You can ignore this disadvantage if your business will not own any significant appreciating assets.

Disadvantage 4: If you die, the tax bases of your S corporation's appreciated capital gain assets (real estate, patents, copyrights, customer lists, and the like) do not get a step up to their date-of-death fair market values. The single-member LLC gives you a step up in basis, and that means lower bills for your relatives when they sell those assets.[4]

You do not have to consider this disadvantage in a service business that will own very few, if any, appreciating assets.

Disadvantage 5: Unlike the single-member LLC, where you can hire your spouse to put in place a Section 105 medical reimbursement plan, you have no such option with the S corporation. The reimbursement aspect of the Section 105 plan is not available to a more-than-2-percent owner of an S corporation. Moreover, the hiring-your-spouse strategy does not get around these rules, as the tax rules attribute your shareholder ownership to your employee-spouse. In other words, if you own 100 percent, your spouse also owns 100 percent for purposes of not qualifying for fringe benefits.

Disadvantage 6: Compared to the sole proprietorship and the single-member LLC, you get far less benefit when your S corporation hires your under-age-18 children to work in the business. Why? On wages paid to the children, the S corporation pays FICA, Medicare, and unemployment taxes. The children pay FICA and Medicare. This combination creates taxes of more than 20 percent that eat mightily into the benefits of the hire-your-child strategy.

Disadvantage 7: Defined contribution retirement-plan benefits are based on a percentage of salary for the corporation. If the corporate salary is low, the defined contribution is low.

Tax law allows sole proprietorships and single-member LLCs to base defined contributions on net business income, a higher number. Thus, sole proprietorships and single-member LLCs produce bigger retirement contributions.

When it comes to choosing a form of business, you need to weigh the aggregate dollar effects of disadvantages with the dollar effects of advantages. Do this right. Get your tax professional's help. The money you pay for this service is truly money well spent.

Now turn your attention to the advantages of the S corporation.

Notes

Notes

Advantage 1: S Corp + ᴹᵒᵈᵉˢᵗ Salary = Lower Taxes

An S corporation makes you both a corporate employee and a corporate shareholder. The corporation will pay you a salary that reflects the work you do for the business.

In 2016, the first $118,500 of salary is subject to a 15.3 percent federal employment tax rate. Of that, 12.4 percent is for Social Security tax and 2.90 percent is for Medicare tax. Half of these taxes are withheld from your salary checks. The S corporation, in its role as your employer, pays the other half directly to the government. You must, of course, pay income tax at your personal level on salary received from the corporation.

On the corporation's annual tax return (Form 1120S), the corporation deducts your salary and the employer's half of Social Security and Medicare taxes. These corporate-level write-offs reduce the taxable income passed through to you on the Schedule K-1 you receive from the corporation. Then all corporate-level taxable income left after deducting your salary and related employment taxes can be paid out to you as a cash distribution without any Social Security or Medicare taxes.[5]

The leftover profit distribution can save you major bucks! Here's why. With a single-member LLC, you pay self-employment taxes (Social Security and Medicare) on essentially all of your business income. However, with the S corporation, the law charges these taxes only on the portion of business income paid to you as salary. The following example illustrates this tax-saving distinction.

Example: Let's say that you have your "choice of entity" decision narrowed down to the single-member LLC and the S corporation. For 2016, you expect to earn $100,000 after paying all expenses, but before you pay any Social Security or Medicare taxes. Let's assume that you choose the S corporation option, and a $40,000 salary is reasonable for your work in the business. The cash advantage to the S corporation is shown below:

	With LLC	With S Corp
Business income	$100,000	$100,000
Corporate salary	N/A	-40,000
Corporate-level SS & Medicare taxes on salary	N/A	-3,060
Unemployment taxes	N/A	-342
Net business profit	$100,000	$56,598
Salary	N/A	40,000
SS & Medicare taxes paid by owner	-14,130	-3,060
Income tax benefits	1,766	851
Cash to owner	$87,636	$94,389
Cash advantage to S corporation		$6,753

The cash advantage here is money in the pocket from tax savings. Nice!

The $6,753 advantage is due solely to the Social Security and Medicare tax savings.

The "income tax benefits" in the example above come from deducting
- 50 percent of the self-employment tax for the single-member LLC, and
- 100 percent of the corporate level Social Security, Medicare, and unemployment taxes.

Also, we did not consider the extra cost for the S corporation tax return. We assumed that lawyer fees were about the same for both the S corporation and the single-member LLC.

Remember: if this were you, you could expect to reap the $6,753 in after-tax cash savings year after year.

Caveats on the Low Salary

Naturally, there are limits on this strategy of using an S corporation combined with a relatively modest corporate salary to slash Social Security and Medicare taxes.

If your business ever gets audited, you must show that your salary level is reasonable for the work you perform. If it's clearly way too low, the IRS could hit your S corporation with bills for back taxes, interest, and penalties.[6] That said, all instances of taxpayers who lost their court cases on this issue involved absurdly low salary levels.[7]

The moral: do not tempt fate by setting your salary so low that it's clearly ridiculous.

Big Advantage 2: Income Splitting

Another major reason some proprietors prefer the S corporation is the income-splitting benefits. If you are in the 35 percent tax bracket and your 78-year-old father is in the 10 percent tax bracket, why not make some of that corporate income available to your father and save 25 percent in taxes? Exactly!

To achieve the savings, you make your father a partial owner of the corporation. You can do this by making gifts of stock. Let's say your father owns 1/3 of the stock and that, after deducting your corporate salary, the S corporation's profits are $63,000. Your father receives $21,000 (1/3 of $63,000) in cash profits from your corporation, pays tax of $2,100,

Notes

Lawmakers have ruined income splitting with most of your children.

and uses the remaining $18,900 for living expenses. As a family, you save $5,250 in taxes with this strategy.

Income splitting has a downside: The father now owns the stock! How do you get it back? Obviously, you need to think about this. It's highly probably that the stock will find its way back to you as an inheritance.

Beware with children: Effective 2008 and later, new kiddie tax rules apply the parents' tax rate to college children under the age of 24. Thus, income splitting with these children is no longer productive.

Summary

There are three reasons to choose the S corporation as your liability-limiting entity.

Reason 1: You want to save Social Security and Medicare taxes. In exchange for this advantage you are willing to live with the extra tax-related paperwork that S corporation status entails compared to sole proprietorship or single-member LLC status.

Reason 2: You want the income-splitting benefits of the S corporation and are willing to live with the extra paperwork.

Reason 3: You want pass-through taxation, and the single-member LLC option is not available to a one-owner business in your state.

Endnotes–Section 36

[1] IRC Section 1361(a)(1); The LLC can elect to be taxed as (1) a C corporation, by filing IRS Form 8832 with the Internal Revenue Service, or (2) an S corporation, by filing IRS Form 2553.

[2] IRC Section 1361(a)(2).

[3] IRC Sections 311(b) and 1366.

[4] IRC Section 1014(a).

[5] See Revenue Ruling 59-221 and *Paul B. Ding v Commissioner*, TC Memo 1997-435 (1997), *affirmed* 200 F.3d 587 (9th Cir. 1999).

[6] See Revenue Ruling 74-44 and Treasury Inspector General for Tax Administration (TIGTA) Report: Audit No. 200130027, Reference No. 2002-30-125.

[7] See for example Joseph M. Grey Public Accountant, P.C. v Commissioner, 119 TC No. 5 (2002); Joseph Radtke, S.C. v U.S., 895 F.2d 1196 (7th Cir. 1990); Spicer Accounting, Inc. v U.S., 918 F.2d 90 (9th Cir. 1990); and Yeagle Drywall Company, Inc. v Commissioner, TC Memo 2001-284.

Section 37

The One-Owner and Husband-and-Wife-Owned C Corporation

In the last section, you learned how the S corporation could protect you from legal liability and put money in your pocket by
- reducing your self-employment taxes, and
- splitting income with family members.

You also learned that you get that legal protection with a single-member LLC and also keep your tax life simple. Further, you learned that, in the right circumstances, the single-member LLC is the best tax-reduction choice compared with the S corporation or the C corporation.

Here you will be happy to learn that, like the single-member LLC and the solely owned S corporation, the solely owned C corporation generally protects your personal assets from exposure to business-related liabilities. Good! (Under applicable state law, you get exactly the same degree of liability protection from either an S or C corporation; the only difference between the two is how they are taxed.)

Historical Disadvantage of Double Taxation

The historical disadvantage of C corporation status is the threat of double taxation. Basically, double taxation means business income and gains get taxed once at the corporate level and again when you receive cash or assets from the company in the form of dividends or liquidating distributions. This double-taxation problem arises because your C corporation cannot deduct these dividends or distributions even though you pay taxes on them at your personal level.

Before the 2003 Economic Stimulus Tax Act, double taxation was an absolutely horrible outcome. Why? Because dividends were taxed at up to 38.6 percent. Now it's not nearly so bad. Under current law, you face a maximum tax on dividends of 23.8 percent (20 percent for the dividends and 3.8 percent for Medicare).[1] Even so, you still want to avoid double taxation whenever you can.

Bad Place for Business Losses

If your business is in the start-up phase or suffering a business downturn, the C corporation puts you at a disadvantage when it generates tax losses.

Notes

When the loss occurs inside your C corporation, the C corporation cannot pass those losses to you. In contrast, with a single-member LLC or an S corporation, the tax losses do pass through to you, and generally you can deduct them immediately on your Form 1040.

So does the C corporation option ever make sense? Yes. It can be a tax-smart choice when you
- don't anticipate tax losses, and
- can avoid double taxation.

In fact, the C corporation can be a great choice in exactly the right circumstances, as you will soon see.

Zero Out Corporate Income to Avoid Double Taxation

Your solely owned C corporation may be able to avoid double taxation simply by *zeroing out* its taxable income every year with deductible payments that benefit you. Such payments can take the form of
- salary and bonuses paid to you for your work in the business,
- rent paid to you for business assets that you lease to the company (copyrights, patents, land and building at the business location, and so forth),
- interest paid to you for money you loan the company,
- payments to a health plan that covers your family health insurance premiums and your uninsured medical costs, and
- company contributions to your personal tax-deferred retirement plan.

If you can zero out the corporation's taxable income every year with these types of payments (all of which benefit you personally), your company won't owe any income tax. So there won't be any double taxation. Of course, you'll owe income tax at the personal level on the salary and bonus payments. All in all, this is a very good deal!

Still, you'll always have the threat of double taxation hanging over your head. If your company gets audited and the IRS decides your purported salary and bonuses were actually disguised dividends, all the apparent advantages of operating as a C corporation can vanish overnight. Not a good deal!

Our take: Relying on the strategy of zeroing out your C corporation's taxable income in order to avoid double taxation is a time-honored practice. It's also risky! In most cases, it's probably not worth the risk of reclassification in the case of an audit, even though your risk of audit is mighty low. When you intend to siphon as much cash as possible out of your business for the benefit of you and yours, we advise against the C corporation and recommend the single-member LLC and S corporation alternatives.

Leave Everything Inside the Corporation to Avoid Double Taxation

Say you are a high-bracket taxpayer. You have a growth business that generates a healthy, but not huge, amount of annual taxable income. To the extent possible, you want to finance your business's growing capital requirements with internally generated cash. You expect to withdraw little or no cash for yourself. Down the road, you plan on selling the business for a big profit.

If you run this operation as a C corporation, you can
- pay income taxes at favorable corporate rates,
- completely avoid double taxation, and
- avoid the dreaded Social Security and Medicare taxes by taking zero cash out of the company.

At the personal level, you'll owe zero income taxes until you bail out by selling your corporate stock to the new owner. When you sell the corporate stock (assuming you've owned the stock for more than a year when you sell), you pay capital gains taxes at the following rates:[2]

Capital Gains Tax Rate	Adjusted Taxable Income Single	Adjusted Taxable Income Married	Adjusted Taxable Income Head of Household
0 percent	Up to $37,650	Up to $75,300	Up to $50,400
15 percent	$37,650 to $415,050	$75,300 to $466,950	$50,400 to $441,000
20 percent	Over $415,050	Over $466,950	Over $441,000

Notes

The 2016 tax bracket numbers on the left were calculated by Thomson Rueters Checkpoint Federal Taxes Weekly Alert, Vol 61-39 based on inflation data. The final tax brackets from the IRS might vary slightly.

In addition, you pay the 3.8 percent Medicare tax when investment income such as capital gains exceeds $250,000 if married, or $200,000 if unmarried.[3]

This can be a good plan; in fact, this plan may be even better than it looks at first blush. The following example illustrates how a C corporation can save major taxes in this scenario.

Example: Save Taxes with Corporate Rates

Under our federal tax system, a C corporation's annual income is taxed according to the following graduated rate schedule:
- 15 percent on the first $50,000;
- 25 percent on $50,001 to $75,000;
- 34 percent on $75,001 to $100,000;
- 39 percent on $100,001 to $335,000;
- 34 percent on $335,001 to $10 million.

Notes

As you can see, the first $50,000 of annual income is taxed at only 15 percent. The first $75,000 is taxed at an average rate of only 18.33 percent. In fact, the first $100,000 is taxed at an average rate of only 22.25 percent.

Those are some pretty low rates—especially when your personal marginal rate is 25 percent, 28 percent, 33 percent, or 35 percent because you have income from other sources.

If you choose for this new business either the single-member LLC or the S corporation, the taxable income it generates passes through to you and gets taxed at your current personal rate. Further, with a single-member LLC, you pay Social Security and Medicare taxes even when you do not take any cash out of the business.

To make this crystal clear, let's look at some easy numbers. Let's assume the business we are talking about will generate $75,000 of annual taxable income. You do not need the cash. You simply leave the cash in the business. Depending on your choice of business entity, your federal tax bill stacks up as follows:[4]

Personal Rate	C Corp	S Corp	SMLLC
25%	$13,750	$18,750	$20,508
28%	13,750	21,000	22,727
33%	13,750	24,750	26,427
35%	13,750	26,250	27,907

Wow! By running this new business as a C corporation, you reap annual tax savings of up to $14,157. Using the 35 percent rate, compare your taxes at the C corporation level ($13,750) with the taxes at the single-member LLC level ($27,907).

In 2016, your individual tax on dividends ranges from a low of zero to a high of 23.8 percnet depending on your income and whether or not you pay the 3.8 percent Medicare tax..

Again, the annual savings accrue because you let the net income ride inside the C corporation. If it does not ride, your result is much different, because you then pay the 15 percent tax on dividends from your corporation. In this example, that increases the net tax on the C corporation profits to $22,937 when you add both the tax the corporation pays and the tax you personally pay on the dividends.

So failure to let the profits ride kills the C corporation strategy.

When you sell your stock in this corporation, you will pay capital gains taxes, say at 15 percent. If you do this early in the game, you also kill the C corporation strategy. But if you can wait for 10, 20, or 30 years, you win with the time value of money, which can be huge.

Summary

The C corporation is seldom the tax-smart choice, but in certain circumstances, it can produce savings. For example, a single taxpayer who needs a medical reimbursement plan might use the C corporation to good advantage. Additionally, if you have all four of the following attributes, you save money with the C corporation.

1. You expect the business to generate annual taxable income of $100,000 or less, and your personal marginal tax rate is 25 percent or higher (meaning you would benefit from the lower corporate tax rates).

2. You don't expect the business to generate tax losses (with a C corporation, you would get no annual flow-through benefit from the losses, and that's a bad thing).

3. You will let the cash profits ride and will not withdraw any significant cash or assets from the business (with a C corporation, such withdrawals generally result in double taxation, a no-no for your cash flow).

4. You will keep the business for a minimum of 10 years and then will effect a tax-deferred transaction or sell at your favorable capital gains rate.

It takes special circumstances to make the C corporation the liability-limiting entity of choice. If you do not have those special circumstances, then a single-member LLC or an S corporation is the best choice for you.

Notes

Notes

Endnotes–Section 37

1. IRC Sections 1(h)(11); 1411(a)(1).
2. IRC Section 1(h)(1)(C).
3. IRC Section 1411(a)(1).
4. This analysis assumes a 2.90 percent self-employment tax rate when the SMLLC option is chosen (over and above the indicated personal marginal tax rate). The federal income tax benefit from the deduction for 50 percent of the self-employment tax is factored into these results.

Section 38

Tactics for Paying the Owner of an S Corporation the Lowest Possible Salary

Seven years ago the IRS hired 5,000 new auditors to look at S corporation salaries and employment tax issues. Why this huge increase? The IRS spotted an alarming trend: Some taxpayers are forming S corporations and cheating on the salary part.

Make sure you get your salary right. If the S corporation gets the salary business wrong, it faces penalties that can exceed 100 percent of the taxes due.[1] In other words, the IRS computes the amount that should have been paid in taxes and then slaps that amount with individual penalties ranging from 2 percent to 100 percent each.

To achieve the S corporation benefits, small business owners try to keep the salaries low so they can realize:

- Social Security and FICA tax savings over what they would normally pay as a proprietorship
- Profits they can split with others in lower tax brackets

For example, say that the bottom line of your Schedule C shows a profit that will make you pay self-employment tax on $90,000 of income for a total self-employment tax of $13,770. If you could form an S corporation and justify a salary of $30,000, you would pay only $4,590 in Social Security taxes.

The $30,000 salary saves you $9,180 in after-tax cash. That's huge!

You can see that you have a powerful motive to keep the salary low. On the other hand, if that salary is too low, you could face the more-than-100 percent penalty problem and your tax reduction strategy could turn into a tax-and-penalty-paying-strategy.

The other reason to keep the salary low is to split profits with relatives in lower tax brackets. If you take a $40,000 salary and earn $100,000, you can split $60,000 with the relatives. But with earnings of $100,000 and a salary of $70,000, you have only $30,000 to split.

If you are in the 40 percent tax bracket and the college freshman you want to split income with is in the 10 percent bracket, your family unit keeps

Notes

30 cents on the dollar for each dollar in profits you split. If you split 1/3 with the freshman, your family saves only $3,000 in after-tax cash with a $70,000 salary, but with $40,000 produces a family savings of $6,000.

Not all S corporations are formed for the purpose of saving Social Security taxes and/or splitting income. However, most proprietorships and 1099 taxpayers that form the S corporation, for other than liability protection, are looking for tax savings.

So how low can you go with the salary? Can the salary be zero? No! If you own the S corporation and you provide services to the corporation, your salary may not be zero.[2] Tax law says that you are an employee of your corporation for Social Security tax purposes, unless exempted from this rule.[3] You are not going to be exempt. As an officer of the corporation, you are exempt only if:
- You do no work for the corporation, and
- You neither receive, nor are entitled to receive, directly or indirectly, any remuneration.[4]

In Spicer Accounting, Inc., the sole shareholder and only worker of this S corporation paid himself dividends, but no salary. The court ruled that all the so-called dividends were salary.[5]

In Revenue Ruling 74-44, two shareholders of an S corporation took zero salaries and claimed all profits as dividends not subject to employment taxes. Wrong, ruled the IRS as it classified the dividends as wages for FICA, FUTA, and federal income tax withholding.

The IRS is not the only government agency that gets upset by zero salary. The Social Security Administration has an interest in this issue. In Ludeking v Finch, the taxpayer incorporated his sole proprietorship as an S corporation. He took zero salary, but received corporate distributions. The court ruled that the Social Security Administration had the authority to change improper dividends to wages for services performed.[6]

The bottom line: Zero salary is out! The IRS wins its cases against zero salary. The Social Security Administration wins its cases against zero salary. The taxpayer pays taxes and penalties.

The IRS won in Radtke. Here, the S corporation paid zero salary. The court ruled that the S corporation had to treat its sole full-time worker as an employee and classify the dividends as wages.[7] In Weiss, the court noted that case law makes it clear that the S corporation may not choose to classify wages as dividends.[8]

The zero salary approach simply does not work. Then what is the proper division between dividends and salary? Is there a formula? Does the IRS provide guidance? No, this is an area where the practice of taxes becomes an art form, not a scientific endeavor.

Thus, rule one: Pay a salary!

The courts have decided many cases on the "no-salary" issue. However, the courts have faced far fewer cases when the IRS attacked as unreasonable the salary paid the S corporation officer.

In Rocco,[9] the IRS lost its bid to allocate S corporation dividends to Rocco's salary. Rocco created an S corporation with a total capital structure of $2,500, kept 4 percent for himself, and sold 96 percent to family members. Obviously, Rocco was looking at some income-splitting benefits.

After Rocco's salary payment, the company distributed big dollars to the shareholders. The IRS thought the small capital structure, small salary, and large dividend too much and took Rocco to court. The Court ruled that Rocco's salary was more than adequate. Rocco and his accountant proved to the court that an outside person could do his job for one-third of what he took in salary.

Planning tip: Rocco not only took a salary, but he also proved that the salary he took was reasonable. Think like this when you plan your salary.

The IRS also lost the Davis case.[10] Davis, an orthopedic surgeon, organized two S corporations: (1) the X-ray company and (2) the physical therapy company. He gave 90 percent of the stock in the two corporations to his three minor children. The IRS tried to allocate all income of the two corporations to Davis as salary. The court said no, absolutely not! Davis spent little time on the two corporations, although most of the patients came from Davis' referrals.

The IRS won a partial victory in the Roob case.[11] Roob offered no evidence to support his low salary. He operated his photo studio as a sole proprietorship. When he incorporated and chose S status, he split ownership equally among himself, his wife, and his eight children.

The IRS got the court to raise Roob's salary and cut the dividends to the shareholders. However, even with the loss to the IRS, Roob came out ahead.

As an S corporation, he made the same money he would have made as a sole proprietor. The court ruled that 55 percent of the income should be wages and 45 percent should be dividends. Thus, Roob had 45 percent of the income:

Notes

Notes

- Not subject to employment taxes
- Split in 10 parts for himself, his wife, and his eight children

Roob could have done better. He presented no evidence to refute the IRS allocation of income to his salary. He should have had evidence of a proper salary based on such factors as:[12]

- Time spent working
- Business size and complexity
- Responsibilities
- Nature of work
- Wages and salaries paid by similar firms

Had Roob taken a little time to create some tax evidence, he could have saved himself considerable time and grief. Also, think of the attorney fees and anxiety he suffered to solve this matter.

If you are looking to save money on Social Security taxes and/or split income with family members, you want to pay a low salary. Make sure you do your homework up front.

If you are the owner and sole employee of the S corporation, your best evidence is wages paid by comparable firms. Then you can justify the dividends based on business goodwill, know-how, location, physical plant, and equipment.

Endnotes–Section 38

1. IRC Sections 6651; 6656; 6672.
2. Revenue ruling. 73-361.
3. IRC Section 3121(d)(1).
4. IRS Regulation section 31.3121(d)-1(b).
5. Spicer Accounting, Inc., v U.S., 9th Circuit, Doc 90-7830, Docket No. 89-35071.
6. Ludeking v Finch, 421 F.2d 699 (8th Circuit 1970).
7. Joseph Radtke, S.C. v U.S., 712 F. Supp. 143, 145 (D.D. Wis. 1989), aff'd No. 89-2199, slip op. (Feb. 23, 1990) (per curiam).
8. Michael Weiss v U.S., United States District Court for SD, FLA, April 12, 1996, 77 AFTR 2d ¶96-762, Doc 96-13157; Docket No. 95-6237-Div-Arononitz.
9. Rocco v Commr., 57 T.C. 826 (1972).
10. Davis v Commr., 64 T.C. 1034 (1975).
11. Roob v Commr., 50 T.C. 891, 898 (1968).
12. Ibid.

Notes

Section 39

Corporation Must Earn the Income; Assignment of Income Fails

The Checks Must Come to the Corporation in the Corporate Name. No Exceptions.

In an effort to save self-employment taxes, some people form corporations and then "assign their incomes" to the corporations. This "assignment method" does not work!

The law says that "gross income" includes all income from whatever source derived, including compensation for services, fees, and commissions.[1] Fundamental to this principle is that the government taxes income to the person who earns it.[2] The person or entity who earns the income is the person or entity who controls the earning of the income.[3]

Truxal assigned his income to a family trust (a separate legal entity). The court ruled that the income belonged to Truxal as an individual because the customers did not deal with the family trust and probably did not know anything about the trust.[4]

Brooks assigned his insurance commissions to his corporation. The court ruled that the insurance commissions belonged to Brooks and should be taxed to Brooks.[5] The insurance contract was between Brooks and the insurance company. The insurance company made the checks in Brooks' name, not the name of the corporation.

Evatt assigned his real estate sales commissions to his corporation. The court ruled that the real estate commissions belonged to Evatt and should be taxed to Evatt.[6] The court noted that the real estate sales contracts were between Evatt the individual and the customers. The corporation was not a party to the contracts.

Notes

Many people form S corporations in an effort to save Social Security taxes. An S corporation does not pay tax. Instead, S corporation profits flow to the stockholders and get taxed to the stockholders as individuals.[7] To save Social Security taxes, the S corporation compensates the person in two ways:

- Salary—earned income subject to self-employment taxes
- Distributions of profits (think of them as dividends), which are not subject to Social Security

In the right circumstances, an S corporation is a wonderful form of business, but you must be careful when commissions are involved. The two cases that follow illustrate what happens when you do it right and what happens when you do it wrong. Jackson does it right by receiving commissions in the corporate name. Isom does it wrong by receiving commissions in his personal name. Jackson and Isom get two completely different results.

Example: Jackson forms Jackson, Inc., an S corporation. Before incorporating, Jackson had Schedule C income of $60,000 and he paid self-employment taxes of $9,180. After incorporation, his corporate/employer and individual/employee FICA and Medicare (the equal of self-employment tax) totals only $6,120 on his $40,000 salary. He pays zero employment taxes on his $20,000 dividend. Thus, with the S corporation strategy, Jackson saves more than $3,000 a year in after-tax cash.

Fly in the ointment: The S corporation strategy to save Social Security works when the law recognizes the S corporation as the legal entity that earns the money. Many companies will not make commission checks payable to a corporation. In such cases, some salespeople hope to get around the problem by simply assigning the income to their corporations. This "assignment" can fail.

Example: Bruce Isom[8] worked as an independent agent for American Family Insurance Co. For several years after Isom incorporated and chose S corporation status, American Family cut commission checks in favor of Isom's S corporation. Then, after a legal review in 1987, American Family stopped cutting checks in favor of Isom's S corporation.

The stoppage upset Isom. He did not want to abandon his S corporation. To keep things going as before, he simply took the checks made out in his name and endorsed them to his S corporation. That worked until the IRS audited Isom's S corporation and declared it a "sham." The court agreed with the IRS and allocated more than $100,000 of the S corporation's income to Isom so that he could personally pay self-employment taxes on this income.

Technical notes: The court noted that Isom's corporation failed the tests for corporate recognition because:
- Isom's corporation did not have the right to direct Isom's activities in some meaningful way, and
- Isom's S corporation did not have a contract to sell insurance with American Family Insurance.

Doing it right: For the corporation to stand up to scrutiny, you want the corporation recognized as the:[9]
- Entity authorized to make sales
- Employer of the agent (you) who makes the sales

Also, you want the checks to arrive in the corporate name.[10]

Summary: To get the benefits of incorporation, you need first to establish that the corporation is a bona fide legal entity. The corporation should:
- Execute contracts
- Receive commissions in its name
- Direct your activities (remember you are the employee—have your "corporate-self" talk to your "employee-self" in writing)

Endnotes–Section 39

[1] IRC Section 61(a).

[2] United States v Basye, 410 U.S. 441, 449 451 (1973); Lucas v Earl, 281 U.S. 111 (1930).

[3] Vnuk v Commr., 621 F.2d 1318, 1320 (8th Cir. 1980), affg. T.C. Memo. 1979 164.

[4] Truxal v Commr., T.C. Memo. 1982-616.

[5] Brooks v Commr., T.C. Memo. 1982-690.

[6] Evatt v Commr., 63 T.C.M. 3194 (1992).

[7] IRC Section 1363(b).

[8] Bruce M. Isom v Commr., T.C. Memo. 1995-383.

[9] American Savings Bank v Commr., 56 T.C. 828 (1971).

[10] Kubik v Comr., T.C. Memo 1974 62; Photocircuits Corp. v U.S., 204 Ct. Cl. 821 (1974).

Section 40

Loans to Your Corporation Could Be Hazardous to Your Financial Health

Once you incorporate your business, you no longer engage in that business. The business now belongs to the corporation.[1] The corporation engages in the business. You are simply the owner of the corporation.

You might work for your corporation. When you work for your corporation, you are an employee of the corporation.

Let's say you own 100 percent of the corporation. This corporation has operated quite well for a number of years but now is having a little financial difficulty. You need to give the corporation a cash infusion.

You make a loan of your personal funds to the corporation. It continues to underperform. You give it another loan, and another. Soon, you have no choice but to take the corporation into bankruptcy.

The trustee liquidates the corporation and gets pennies on the dollar. There's no cash for you; the lawyers get the pennies. You want to write off the bad loans on your taxes. You are out the cash. How is the write-off going to work? In a word, badly.

You made the loans to the corporation in your capacity as an employee of the corporation. At the time you made the loan, the tax law considered you in the business of being an employee.[2] Thus, your deductions for the bad loans are going to be bad-debt miscellaneous itemized deductions, subject to the 2 percent of adjusted gross income floor. The 2 percent of adjusted gross income subtraction from your miscellaneous deductions is not great, but this could be minor compared with the real problem.

The real problem is that for alternative minimum tax (AMT) purposes, you get zero deduction for the bad loans.

As we have stated many times before, the AMT is a truly unfair tax: It taxes the deductions lawmakers grant you on your regular tax return.

In this case, your bad loans are bad-debt deductions that tax law allows in the miscellaneous itemized deduction section of your Schedule A, Form

Notes

1040—the part subject to the 2 percent of adjusted gross income floor. But when you compute the AMT, you get no deduction whatsoever for any miscellaneous itemized deductions subject to the 2 percent of adjusted gross income floor.

Example. On your regular taxes, you claimed a $100,000 bad-debt deduction based on the money you lost when you made the loan to your corporation. For AMT purposes, you get a zero deduction for the $100,000. Further, the AMT does not allow you to carry over the lost $100,000 deduction. The AMT makes the $100,000 deduction disappear forever. Yikes!

Planning tip. If your business needs a loan, ask yourself and answer truthfully: Is the business going to make it? If not, don't make the loan. That's hard, no question. But face it; if the business isn't going to make it, the loan only delays the inevitable.

If the business is going to make it, then make the loan, put the terms in writing, and live by the repayment terms. Don't fool around with this. Remember, you get the short end of the stick when you are an employee of your corporation and the loan you make to your corporation goes sour.

This loan problem is one of the disadvantages of incorporation that you need to consider when choosing your operating entity.

Planning tip. If you think the business is going to fail but, against your better judgment, you still want to make the loan, consider an additional investment in the corporation, called an *additional contribution to capital*. If you do this and the business fails, you generate a capital loss. Although the limit on net capital losses (after offsets with gains) is $3,000 a year, that's certainly preferable to no deduction at all.

Endnotes–Section 40

[1] Graves v Commr., 99 AFTR 2d 2007-950, 2/8/2007.

[2] Ibid.

Section 41

What Your Corporation Can Reimburse to You and Its Other Employees and Why That's Very Important

Who owns the business car, you or your corporation? If it's you, you can often pocket considerably more after-tax cash when you know the reimbursement rules.

The IRS says that the corporation (an employer) may reimburse an employee for business expenses which include, among others,[1]
- trade or business expenses,
- interest expenses,
- taxes,
- losses,
- bad debts,
- depreciation,
- cost recovery,
- research and development,
- amortization of lease acquisition costs,
- Section 179 expensing,
- deductions for clean fuel vehicles,
- amortization of costs for removing barriers to handicapped workers,
- start-up expenditures, and
- goodwill.

The employee must incur these expenses in the performance of duties for the corporation or other employer.[2] Further, the employee must substantiate the expenses to the corporation in accordance with any specific conditions imposed by the Internal Revenue Code.[3]

For example, if the corporation or other employer reimburses travel, entertainment, automobile, computer, or airplane expenses, the employee must submit the documents that support these deductions in accordance with the rules for these deductions. Thus, for travel, the employee must submit receipts for expenses of $75 or more, and justify the business reason for the trip, etc. For automobile, the employee must prove the business use of the vehicle, like keeping a three-month log of use, and have receipts for expenses of $75 or more.

Notes

If the employee is reimbursed for the home-office deduction, the employer must demand proof that substantiates administrative use, regular use, and exclusive use. In other words, the employer acts like an auditor for the IRS making sure that the expenses meet the requirements of the law.

If the employee fails to submit adequate proof, the employer must include the expense reimbursements in the W-2 of the employee.[4] Yikes! No one wants that.

Avoid the W-2. Submit proper proof. With proper proof, the corporation or other employer gets the tax deduction and the employee who gets the reimbursement has no taxable income.[5]

This is the result you want. You do not want to claim the expenses personally as employee business expenses on your IRS Form 1040. If you do claim employee business expenses, two bad things attack your deductions,
- the 2 percent of adjusted gross income floor, and
- the alternative minimum tax.

The IRS regulation includes depreciation and cost recovery as reimbursable expenses.[6] A while back, Ralph M. Parsons Company reimbursed Milton Lewis $14,007 to cover 60 percent of the depreciation and maintenance expenses on the home that he used for business entertainment.[7] (The law authorizing the deduction for depreciation of a home used for home entertainment has been eliminated for some time now, but this case illustrates the depreciation reimbursement). IRS Private Letter Ruling 6406174570A states that a college can reimburse a professor for his home-office expenses, including depreciation.

Failure to Ask S Corp. for Reimbursements Costs Travel Deductions

Tibor Horwath and his wife owned 100 percent of their S corporation. Tibor also operated his consulting business as a sole proprietorship and periodically consulted with the S corporation.

The S corporation got a contract from Primex. The S corporation contracted with Tibor for some consulting on its Primex contract. Tibor incurred $16,812 of legitimate travel expenses while performing the contract, but he made a fatal error: he did not submit the travel to his S corporation for reimbursement. Instead, he deducted the travel on his Schedule C sole proprietorship return.

The court ruled that Tibor gets no deductions for this travel.[8] His contract said to submit the travel to his S corporation. Tibor's failure to submit the travel for reimbursement destroyed his proprietorship deduction. But this gets worse.

The S corporation also gets no deduction because it did not claim the expenses on its original tax return and now more than three years have passed, making it too late for the S corporation to amend its tax return.

Planning note: When you operate all or some of your business as a corporation, you must pay attention to the separate legal status of the corporation. You also have to honor the agreements you make with your corporation, even when you own 100 percent of the stock.

AMT Destroys Employee Business Expenses

Elmer Hopson suffered a shock to his tax return. He claimed $38,062 in employee business expenses as itemized deductions against his wage and salary income of $69,432. After other deductions, he calculated his regular income tax at $1,526.

But, as the IRS pointed out, Elmer made a tragic mistake. He failed to calculate the "alternative minimum tax" (AMT). In the AMT calculation, his $38,062 of employee business expenses disappear and turn to a zero deduction.

The AMT changed his taxes from $1,526 to $5,341. Shocked, Elmer amended his tax return and took the IRS to court, where he promptly lost and paid the AMT as required by the law.[9]

Planning note: Regular business expenses reduce your taxes, both regular taxes and AMT taxes. Employee business expenses do not reduce your AMT taxes. Avoid this problem. Have your corporation reimburse your expenses or have the corporation pay the expenses directly.

Notes

Endnotes–Section 41

[1] Reg. Section 1.62-2(d)(1) allows as reimbursements the expenses in Part VI, Subchapter B, Chapter 1 of the Internal Revenue Code.

[2] Reg. Section 1.62-2(d)(1).

[3] Reg. Section 1.62-2(e).

[4] Reg. Section 1.62-2(c)(5).

[5] Reg. Section 1.62-2(c)(4).

[6] Reg. Section 1.62-2(d)(1) allows as reimbursements the expenses in Part VI, Subchapter B, Chapter 1 of the Internal Revenue Code.

[7] Milton Lewis, T.C. Memo. 1974-59.

[8] Tibor Guenther Horwath v Commr., T.C. Memo 2004-213.

[9] Elmer J. Hopson v Commr., T.C. Summary Opinion 2004-25.

Section 42

Tax Tips to Save Your Social Security Benefits

Are you collecting or about to collect Social Security benefits before you reach full retirement age of 66?

Are you going to have business income while collecting Social Security?

If you said "yes" to both questions, you could pay taxes equal to 97.99 percent on your Social Security benefits. We suspect this would not make you happy.

Whoo, Explain that 97.99 Percent Tax

Jan Smith, age 62, is married to Fred Smith. They are in the 25 percent income tax bracket and file a joint tax return.

Ms. Smith is self-employed, earning $25,720 in net self-employment income for the year. The $25,720 is $10,000 more than the $15,720 maximum early retirement earnings allowed by Social Security. Watch how Mr. and Mrs. Smith part with 96.14 percent of this $10,000 in excess earnings:

1. Because Ms. Smith earns $10,000 more than the $15,720 lawmakers allow in earned income for early Social Security retirement benefits, she must return 50 cents on each excess dollar.[1] She has $10,000 in excess dollars so she can say goodbye to the $5,000 she has to return.[2]

2. Ms. Smith also pays $1,413 in self-employment taxes on the $10,000 excess earnings.[3]

3. The $10,000 in excess earnings triggers $2,323 in net income taxes on this $10,000 of self-employment income.[4]

4. Finally, the stealth income arrives. Because Mr. and Mrs. Smith earn more than $44,000, Ms. Smith must include 85 percent of her Social Security benefits in taxable income. The net amount left from the original $10,000 in excess earnings is $5,000. The tax on 85 percent of this $5,000 is $1,063.[5]

Notes

Total tax. $9,799! Wow, that seems awfully unfair. On this $10,000 of additional income, Ms. Smith keeps $201.

What Do You Think?

When you pay into Social Security, you probably think you are

- earning your Social Security benefit,
- entitled to your Social Security benefit, and
- going to receive your Social Security benefit.

That's what Ms. Smith thought.

She needs to do some tax planning.

Taxes to Consider

1. If you under full retirement age drawing Social Security benefits and you earn more than $15,720, your Social Security benefits are cut 50 cents on the dollar for each dollar of earnings in excess of $15,720.[6]

2. If you are drawing Social Security benefits and earn more than $41,880 in the months before the month in which you reach the month of your 2016 full retirement age of 66, your Social Security benefits are cut by $1 for every $3 of earnings in excess of $41,880.[7]

3. Regardless of retirement age, your Social Security benefits are subject to the income tax.

Income Tax on Social Security Benefits

To determine whether Social Security benefits are subject to income taxes, you first have to find your inclusion category, which tells you how much of your Social Security is subject to the income tax. There are three possible inclusion categories:

- Zero.
- 50 percent of your Social Security benefits over the threshold.
- 85 percent of your Social Security benefits over the threshold.

First Step

The first step in finding your inclusion category is to find your threshold amount by adding together all of the following:[8]

- Adjusted gross income from your Form 1040
- 50 percent of your Social Security benefits
- Tax exempt interest
- Student loan interest deduction
- Tuition and fees deduction[9]
- Domestic production activities deduction[10]
- Exclusion of interest from Series EE and I U.S. Savings Bonds issued after 1989[11]
- Exclusion of foreign earned income or housing[12]
- Exclusion of income for bona fide residents of American Samoa[13]
- Exclusion of income for bona fide residents of Puerto Rico[14]
- Exclusion for employed-provided adoption expenses[15]

Above

If your threshold total from the above exceeds[16]

- $44,000 for married taxpayers, or
- $34,000 for single taxpayers,

you include and pay tax on 85 percent of the Social Security benefits that exceed the threshold amount.

Below

If your inclusion total falls in the range from[17]

- $32,000 to $44,000 for married taxpayers, or
- $25,000 to $34,000 for single taxpayers,

you include and pay tax on 50 percent of the benefits to the extent such benefits fall in the range.

Notes

Use a C Corporation to Avoid the Taxes

If you do *not* operate a tax-defined personal service business, you could incorporate your business and operate as a C corporation to

- shelter income inside the corporation until you reach full retirement age;
- hoard up to $250,000 in corporate income with no plan for this money;[18]
- adopt a retirement plan to reduce and defer income until after full retirement age;[19]
- keep your earned income (salary) at a level that does not trigger taxes on your Social Security and/or does not trigger recapture of benefits;[20]
- defer income by using a fiscal year that ends in January;[21]
- grant you fringe benefits, like group term life insurance and a 100 percent medical reimbursement plan.

Caution for Personal Service Corporations

The strategies above work for corporations that are not classed as personal service corporations. In general, your corporation is a personal service corporation if you are the one who does the work and you do that work in one of the following fields:[22]

- Health
- Law
- Engineering (including surveying and mapping)
- Architecture
- Accounting
- Actuarial science
- Performing arts
- Consulting

Sales are not consulting.[23] If your remuneration depends on the consummation of a transaction—as in insurance, financial planning, or real estate—you are not a consultant. You are in sales, and you may form a corporation without it being classed in the unfavorable "personal service" group.

If you are in the personal service corporation group, consider the S corporation strategy.

Use an S Corporation to Avoid Taxes

The S corporation is a regular corporation, but the shareholders (for example, you) elect to be taxed as individuals.[24]

Think of the S corporation as a funnel with two spouts. In the top of the funnel, you put all your income and expenses—just as you would with a sole proprietorship. However, out of the two spouts you receive

1. salary (earned income), and
2. distributions (like dividends, which are not earned income).[25]

Further, on the distributions that your S corporation makes to you, you do not pay FICA or Medicare taxes. Thus, the S corporation can help you

- avoid the loss of Social Security benefits before you reach full retirement age, and
- avoid paying Social Security taxes into the system.

Example. Let's say that Ms. Smith from the example above forms an S corporation and now earns a $15,480 salary and receives a $10,000 distribution. Assuming that the salary is reasonable, Ms. Smith's corporate form

- saves $1,413 in FICA and Medicare taxes;
- saves $5,000 in Social Security benefits; and
- spends an extra $1,063 on the additional $5,000 in Social Security income of which 85 percent is subject to income taxes. (The extra $5,000 comes from the fact that Ms. Smith does not have excess earned income over the $15,480 and thus does not have to return half of the $10,000 to the government like she did earlier.)

Her net savings with the S corporation form of business are $5,350 or 54.6 percent of what she lost in the earlier example.

Final Thoughts and Pointer

Somehow, it just doesn't feel right when you have to plan to save your Social Security benefits. After all, you'd think that your Social Security is yours.

If you are planning on receiving your Social Security benefits before full retirement age, this is a good time to start thinking about your plan.

Notes

Regardless of your current form of business, you need to examine what you plan to do with Social Security. There are several parts to this equation as you learned in this section. We recommend spending a few moments with your tax advisor to get the best strategy in place.

This section gives both you and your advisor some of the basics to consider, but the planning part is a put-pencil-to-paper exercise to produce the best results.

If you are already receiving early retirement Social Security and taking a licking, it's not too late to get your plan in place and start saving your money.

Notes

Endnotes–Section 42

1. http://www.ssa.gov/news/press/factsheets/colafacts2016.html

2. Technically, this is not a tax—just a return of benefits. But since she loses the money to the government, we are calling this a tax. Also, she does not write a check to return the excess benefits, she simply suffers a reduction in future benefits. But the bottom line is that she is suffering a $5,000 loss in income.

3. 2016 self-employment tax rate of 15.3 percent times .9235 times $10,000 equals $1,413.

4. 25 percent times ($10,000 minus $707—the 50 percent of the employer's portion of the self-employment tax) equals $2,323.

5. 25 percent times $5,000 times 85 percent equals $1,063.

6. The 2016 full retirement age is age 66. Self-employment earnings and wages in excess of the $15,720 limit reduce Social Security retirement benefits.

7. http://www.ssa.gov/news/press/factsheets/colafacts2016.html

8. IRC Section 86.

9. IRS Form 8917.

10. IRS Form 8903.

11. IRC Section 135; IRS Form 8815.

12. IRC Section 911; IRS Forms 2555; 2555-EZ.

Notes

[13] IRC Section 931; IRS Form 4563.

[14] IRC Section 933.

[15] IRC Section 137; IRS Form 8839.

[16] IRC Sections 86(a)(2); 86(c)(2).

[17] IRC Sections 86(a)(1); 86(c)(1).

[18] IRC Section 531.

[19] IRC Section 404.

[20] Ms. Smith would take a salary of $15,480.

[21] You may pick any period; we picked January for maximum deferral; see IRC Section 441; Revenue Ruling 57-589.

[22] Reg. Section 1.448-1T(e)(4)(i).

[23] Reg. Section 1.448-1T(e)(4)(iv).

[24] IRC Section 1363(b).

[25] Technically, tax law calls the S corporation dividend a distribution. The distribution or dividend is not earned income—see Revenue Ruling 59-221. Also, see Social Security Handbook Section 1811(A)—"earnings" includes wages for employment covered by Social Security.

Section 43

Avoiding and Coping with the Dreaded IRS

Who audits the returns: Ignoring the computer inquiry or correspondence audit, your initial return examination will be conducted by a:
- Tax auditor, or
- Revenue agent.

Tax auditor: If you go down to the IRS to present your side of the story, you generally visit with a tax auditor. Don't expect a tax expert. The IRS requires a tax auditor to have a four-year college degree (in any field, for example, history). Tax auditors advance above the mid-salary range by completing six semester hours of accounting (such as the basic introduction courses: Principles of Accounting I and II). CPAs refer to the Principles courses as "bookkeeping" courses.

No interpretations: Tax auditors do not interpret IRS guidelines or engage in tax research. A "classifier" defines the auditor's scope for the audit and the auditor follows a set of questions regarding the items the classifier identified. Often, the auditor looks at your return for the first time when you walk through the door and take your seat for the audit.

The adding machine: Tax auditors like to take your receipts, add them up, compare them to your return, and disallow any shortage. Tax auditors are not trained to know that you do not need receipts for travel and entertainment under $75.00.

Go to the audit naked: If your return is audited by a tax auditor who knows little about tax law, you may want to go to the audit by yourself (after consultation with your tax advisor). After all, why send a technical tax person who speaks a language that the IRS auditor will not understand?

Revenue agents: Revenue agents must have four-year college degrees and a minimum of 24 semester hours of accounting education or the equivalent in experience. The revenue agent learns tax law from the IRS and handles your return the IRS way.

Don't go naked: You need your tax advisor to speak the agent's language and to ensure that you do not lose rightful deductions. Your tax advisor should attend the initial meeting when you deal with the revenue agent.

When to Get Help for the Audit

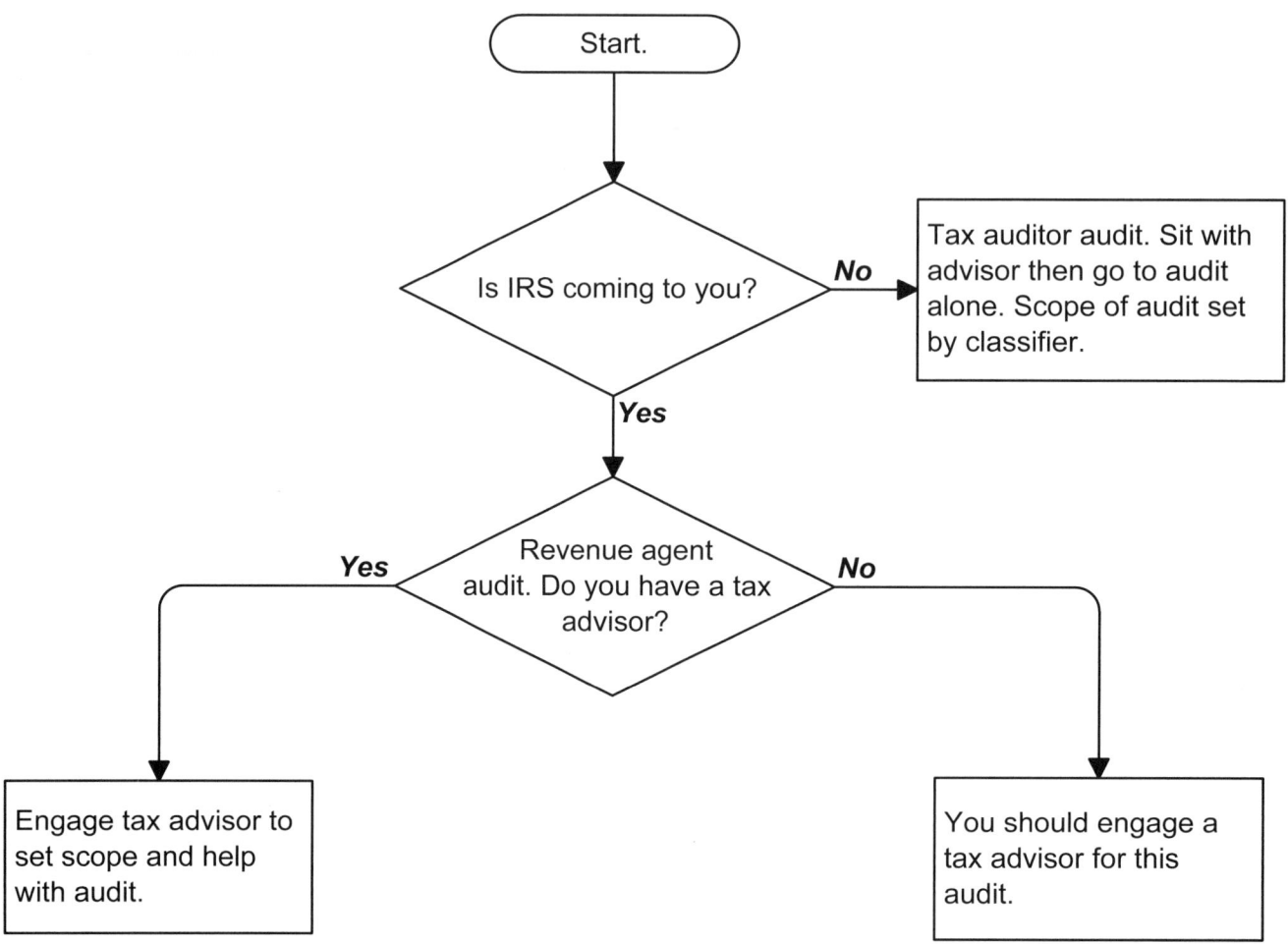

During that meeting, your advisor will agree, preferably in writing, to the rules and procedures for your audit, including:
- Business hours to be observed
- Where the agent will work
- Agent access to machines, such as copiers
- Agent access to personnel, like your bookkeeper

Most good tax advisors limit the agent's access to machines and people. Generally, your advisor gets the agent to explain what documents he or she needs and then acts to satisfy those needs.

Protect your documents: You should make two copies of all documents you give to the IRS (one for you and one for the IRS). That gives you a trail that you can follow later should that need develop.

Restrict access to machines: You should not give the IRS free access to the copy machine and you should not allow the IRS to bring its own copy machine.

Restrict access to people: You do not want the agent speaking in tax jargon to your bookkeeper. If the agent has questions for the bookkeeper or other employee, try to get the questions in writing. Then have your bookkeeper answer the questions in writing, after review by your tax advisors so that there are no mistakes understanding the tax jargon. If the written response is not appropriate, your tax advisor should be present for the question-and-answer session to make sure your employee answers the questions that the IRS asks.

Beware of informants: Recently, the IRS paid a record $5.3 million in informants' fees to recover $172 million in taxes. A good return on investment, don't you think? That year, the IRS paid an average reward of $6,340. More than 90 percent of the informants do not collect any money. For the $6,340 average, the IRS paid only 7 percent of the 11,393 informants. Most informants do not collect because they do not snitch for the money. They are mad at their employers, past employers, spouses, past spouses, or neighbors. The IRS does have about 800 controlled informants, of whom about 40 are accountants.[1]

As you would expect, the IRS makes informants pay tax on rewards as income for services rendered.[2] As you can tell from the average award, the IRS is not a big spender. It places limits on most awards and sets the following guidelines:[3]
- For responsible information that results in recovery of tax, the reward is 10 percent of the first $75,000 recovered, 5 percent of the next $25,000, and 1 percent of the balance (not to exceed a reward of $100,000).

Notes

- For information of value in recovering tax, the reward is 5 percent of the first $75,000 recovered, 2.5 percent of the next $25,000, and 1 percent of the balance (not to exceed a reward of $100,000).
- For information that caused an investigation but had no value in finding the tax due, the reward is 1 percent of the first $75,000 recovered and 0.5 percent of the balance (not to exceed a reward of $100,000).

You can negotiate snitch fees greater than the guidelines.[4]

Strategy for the Audit

Overview: Obviously, you should be ready for an IRS audit on the day you file your tax return. Your information should be complete, organized, and readily accessible. You should have notes and technical memoranda to support unusual or aggressive positions.

Tips for the audit: Once the audit is under way, you should abide by the following guidelines:

- Bring organized information that you can retrieve rapidly.
- Control the scope of the audit by bringing only those records requested.
- Do not volunteer information.
- Do not answer questions that the IRS did not ask.
- Stick to the subject and make sure you answer the examiner's questions.
- Do not claim that the income tax is unconstitutional.
- Do not claim that the only legal tender is gold, therefore you do not owe any paper dollars in taxes.
- Give the examiner only the information he or she needs to answer the question.
- Do not take charge of the audit! Let the examiner ask the questions and decide which issues to cover.
- Allow the examiner to decide which adjustments, if any, to propose. If he or she proposes adjustments, you should try to use additional documentation to eliminate the adjustments.
- Do not panic before, during, or at the adjustment stage.
- Deliver your records with a smile (because you know that the burden of proof is on you).
- Do not chitchat or engage in small talk.
- Ask for the auditor's supervisor if you know he or she is wrong on a technical point.
- Dress normally.
- Do not plead poverty or ignorance.
- Be early for all appointments.
- Never say: "I have always done it that way."
- Do not praise the agent.
- Be businesslike.

- Be prepared to answer economic questions regarding where you get the money to support your lifestyle.
- Do not give in to audit adjustments.

Planning tip: The *IRS Audit Manual* states: "Hasty agreement to adjustments and undue concern about immediate closing of the case may indicate a more thorough examination is needed." If you appear soft, the IRS will try to get more from you.

Review needed: Most important, you need to review all proposed adjustments. The IRS easily could be wrong. Look at technical books to make sure of the law. Ask your tax advisor about the proposed adjustments.

Reducing Your Chances of IRS Audit

TCMP audits: Currently the IRS is not conducting any Taxpayer Compliance Measurement Program (TCMP) audits. This could change anytime. Your return could be selected at random for the worst of all possible audits, the TCMP audit. The IRS uses this audit to develop statistics for its audit selection process. In the TCMP audit, the IRS examines every detail. It is time-consuming, costly, and an overall terrible experience for the taxpayer. Your odds of a TCMP audit are very small.

Reduce chances of audit selection: You can reduce your odds of regular audit selection by:
- Mailing your tax return by registered mail, return receipt requested.
- Mailing your return the day before the due date. Take no chance that the United States Post Office turned its postage meters ahead to the next day. They do that in Houston. At 8:00 p.m., the Houston Post Office turns its postage meter to the next day.[5]
- Writing the registered mail receipt number on the original return before you copy and mail it to the IRS.
- Adding supporting statements and photocopies of canceled checks, appraisals, and police reports to any claim of casualty or theft loss. (You should try to satisfy the IRS's audit requirements for a casualty or theft deduction before you file your return.)
- Sending your changes of address to the IRS so that IRS notices arrive in a timely manner.
- Filing your return on time (extension dates are okay, but filing late for a regular return or for an extended return is a major problem).
- Having a qualified tax advisor sign your return, such as a CPA or enrolled agent.
- Never using a dishonest tax return preparer (the IRS has a list).
- Reporting all income.
- Reporting some small miscellaneous income that displays your honesty.

Notes

Notes

- Not claiming unallowable deductions.
- Not claiming more than 14 withholding allowances.
- Answering audit questions in advance.

Work for the IRS: If you have an unusually high deduction or expense, you should add a supporting schedule that reveals the details. Next, you should answer audit questions in advance. You can look at the *IRS Audit Manual* to find the questions. The manual is a public document and your tax advisor probably has a copy. By answering the questions in advance, you reduce the chances of a face-to-face visit with the IRS.

After the Audit

Settle quickly: If you survive the audit with no adjustments or the government owes you money, settle quickly.

Disagree: If the IRS wants money from you, you should disagree with the auditor's findings and respond to the IRS's 30-day letter. It takes a while for the IRS to send you your letter. The 30 days refers to the time you have after you receive the letter demanding adjustment, not how long it takes the IRS to send it to you.

Protests: Depending on the size of the audit adjustment, you protest the audit findings to a supervisor or appeals officer. You must arrange or file your protest during the 30-day period after receipt of the so-called 30-day letter. When responding to any IRS notice by telephone, make sure you send a confirming letter to the IRS by registered mail, return receipt requested.

Notice of Deficiency: If you do not agree with the IRS while discussing the 30-day letter, the IRS will send you a Notice of Deficiency, also known as the 90-day letter. In this notice, the IRS tells you that at the end of 90 days it will assess the tax due. Thus, for you, the 90-day is an ultimatum. You may either pay the tax or take the IRS to court.

Legal fees: If the IRS took an unreasonable position that forced you to take the IRS to court to win your deductions, you may recover legal fees. The courts generally award up to $200 an hour for attorney fees plus expenses when you can prove that the IRS position was not substantially justified.[6] In special circumstances, and sometimes in more expensive areas, the courts award more than $200 an hour for fees. You may not recover legal fees if your net worth exceeds $2 million.

Your rights: You have rights as a taxpayer. Congress passed the Taxpayer Bill of Rights and those rights include, among others, the following:
- The IRS must explain your rights before starting the audit[7] (such as by giving you a copy of the IRS publication on your rights).
- You have the statutory right to representation during the audit.[8]
- The IRS must stop the audit and let you consult your representative when you make the request.[9]
- The audit must take place at a reasonable time and place.[10]
- You may record the audit interviews.[11]
- The IRS must forego tax and penalties that arise from inaccurate "written" advice it gave you.[12]
- The IRS may not use quotas to evaluate the performance of collection employees.[13]
- If the IRS is unjustified, you may collect attorney fees and litigation costs.[14]
- You may sue the IRS for its agents' reckless or intentional disregard of tax law.[15]

Some Final Thoughts

Unclaimed deductions: While working on your audit evidence, it is likely that you will find some unclaimed deductions. Do not report them to the IRS when you find them. Wait until the end of the audit. That way the IRS will not be interested in trying to find more problems in your return to offset your new findings.

Never ignore an IRS notice: Respond promptly to all notices and make sure you can prove that you responded by using registered mail.

Always file a tax return: The penalties for failure to file far outweigh the penalties for failure to pay. Thus, even if you are short of money, you are better off filing.

Offer in Compromise: If you failed to file in the past, meet with a tax advisor to discuss an "Offer in Compromise" that you can send to the IRS. Since this is a compromise, you obviously offer less than you owe and the IRS might accept it. You need to get the offer ready before you let the IRS know what you intend to do. Thus, find a good advisor who has experience with such offers.

Notes

Endnotes–Section 43

1. Lexis, 47 Tax Notes 965.
2. IRC Section 61(a)(1); Reg Section 1.61-2(a)(1); Rev. Rul. 76-374, 1976-2 CB 19.
3. IRS Pub. 77, Rewards for Information Provided by Individuals to the Internal Revenue Service.
4. IRC Section 7623.
5. 65 Tax Notes 1182.
6. IRC Section 7430(c)(1)(B)(iii); Rev Proc 2014-61.
7. IRC Section 7521(b)(1).
8. IRC Section 7521(b)(2).
9. Ibid.
10. IRC Section 7605(a).
11. IRC Section 7521(a)(1).
12. IRC Section 6404(f).
13. P.L. 100-647, 100th Cong., 2nd Sess, S 6231.
14. IRC Section 7430.
15. IRC Sections 7431-7434

Section 44

IRS Makes Deducting Start-Up Expenses Easier

Before explaining how the IRS just made your life easier, let's briefly review what defines a "start-up expense." Basically, a start-up expense is an expense that would not be deductible without this special tax break which allows you to deduct both your "thinking about getting into business expenses" and your "getting your business started expenses."

Start Up of a New Business

You probably had not thought about deducting your "thinking about getting into" business expenses. Most people don't. But in the start-up classification, the "thinking about it" expenses qualify.

If you started a business during the last three years, ask yourself these questions: Before beginning the business and while thinking about getting into this business, did you

- travel to meet with and learn from others who are in the business?
- go to lunch, dinner, movies, theater, or play golf with friends and business acquaintances to find out about the business and learn if you might be good at the business? (If you paid only for yourself at these entertainments, your Dutch-treat cost qualifies for deduction just as if you had picked up the tab.)
- take classes in or out of town to learn more about the business?
- spend money analyzing the market and how it looks for the future?
- buy books and magazines to find information about the market?
- use your car to make prospecting and other calls before getting your license or meeting the other qualifications necessary to enter the business?
- obtain training for the new business (excluding the training to qualify for entry into the new business)?
- make long-distance telephone calls to others to learn more about the business and how you might fit into the business?

These types of costs qualify as start-up expenses. The list clearly reveals that without this special write-off provision you would get nothing. This is one of those tax-law rules that makes you like lawmakers.

Notes

Start-up expenses also include expenditures you make for any of the following:[1]

- Surveying or analyzing potential markets, products, labor supply, transportation, and other aspects of the business
- Advertisements for the opening of your business
- Salaries and wages for employees you train and their instructors
- Travel and other necessary costs for securing prospective distributors, suppliers, or customers
- Salaries and fees for executives and consultants, or for similar professional services

How Things Got Easier

Now, in addition to thanking lawmakers for start-up deductions, you have the regulatory IRS to thank for making it easier to realize the cash benefits from your start-up deductions. Beginning with start-up expenses incurred after September 8, 2008, you no longer have to make that exacting election under Section 195 to qualify start-up expenses for deduction.[2]

Don't let that September 8 date throw a road block in your path. The "no election needed" requirement is also effective for your prior open tax years.[3] Therefore, if you failed to make the election in a prior year, you can use the new rules in effect after September 8 to amend that prior year if that prior year is an open tax year (generally, the year is open for three years from the day you mail the return to the IRS).

Under the new rules, you do not make an election to write off your start-up expenses. Instead, the regulations make that election for you automatically. You have to love this: the new regulations "deem" that you made the start-up election unless you expressly elect out of these tax-favored start-up write-offs.[4]

Planning tip: We can think of no logical reason not to write off your start-up expenses.

How the Write Off Works

The Small business Jobs Act increased the $5,000 to $10,000 and the $50,000 to $60,000 for tax years beginning in 2010 only (IRC Section 195(b)(3).

Under the new rules, the write-off method of deducting start-up expenses remains as is. In the taxable year you begin an active trade or business, you deduct the lesser of what you spent on start-up or $5,000 reduced (but not below zero) by the amount by which the start-up expenditures exceed $50,000.[5] You deduct the remainder using straight-line amortization over the 180-month period beginning with the month in which your active trade or business started.[6]

Example: You spend $21,740 on start-up. You write off $5,000 on the day the business starts and amortize the remaining $16,740 at $93 a month over 180 months.

If you sell or discontinue the business before the 180 months expires, you write off the unamortized start up at that time.

Now that you know about this new and easy-to-use write-off of start-up expenses, ask yourself these questions:
- Did you deduct your start-up expenses?
- Did you incorrectly claim start-up expenses as business expenses?

If you got either of these wrong, now is the time to get these corrected.

When Does the Business Start?

You begin deducting start-up expenses in the month your business begins. In determining what month your business begins, a good rule of thumb is the month you start making your first sales calls, see your first patients, or have customers come into your place of business.[7]

Example: Sam Jones spent $150,000 over three years to develop a service-assessment system. He deducted the $150,000 on Schedule C. In case the expenses were not deductible, he added a note to his tax return saying that the expenses may be start-up expenses. Jones made zero sales and was constantly changing his product. In technical advice, the IRS ruled that Jones may neither deduct the $150,000 nor treat it as a start-up expense, because he never actually started the business.[8]

Planning note: Had Jones created one product or service then worked at selling that one product or service, he would have had a business and his $150,000 tax write-off, even if he never made any sales.

If you do not qualify to be in business or the law prohibits you from starting the business, you are not in business.[9] A suspended broker did not incur tax-deductible costs when seeking reinstatement, because he was not in business.[10]

Robert L. Duecaster, a high school teacher, attempted to deduct his law school tuition and other costs as start-up costs for his law practice. Wrong! The court ruled that Duecaster gets no deduction for the educational expenses because the education was necessary to qualify him to practice law, not to start a business.[11] The law school expenses were personal.

Ignoring the fact that you cannot deduct your costs of getting the credentials necessary to get into your business, think of how this start-up law

Notes

grants you benefits for thinking about and investigating the beginning of your business. Lawmakers have made it clear that they want you to get into business and help grow this economy.

What Happens to the Costs of an Unsuccessful Search?

When a corporation abandons an unsuccessful search for a new business, it may deduct the costs of investigating the venture as a loss.[12]

Planning tip: If this loss puts the corporation out of business, your stock in the corporation becomes worthless, and you may claim the worthless stock as a capital loss. In general, stock losses produce capital losses. However, with a Section 1244 election on small business stock, your loss on this stock is a more favorable ordinary loss.

If you, as an individual, abandon your search, you do not receive such favorable treatment.[13] The IRS ruled that individuals may deduct losses for a new business search only when they do more than investigate. You must enter a transaction for profit and later abandon the transaction.[14] The IRS has ruled that you enter a transaction for profit when you go beyond a general investigatory search and focus on the acquisition of a specific business investment.

Thus, you may deduct costs incurred in an unsuccessful search when you identify and focus on a specific business.[15] Documents that help you prove identification include agreements, profit-and-loss projections, and advice from professionals about a specific business.

Planning tip: You may not deduct losses incurred in the general investigatory search.[16] The IRS declares that such a loss is personal.

Expansion of Existing Business

You may deduct as current expenses the costs of expanding your existing business.[17] Obviously, the key is to have an existing trade or business that you can expand.[18] The IRS and the courts have ruled that the following costs are deductible as business-expansion expenses:
- Developing a new sales territory[19]
- Promotional activities to increase sales[20]
- Start-up of new equipment for existing business[21]
- Expenses of a residential developer investigating development of industrial sites[22]
- Addition of new branches by a bank[23]

If you start a new line of business, you treat the expenses of start-up under the start-up rules.[24] Defining a new line of business is a question of fact that is not always easily resolved.

Example: Fragrance, Inc., manufactures and imports fragrances and cosmetics. At first it sold its goods only at the wholesale level. Later, to broaden its base, the company opened a retail boutique. The store was a great success. The company then opened 11 more retail stores.

IRS Ruling: In technical advice, the IRS ruled that[25]
- the company's first retail boutique was a new business; and
- the 11 additional boutiques were simply an expansion of an existing business.

Thus, the company would treat the costs of opening the first boutique as start-up expenses; however, the costs of getting the other 11 boutiques up and running are those most tax-favored ordinary business expenses, deductible as incurred.

Three Cautions for Start-Up Expenses

Caution 1. Purchasing an Existing Business

When you start or enter a business from scratch, you can easily identify start-up expenses as those incurred before you make your first sales calls or list your property for rent. However, when you take over an existing business, your tax life is more complicated. For an existing business, start-up costs include only the costs that help you seek a business, review businesses, and decide which one to purchase. Once you have identified your target, you incur capital acquisition costs that do not qualify for start-up treatment.[26]

Example: You hire an accounting firm and a law firm to assist you in the potential purchase of Jimmy Company. The firms research the industry and analyze the financial projections of Jimmy Company. On the basis of this information, you have the law firm prepare and submit a letter of your intent to buy Jimmy Company. The letter states that a binding commitment will result only after a purchase agreement is signed. The law firm and accounting firm continue to provide services, including a review of Jimmy Company's books and records and the preparation of a purchase agreement. After the review, you sign the agreement to buy Jimmy Company.

You have start-up costs only to investigate the business before submitting the letter of intent. Once you submit the letter of intent, your legal, ac-

Notes

counting, and other expenses to purchase this existing business are capital costs.[27]

Caution 2. Failure to Identify and Buy the Business

The expenses are personal if you (1) did not identify or (2) did not buy a specific business. You get no deductions because[28]
- no business exists to produce start-up deductions, and
- no loss exists because you did not identify a specific acquisition.

Caution 3. Investments, Corporations

You must spend money to investigate or create an "active" trade or business. Money you spend to look into investments does not qualify for tax-favored start-up treatment.[29]

In the case of rentals as active businesses, the Senate has said that, in general, your operation of an apartment complex, office building, or shopping center qualifies as an active business.[30] The Senate further stated that rentals in which you furnish significant services incident to the rentals constitute an active business.[31]

The word "active" means that you, your corporation, or your partnership participates in the management of the trade or business.[32] The special treatment of start-up expenses goes to the taxpayer who incurs the start-up costs and enters the trade or business.[33]

A sole proprietor claims start-up costs on his Schedule C for a new business.[34]

A C corporation or an S Corporation claims its start-up expenses on its corporate return.[35]

In general, if you're starting a business using a corporation, you need to differentiate clearly among investment, start-up, and organization expenses. Start-up and organization costs both qualify for the $5,000 and 180-month amortization, but investment expenses are capital expenditures.

Also, keep in mind that the corporation is a legal entity separate from you. You may not deduct expenses paid on behalf of another, so make sure the corporation pays the corporate expenses. If you pay any of the corporate expenses, make sure that the corporation reimburses you for the expenses.

Notes

Endnotes–Section 44

1. *IRS Publication 535, Business Expenses (2011)*, p. 26.
2. TD 9411.
3. Ibid; Reg. Section 1.195-1T.
4. Reg. Section 1.195-1T(b).
5. Reg. Section 1.195-1T(a).
6. Ibid.
7. Marketing efforts are important for deciding when the business starts. In general, if you are consistently making sales calls, you are in business. See Richmond Television Corp. v. U.S., 345 F2d 901 (4th Cir 1965); Technical Advice Memorandum 9027002.
8. Private Letter Ruling 9310001.
9. Owen v. Commr., 23 T.C. 377 (1954).
10. Munroe v. U.S. 65-2 USTC ¶ 9495, 16 AFTR2d 5170.
11. Robert L. Duecaster v. Commr., T.C. Memo. 1990-518.
12. Harding v Commr., T.C. Memo 1970-179; Revenue Ruling 73-580.
13. IRC Section 165.
14. Revenue Ruling 57-418.

Notes

15. Revenue Ruling 77-254.
16. Ibid.
17. IRC Section 162(a); Briarcliff Candy Corp. v Commr., 475 F2d 775 (2nd Cir 1973).
18. Revenue Ruling 56-181; Briarcliff Candy Corp. v Commr., 475 F2d 775 (2d Cir 1973).
19. Briarcliff Candy Corp. v Commr., 475 F2d 775 (2d Cir 1973).
20. Revenue Ruling 56-181.
21. Cleveland Electric Illuminating Co. v U.S., 7 Cl Ct 220 (1985), 85-1 USTC ¶ 9128, 55 AFTR2d 85-652.
22. J. W. York v Commr., 261 F2d 421 (4th Cir 1958).
23. NCNB Corp. v U.S. 684 F2d 285 (4th Cir 1982), 50 AFTR2d 82-5281.
24. Godfrey v Commr., 335 F2d 82 (6th Cir 1964), 14 AFTR2d 5338, Cert Denied 379 US 966.
25. Private Letter Ruling 9331001.
26. Revenue Ruling 99-23.
27. Ibid.
28. Senate Finance Committee Report on P.L. 96-605.
29. Ibid.
30. Ibid.
31. Ibid.
32. Ibid.
33. Ibid.
34. Ibid.
35. Ibid.

Section 45

Tax Planning in the Event Your Business Loses Money

Overview: Should you incur a tax loss in any tax year, you want that activity classed as a business activity so that you can deduct your losses. Tax law gives no loss deductions for activities not carried on to make a profit.[1] Activities you do as a hobby, or mainly for sport or recreation, come under this limit.[2]

Application of the hobby rules: The limit on not-for-profit losses applies to individuals, partnerships, estates, trusts, and S corporations.[3] It does not apply to corporations other than S corporations.[4]

Planning tip 1: Incorporate to avoid the hobby-loss rules.

Planning tip 2: Invest money in the corporation up front and treat the stock as Section 1244 stock to avoid problems. Then, if the business fails, you can deduct your initial investment on your personal return not as a capital loss limited to $3,000 a year, but as a fully deductible ordinary loss.

Planning note: The 1244 election that produces ordinary losses applies only to the original investment. Your additional investments produce capital losses subject to the $3,000 annual limit.

Best bet: Schedule C losses are fully deductible business losses. You can have a Schedule C loss deduction if you can prove that your activity is a business and not a hobby. You prove business activity by meeting some of the tests that follow (the more you meet the better your proof).

Expectation of profit: Although the IRS does not require a "reasonable expectation of profit," your facts and circumstances must show that you entered the activity, or continued the activity, with the objective of making a profit.[5] The IRS grants a profit motive if you prove that you have a small chance of making a large profit.[6]

Intent: Whether your business meets the test to be a business is a question of fact that depends on an analysis of your intent as determined from all facts and circumstances.[7]

Desire income: To be a business, you must be involved in your activity with continuity and regularity and your primary purpose for the activity must be for income or profit. A sporadic activity, a hobby, or an amusement diversion does not qualify as a business.[8]

Notes

Presumption of profit: The IRS presumes you carry on your activity for profit if it produces a profit in at least three of the last five tax years, including the current year.[9] You can rely on this presumption every time, unless the IRS shows it is not valid.[10]

Proving profit intent when you have losses: If you fail the three-out-of-five test, you may still deduct losses if you can prove that your activity operated as a business. The IRS lists nine factors that may be important in establishing a profit motive.

1. Businesslike manner: The fact that you carry on your activity in a businesslike manner and maintain complete and accurate books and records may show that the activity is engaged in for profit.[11] You look more businesslike when you:
- Have a separate business checking account
- Have a separate business credit card
- Keep monthly financial statements
- Prepare an annual budget for the business

2. Expertise: You help your profit motive when you study accepted business practices for your activity and consult with those who are expert therein.[12] You especially help your cause when you carry on your activity as directed by the experts. Failure to follow expert advice suggests lack of profit intent, unless you can show that your new or superior techniques may produce profits.[13]

3. Time and effort: The fact that the taxpayer devotes much of his time and effort to carrying on an activity, particularly if the activity does not have substantial personal or recreational aspects, may show an intention to derive a profit.[14] If you depend on income from your activity for your livelihood, you show strong intent to make a profit.[15]

Planning note: Almost anything you do for the sole purpose of putting food on the table makes a for-profit endeavor.

4. Asset appreciation: The IRS accepts profit from appreciation as part of your profit motive.[16] In other words, if you expect to lose money on rents, but make money on the increase in value of the property, you have a profit motive.

5. Prior success: The fact that the taxpayer has engaged in similar activities in the past and converted them from unprofitable to profitable enterprises may show that he is engaged in the present activity for profit, even though the activity is presently unprofitable.[17]

6. Income and loss history: A series of losses during start-up does not mean your activity is not engaged in for profit.[18] However, when losses continue beyond the period ordinarily required to make the activity profitable, that excess period may suggest that your activity is not being engaged in for profit.[19]

Planning note: A series of years when your activity produces net income would, of course, be strong evidence that the activity is engaged in for profit.[20]

7. Occasional profits: An occasional small profit compared to large losses does not show that you engaged in the activity to make a profit.[21] However, substantial profit, though only occasional, suggests that an activity is engaged in for profit.[22] Moreover, an opportunity to earn a substantial ultimate profit in a highly speculative venture indicates that the activity is engaged in for profit even though you generate only losses.[23]

8. Your other income: If you attempt to make a living from your activity, you usually establish a profit motive and can deduct your losses. Substantial income from sources other than your activity may suggest that you engaged in a not-for-profit activity, especially if that activity involves substantial personal or recreational elements, like golf.[24]

9. Personal pleasure or recreation: Your personal motives for the activity may suggest that the activity is not engaged in for profit, especially when it involves recreational or personal elements.[25] On the other hand, an activity that lacks any appeal other than profit suggests a profit motive.[26] However, your intent to derive profit *does not* have to be your exclusive or sole intent.[27] You can have a for-profit motive combined with purposes or motivations other than solely to make a profit.[28] Also, the fact that you derive personal pleasure from the activity does not make the activity not for profit if you engaged in it for profit as evidenced by other factors, whether or not listed above.[29]

Planning note: If your activity involves recreation, you must pay attention to the profit motive or the IRS could take your deductions under the personal-pleasure motive.

Hobby-loss limits: If tax law classes your activity as a hobby:
- The law limits your deductions to no more than your income from the hobby[30]
- The law reduces your deductions by 2 percent of adjusted gross income—because you report your hobby on Schedule A[31]

Moreover, you may not carry over any unused losses from the current year to any future year.[32] You want to avoid the hobby results because the results are truly ugly.

Planning tip: Make your activity a business, have fun, and enjoy your profits. That way, should you experience a few loss years, you secure your loss deductions.

Filing tip: Do not agree to make a profit in three of the first five years by filing IRS Form 5213. Instead, make your activity a business, keep good records, and attempt to make a profit. Unlike a hobby, if you fail to make a profit in your business, you may deduct your losses.

Notes

Working example: Horses are not a hobby for a computer programmer. Michael Shane worked full time as a computer programmer. In addition, he raised, bred, and raced horses. His horse activities lost money and the IRS classed the activity as a hobby. Shane won his loss deductions in court because he:[33]

- Conducted his horse activity in a businesslike manner
- Saved money by operating the horse activity from his personal checking account (generally, you should have a separate business account to make your activity look like a business)
- Redirected operations in attempts to stop losing and start making money
- Developed expertise in horses and racing
- Spent substantial time and effort on his horses and racing
- Expected his horses to appreciate
- Allowed no one, not even himself, to ride his horses other than qualified jockeys

Lesson: Shane had a business because he conducted his activity as business, even though it gave him great personal pleasure. Get maximum benefit and personal pleasure—conduct your activity as a business!

Endnotes–Section 45

1. Reg. Section 1.183-2(a).
2. Ibid.
3. Reg. Section 1.183-1(a).
4. Ibid.
5. Reg. Section 1.183-2(a).
6. Ibid.
7. Hibbins v Commr., 312 U.S. 212 (1941).
8. Commr. v Groetzinger, 480 U.S. 23 (1987).
9. IRC Section 183(d).
10. *IRS Pub. 535, Business Expenses (2011)*, p 5.
11. Reg. Section 1.183-2(b)(1).
12. Reg. Section 1.183-2(b)(2).
13. Ibid.
14. Reg. Section 1.183-2(b)(3).
15. Reg. Section 1.183-2(b)(8).
16. Reg. Section 1.183-2(b)(4).
17. Reg. Section 1.183-2(b)(5).
18. Reg. Section 1.183-2(b)(6).
19. Ibid.
20. Ibid.
21. Reg. Section 1.183-2(b)(7).
22. Ibid.
23. Ibid.
24. Reg. Section 1.183-2(b)(8).
25. Reg. Section 1.183-2(b)(9).
26. Ibid.
27. Ibid.
28. Ibid.
29. Ibid.
30. IRC Section 183(b).
31. IRS Pub. 535, Business Expenses (2011), p 5.
32. IRC Section 183(b)(2).
33. Michael T. Shane v Commr., T.C. Memo. 1995-50

Section 46

Answers to Questions

179 Deduction for S Corporation Produces Less Cash Benefit

Every year, I buy about $50,000 of equipment for my business. I always claim the Section 179 deduction for the entire $50,000. I incorporated my business last year and claimed the Section 179 deduction on the S corporation return. This seemed to produce less of a tax benefit than when I claimed the deduction on my personal return. Where is the best place for the Section 179 deduction?   (T.B.M., Watsonville, CA)

When you had the business personally, you claimed the income and expenses on Schedule C of your IRS Form 1040. Say you had income of $100,000 last year and you claimed a $50,000 Section 179 deduction. The deduction would produce a tax benefit of $19,182.

With your S corporation, the Section 179 deduction comes to your personal return as a K-1 line item, which offsets your income. With $100,000 of S corporation income, your Section 179 deduction would produce a tax benefit of only $13,259.

Why the $5,923 cash difference? For an individual businessperson reporting on Schedule C of your Form 1040, the Section 179 deduction reduces both your income and self-employment taxes. The K-1 reduces only your income tax.

Planning tip: Before incorporating, consider all the benefits and drawbacks. Your best bet is a side-by-side analysis of dollar savings and losses by incorporating. This is a great exercise for your tax advisor and a worthwhile expenditure of tax advisory fees by you.

W-2 for Section 105 Plan

Do I have to report the Section 105 medical reimbursements on a Form W-2?   (L.F.P., Carmel, IN)

No. IRS Publication 15, *(Circular E) Employer's Tax Guide*, states that reimbursements under an employer's self-insurance plan are not wages.

Further, the W-2 specifically excludes a block for reporting this nontaxable fringe benefit.

Both CPA and IRS Wrong

Thank goodness I have taken your course. Last week, I took my CPA along as I marched down to the IRS office for an audit. During the audit, the IRS rejected my home-office deduction because I have a shared office at the Coldwell Banker real estate office where I am an agent. My use of the Coldwell Banker office consists of floor duty once every other week and attendance at sales meetings twice a month. All my other work is done at my home office, including all my administrative and management duties. I use my home office exclusively for business on a regular basis.

As you can see, I know the rules for the home office. Well, here is what happened. First, my CPA agreed with the IRS that I should not get a home-office deduction because Coldwell Banker gives me an office. Second, they both agreed that *Soliman* (the case where the anesthesiologist worked at three hospitals and lost his home office) controlled my deduction. I think both my CPA and the IRS are wrong. Can you help me out here?   (F.W., Pahoa, HI)

Your CPA is a disappointment. He or she has not been keeping up with the rules. Because they found *Soliman* truly unfair, lawmakers changed the rules in 1997. However, because of a lack of money, lawmakers made the new rules effective on January 1, 1999. The rules that became effective in 1999, six years ago, explicitly authorize more than one office.[1]

To see this authorization and gather some ammunition for your audit, go to the IRS website at www.irs.gov and retrieve IRS Publication 587, *Business Use of Your Home*, in PDF format. Go to page 3 and look in the lower righthand column under Principal Office and you will find these words: *You can have more than one business location, including your home, for a single trade or business.*

Thus, right from the IRS's own publication, you have your position in writing. You may want to offer both your CPA and the IRS auditor the opportunity to eat their words on the more-than-one-office rule. But hold on—we have more for you.

Stay right where you are in this IRS publication and move down this column about an inch or so, and you will find these words: *Your home office will qualify as your principal place of business if you meet the following requirements.*

You use it exclusively and regularly for administrative or management activities of your trade or business.

You have no other fixed location where you conduct substantial administrative or management activities of your trade or business.

These words were enacted to overturn the harsh and unfair results of the *Soliman* case. On page 5 of this publication, you will find Paul, an anesthesiologist, who has exactly the same attributes Soliman had when he lost his case in the Supreme Court in 1993. But now, because lawmakers found *Soliman* unfair, Paul wins his deductions.

In summary, you win your home-office deduction. Both your CPA and the IRS are dead wrong and definitely behind the times with their outdated information. Obsolete knowledge is not uncommon, even among professionals; that's why it's important to protect yourself with your own solid base of tax knowledge.

Deducting Golf

How do I deduct the golf when I have a business discussion on the golf course with a prospect? (Z.H. Venice, FL)

If you want to deduct the golf, you need to move the business discussion to the clubhouse. Discussing business only on the golf course puts your golf deductions in jeopardy because you are in direct conflict with IRS regulation 1.274-1(c)(7), which says that it presumes the distractions on the golf course are too great to qualify your discussion during the golf game as an entertainment deduction.

You'll like the solution. It's easy. Have a business discussion with the prospect over lunch or snacks in the clubhouse before, or after the golf. Document that discussion in your diary. You want this discussion to have the possibility of giving you a specific business benefit (like turning the prospect into a customer). In your diary documentation, be specific about the business-benefit intent.

By doing this in the clubhouse, you put yourself on the right side of two different IRS regulations, either of which is going to grant you a "directly related" entertainment deduction for the meal or snack consumed during the discussion. Now that you have this directly related entertainment deduction, you can precede or follow it with golf that qualifies for deduction as associated entertainment.[2] In other words, the golf is deductible because it is connected with the discussion in the clubhouse.

Notes

105 Medical Plan

My wife is going to hire me to work in her proprietorship. My medical plan is through Kaiser. To get the best pricing, I am buying one plan to cover my wife and child and a separate plan to cover myself. Kaiser will bill me for the premiums. Once a month, I am going to turn in all the family medical bills to my employer-wife, who is going to reimburse me for the medical. Is this an acceptable setup to make my employer-wife's Section 105 medical plan deductible on her tax return? (M.S., Santa Rosa, CA)

Yes, more than acceptable—this looks about perfect.

Your wife (the employer-spouse) reimburses you (the employee) for all medical. She will have proof that she is reimbursing medical based on the invoices, copies of paid checks, and so on. That's excellent.

All insurance is in your name—you, the employee. She is simply a member of the family for purposes of the insurance, which is in your name. Again, excellent!

Selling the Corporate-Deducted Home

When I sell the home for which I received corporate reimbursement for home office use, do I owe the business any money? Do the rules work just as if I had deducted the home personally? (M.W., Enfield, CT)

You owe the corporation nothing. Your position at the time of sale is identical to the position you would be in had you claimed the deduction for a home office personally.

Wages and 105 Plan

My CPA told me that I have to pay my wife a wage if I want to cover her with the Section 105 plan. Is this true? (G.S., Burnsville, MN)

No. In fact, this confuses many people. In Section 16 of this course, we discusssed the *Speltz* case,[3] in which Maureen Speltz won her Section 105 medical plan deduction.

Two points from your question are answered in *Speltz*:
- Maureen Speltz paid her husband Peter a zero cash wage.
- The court ruled that the fringe benefit of the 105 plan was reasonable compensation for the services provided by Peter Speltz.

To see if your wife's compensation is reasonable, divide the cost of your 105 fringe benefit by the number of hours your wife will work. For example, say your wife is going to work 350 hours during the year and the cost of your 105 medical plan is $8,500. That produces an hourly rate of remuneration of $24.29. If that's too high, find more work for your wife. You want this benefit to represent a reasonable rate of pay.

Keep in mind that you are paying a zero cash wage to your wife. This is great. You and your family get the medical benefit and you avoid having a payroll, payroll taxes, and all that related payroll mess.

IRS Inspects Home Office

Does the IRS ever make a physical inspection of the home office as part of an audit? (C.O.T., Traverse City, MI)

Internal Revenue Manual (the IRS audit guide) Section 4.10.3.3.5.1, *Inspection of the Business in the Home*, states:

When determining the validity of office in the home deductions, the office or business should be toured as any other business site. In order for any portion of a personal residence to qualify, it must be used <u>exclusively</u> for business purposes. This can only be determined by inspecting the business portion of the residence.

So the answer to your question is yes, the IRS tells its examiners to look at home offices. Ask yourself how your office would look in a viewing by the IRS. Does it look like an office exclusively used for business? It should.

If you no longer own the home, how would you prove exclusive use? Photographs of your home office are always valuable. Take them annually and note the date they were taken.

Home Office for Corporation

What does the IRS audit manual say about the home office for an individual who operates her business as a corporation? (S.T.A., Tallahassee, FL)

You will be interested in two boilerplate explanations from the Internal Revenue Manual that examiners use to explain why the IRS is denying the home-office deductions:[4]

1. *We (the IRS) have disallowed your deductions for office in the home expense because you have not established that it was for the convenience of your employer. Voluntary, vocational, or incidental use of part of your home in connection with your employment does not entitle you to a business deduction.*

Notes

2. *If you rent all or part of your residence to your employer and use the rented portion when performing services for the employer, you cannot deduct home-office expenses attributable to the rental.*

If you want to avoid the disallowances above and achieve a full deduction for the home office, follow these directions:
- Make your corporation write you a letter stating that you must find office space and that space may be in your home.
- Do not rent the office in your home to your corporation.
- Complete IRS Form 8829 showing your home-office expenses for the year. Do not file this form with your tax return. Instead, give the form to your corporation as the basis for corporate reimbursement to you for the home-office expenses.
- Do not report reimbursed employee expenses as taxable income.

Your corporation gets the deduction for its reimbursement of your employee expenses. But with this deduction comes the need for proof. Make sure you submit proof that backs up the deduction to your corporation; for example,
- receipts for expenses,
- photos that show the office set up for exclusive business use, and
- a log book, for at least a sample period, that shows use of the office for more than 10 hours a week.

Business Airplane

I purchased a Cessna 182-92895 for $80,000 on December 30 and used it for business that day. I am a licensed real estate professional, paying dues to a variety of real estate boards and associations in North Carolina and Florida. I plan to use the plane to take photos of properties for sale and to show prospects properties from the air. My accountant does not like my airplane. What do you think? (H.L. Sanford, NC)

We like your airplane. Your accountant should like your airplane too. It allows you to do what you like best: play while you work and get deductions for the work.

The airplane is Section 179 property eligible for expensing. Thus, you have several choices: Write it all off or write some of it off and depreciate the remainder at rates of 20 percent in year one, 32 percent in year two, and so on. (You write off the business percentage only.)

You need to keep a flight log for the next six years on this plane to prove your business use.[5] You could have 100 percent this year and 60 percent business use next year without worrying about recapture of any Section 179 deductions. Thus, if you wrote the whole thing off this year and then had 60 percent business use next year, no problem. But if you had only 45 percent business use next year, you would have to recapture the original write-off and depreciate the airplane using the straight-line method.

It seems that you have plenty of opportunities for business use, such as
- searching properties from the air;
- taking photos of properties and neighborhoods;
- taking prospects up to view properties from the air;
- showing, taking photos, and viewing damage after floods, tornados, and hurricanes; and
- traveling to educational courses anywhere in the tax-defined North American area.

As for the *Tax Strategies for the Self-Employed* course, we are delighted that you are realizing the benefits and getting a lot from our program. That was our intent. Thanks for the feedback.

C Corporation Golf Problem

Because I don't keep the best records, I decided that I would operate as a C corporation. I am in discussions with the IRS regarding my documentation of entertainment that involved playing golf. I did not write anything down at the time I played golf, but I explained that I discussed business on the golf course with these people. What do you think is going to happen? (A.N., Livonia, MI)

You are going to be miserable!

Two bad things are going to happen. First, your corporation is going to lose the golf deductions because you did not follow the rules. You were supposed to write down your business reason for the entertainment within one week of the expenditure. Also, your discussions failed the business-setting test. So, for these reasons your corporation is going to lose the deduction. But this is only the first of your two problems.

Your second problem is that the IRS is going to claim that you got personal benefit from the golf; therefore, the IRS is going to make your corporate-paid golf expenses a constructive dividend to you.

Your documentation failure makes the law bite you in two ways. First, your corporation loses the deduction and must pay taxes on this lost deduction. Second, the lost golf deduction is a constructive dividend, giving you taxable-dividend income.

Notes

Your misery is complete. You have been double-taxed for this mistake.[6]

Hopefully, this is a lesson. From this moment forward, keep contemporaneous records.

Letter Requiring Home Office

Do you have a sample letter I can use to have my corporation require me to use a home office? (M.W., Enfield, CT)

No, we don't have a sample letter, but this answer will give you what you need. Also, remember, you would not need any type of letter if you reported your income and expenses as a proprietorship on Schedule C. What triggers your need for the letter is your employee standing with your corporation.

You might have a variety of reasons for having the corporation require you to work at home. For example, some office buildings do not operate the heating or cooling on weekends or after hours. You may need to work during these times, and that could be a reason for the corporation to require you to have another office.

Similarly, your business neighborhood may not be the safest place after dark. Your corporation could deem it necessary that you work after dark.

Your corporation may deem it inappropriate for you to do your administrative work at the office, because it wants sales production during business hours. Therefore, the corporation requires you to do your administration at another location, like an office in your home.

When composing the letter, try to keep two things in mind. First, you want a good reason why you, the employee, should work at home. Second, you want this reason to make your work at home a convenience for your corporate employer.

Your letter from your corporation to yourself might go like this: "The corporation desires the services of M.W. more than eight hours a day and further desires that M.W. spend his time inside the corporate walls only attending to sales and production activities. This will encourage the other workers to model after M.W. and be more productive. Therefore, the corporation requires that M.W. obtain an administrative office outside the corporate walls, and the corporation shall reimburse M.W. for these expenses."

This letter should satisfy the requirement set forth in the code and by the IRS in its home-office publication, which states that "your business use must be for the convenience of your employer."[7]

The easy way to seek reimbursement from the corporation is to complete IRS Form 8829 and submit it to the corporation for reimbursement. IRS regulation Section 1.62-2(d)(1) allows the corporation to reimburse the employee for all the expenses that appear on the home-office deduction form. Because these are reimbursed employee expenses, the employee does not report them as income.

Proper accounting by the employee includes reducing the itemized deduction for mortgage interest and property taxes to the net expense incurred after receiving the corporate reimbursement. For example, if mortgage interest for the year is $20,000 and the corporation reimburses $2,000, the employee should claim only $18,000 as a mortgage interest deduction on the return.

Medical When You Have Two Businesses

We have two corporations: one in Texas and one in Nevada. The Texas corporation has five employees besides my husband and myself. The Nevada corporation has only my husband and me as employees. Can we establish a Section 105 medical reimbursement plan in the Nevada corporation without granting a similar benefit to the employees of the Texas corporation? (P.O. El Paso, TX)

No. For purposes of the medical discrimination rules, tax law does a huge roundup of all your businesses and all your spouse's businesses, including corporations, proprietorships, and LLCs, and makes them one business.[8] Thus, if you want a medical reimbursement plan at the Nevada corporation, you must provide the same medical reimbursement plan at the Texas corporation.

Doctor-Prescribed Golf

I have played golf for years, and now I would like my doctor to prescribe golf as the exercise I need for my heart. If I can get such a prescription, which I am sure I can, may I then deduct the golf as a medical expense? (S.F., Wayne, IN)

No, forget it. You have two problems. First, you are already a golfer, so the prescribed treatment would require nothing new on your part. Second, you have no medical reason that makes golf the exercise needed for your heart.

Notes

Notes

The courts distinguish personal expenditures beneficial to your general health from expenses for the prevention or alleviation of a physical defect or illness. In *Seymour*, the court noted that the physician prescription does not, by itself, make for a medical expense deduction.[9]

Leon Altman tried to deduct his trips to the golf course because two physicians recommended golf for his pulmonary emphysema, which had totally disabled him. No deduction, ruled the court. Altman had played golf before he became disabled, and thus the court could find no direct correlation between the golf and the medical need.[10]

105 Deduction for Back Chair

I hurt my back. For the past year, I have seen doctors and chiropractors and have gotten some relief. But I still have pain almost daily. I recently bought a fancy back chair for $1,800, and it seems to help with the pain. As a piece of furniture, this chair is useless. The front sticks out so that you trip walking by. Getting in and out of the chair is a trick. Is the cost of this chair (which my wife hates, but I love) deductible as a medical expense? If it's deductible as a medical expense, can I have my Section 105 plan reimburse the cost to me (thus making this chair a business expense)? (A.P., San Rafael, Calif.)

Maybe. Revenue ruling 58-155 said that the cost of a reclining chair intended to give rest to a taxpayer with a cardiac condition was deductible if the taxpayer could prove that the chair

- was prescribed by the cardiac specialist;
- served no purpose other than the mitigation of the physical condition of the patient; and
- was not to be used generally as an article of furniture.

If you can meet the criteria laid out in this revenue ruling, you would have a lock on the deduction.

Thus, we recommend that you get a prescription or a least a written recommendation for the chair from either the physician or the chiropractor, and that you build proof that this chair would not be used generally as an article of furniture. Perhaps you are the only one in the family that reclines in it.

Deduction for Family Wedding

I am planning to travel to a family wedding in New York. While there, I plan to discuss business with one or more people. Are all the trip

expenses deductible? Are travel expenses 100 percent deductible? What about the meals in connection with the travel? (A.L., Fremont, CA)

First, travel to a family wedding is probably not going to be deductible, regardless of the time spent discussing business at the wedding. So forget that. But let's see how you can get a deduction and attend the wedding, too.

First, you have to prove that your trip to New York is primarily for business purposes.[11] Say you travel from California to New York on Wednesday. On Thursday, you adjust for the time change. On Friday, you go to a sales seminar that lasts a minimum of four hours and one minute.[12] You do the same on Monday. On Tuesday, you travel home.

On Friday night, you attend the rehearsal dinner.

On Saturday, you attend the wedding.

The result: You deduct Wednesday, Thursday, and Tuesday as business travel days.[13] You deduct Friday and Monday as business training days. You deduct Saturday and Sunday as necessary business stay-over days.[14] You have made all your days business days. On a business day, you deduct breakfast, lunch, dinner, lodging, and all other costs of sustaining life on the road.

This is how you can get legitimate deductions for your trip and attend the wedding festivities, too.

Coffee for Employees

May I deduct the cost of coffee and sodas I provide for my employees? If so, is this subject to the 50 percent cut? (T.E., Lexington Park, MD)

Yes, you may deduct the cost of the coffee and sodas as a *de minimus* fringe benefit.[15] In fact, you deduct the full cost. The 50 percent cut on business meals and entertainment does not apply to the coffee-and-sodas fringe benefit.[16]

Notes

Endnotes–Section 46

1. Commr. v Nader Soliman 71 AFTR 2d 93-463 (1993, S Ct); results of this case reversed by PL 105-34, 8/5/97.
2. Reg. Sections 1.274-2(c); 1.274-2(d).
3. Peter F. Speltz v Commr., TC Summary Opinion 2006-25.
4. IRM 4.10.10.2 (04-04-2008) Standard Explanations for Report Writing, 4809, 4816.
5. Reg. Section 1.274-5T(b)(6).
6. Henry Boler v Commr., TC Memo 2002-155.
7. IRC Section 280A(c)(1).
8. IRC Sections 105(h); 106; 318(a); 414(b); 414(c); 414(m); 414(m)(6)(B); 1563(a); 1563(e)(5). See the *General Explanation of the Tax Reform Act of 1986 (Blue Book)* prepared by the staff of the Joint Committee on Taxation, pp. 780–781, for the reasons Congress enacted the Section 89 rules against discrimination, which were repealed in 1989 by Title II of the Debt Limit Extension Act.
9. John L. Seymour v Commr., 14 TC 1111 (1950).
10. Leon S. Altman v Commr., 53 TC 487 (1969).
11. Reg. Section 1.162-2(b)(2).
12. Reg. Section 1.274-4(d)(2)(iii).
13. Reg. Section 1.274-4(d)(2)(i).
14. Reg. Section 1.274-4(d)(2)(v).
15. IRC Section 132(e).
16. IRC Section 274(n)(2)(B).

Notes

Notes